The European Union - bad for Britain - a trade union view

Will Podmore
and
Doug Nicholls

Printed and Published by
Bread Books
P.O.Box 1806
Coventry
CV6 1YJ
www.breadbooks.com
Copyright © Will Podmore and Doug Nicholls 2005

ISBN: 0-9542112-5-1

Legal Notice

All rights reserved. No part of this book may be reproduced, stored in a retrieval system, or transmitted in any form, or by any means, electronic, photocopying mechanical, recording, or otherwise without the prior written permission of the author.

Requests to publish work from this book must be directed to Bread Books.

Will Podmore and Doug Nicholls have asserted their rights under Section 77 of the Copyright, Design and Patents Act 1988 to be identified as the authors of this work.

Contents

	Introduction	1
1	The European Union 1945-1992	3
2	The European Union 1992-2002	45
3	The drive towards a single EU state	90
4	The EU and its institutions	130
5	The costs of EMU - lower growth, lower wages, fewer jobs	168
6	Industrial inspiration	207
7	Agriculture, fisheries and services	240
8	Yes to independence - out of the EU	272
	Index	304

The EU Bad for Britain

Introduction

We want to make poverty history. Seeing the President of the European Union (EU) at the recent G8 summit gave perhaps the impression that he was a new head of State. Perhaps it should have been called G9. It was precisely against the formation of a new superstate called the EU, that French and Dutch workers and trade unions led the successful campaigns in their countries against the proposed EU Constitution for Europe.

Countries in the EU have collaborated to plunder not just Africa, but others in eastern Europe and the remaining organised and skilled workers of western Europe. The gap between the rich and poor at home has never been greater. The EU widens it.

We want peace, yet since the vicious war on Yugoslavia, we have seen the EU fostering ethnic divisions and supporting invasions, economic and military of previously sovereign nations.

We want industry and science, yet we have seen the EU wreck manufacturing based economies.

We want thriving public services, yet in the decline of the wealth creating base of industry, we have seen the EU run down and privatise utilities and industries needed by us all.

We want democracy, yet we have seen the highly centralised EU bureaucracy take power further and further away from the workplace and neighbourhood.

We want investment in British industries, transport, public services, technology and agriculture. Yet we pay £3.5 billion a year into the EU which ends up subsidising and getting lost in widespread fraud and corruption. Trade Unions would be penalised if their annual accounts were suspect. The EU auditors have refused to sign off its accounts for the last 10 years so flagrant is the corruption.

We want to elect leaders who we can influence, yet we have been ruled under the EU by the unelected and unaccountable.

We want socialism, a planned economic system with human beings at the centre of policy. Yet we have seen the EU promote the hidden hand of the market, its main aim being the free movement of capital and labour.

We want state control and social values and laws aligned to our aspirations for growth, social solidarity and secular respect. Yet we have seen the EU introduce totalitarian laws under the guise of liberal sentiments.

We want cheaper food, yet the EU arrangements guarantee every family in Britain pays massively over the odds for their basic food requirements.

We want decent pensions and long retirements. The EU's hostility to our pensions system and its directions to end final salary schemes have caused the biggest pensions crisis in our history.

We clearly as a trade union movement have not wanted the euro, nor the Constitution for Europe, yet we have remained tolerant or ignorant of everything else the Euro federalists have thrown at us.

The Tory Prime Minister Ted Heath lied to the nation when he took us into the European Economic Community. Harold Wilson lied to keep us in it at the time of the referendum thirty years ago. Margaret Thatcher lied to get Parliament to sign the Single European Act which drastically reduced the power of an elected British government. John Major lied to sign us up to the Amsterdam Treaty. Tony Blair lied to us to sign the European Constitution.

We have written this book to expose the lies and assert what we as a trade union movement want. Practically every motion passed at the TUC each year would lead us in campaign against the EU if we were really serious about implementing them. We try to show how the EU root and branch, tooth and claw is not in our interests. We seek to provide the facts that lead inescapably to the conclusion that the EU is bad for workers, and therefore bad for Britain. It is time to leave this employers' institution and there are more opportunities for growth and development and trade union advance outside than inside the EU.

With the recent French and Dutch no votes on the Constitution the tide is turning against the employers' vision of Europe which has been the EU. We believe that British workers have an important role to play in accelerating the process of reclaiming our nation. This is an important internationalist role in an increasingly dangerous world. The EU represents heavily armed globalisation on our doorstep. It represents low growth and high unemployment. It offers no model for British workers.

Will Podmore Doug Nicholls August 2005.

Chapter 1 The European Union 1945-1992

1: Britain and the European Union, 1945-1986

2: The Single European Market (1986)

3: Inside the European Exchange Rate Mechanism (1990-92)

4: What is Economic and Monetary Union?

5: The Maastricht Treaty (1992) and EMU

6: What is the political aim behind the euro?

*   In 1975, the Labour government stated, "There was a threat to employment in Britain from the movement in the Common Market towards an Economic and Monetary Union (EMU). This could have forced us to accept fixed exchange rates for the pound, restricting industrial growth and so putting jobs at risk. *This threat has been removed.*"

*   EMU would mean worse working conditions and social services and lower wages and benefits. Bill Morris, ex-General Secretary of the TGWU, said, "I am not prepared to have a situation where we say, hello the euro, bye-bye the public services, because that's the choice we have to make."[1] He warned of the danger of 'a headlong rush into the single currency, bringing huge cuts in public spending and public service'. He said that in EMU, "National governments would declare themselves powerless to do anything, while decisions would be taken by a bankers' committee insulated from any form of accountability or popular pressure."

1: Britain and European Union, 1945-1986

The idea for European Union did not come from any of the peoples of the EU member states. Ever since the fall of the Roman Empire, small elites have tried to force unity upon Europe's states. An early forerunner was the Holy Roman Empire, which, as Voltaire famously observed, was neither Holy, nor Roman, nor an Empire. Napoleon tried to enforce unity and failed. In the 19th century, high-minded pacifists, liberals and republicans, opposed to the obsolete absolute monarchies of backward Eastern Europe and to the aggressive nationalisms of Western Europe's states, advanced the slogan of the 'United States of Europe'. In the early 20th century, some thought that the European imperialist powers, rather than fighting each other, should combine to exploit the colonies, challenge other countries with imperial ambitions and, after 1917, attack the Soviet Union. The first political party in Britain to raise the call of European unity was Oswald Mosley's British Union of Fascists.

Hitler also wanted a United Europe: for instance, in March 1943, his Foreign Minister Joachim von Ribbentrop proposed setting up a Staatenbund, a European Union of States. (Paul-Henri Spaak, one of the EU's founders, described himself in 1938 as a 'national socialist' and praised Hitler's 'magnificent achievements'.) Europe's nations only saved their independence by defeating Hitlerism. Some have claimed that the idea of a united Europe came from the Resistance, rather than from the Nazis. But resistance support for federalism was not at the head of their programme. By 1943 many Axis sympathizers were keener 'Europeans' than their opponents.[2]

At the end of the Second World War two visions competed for prominence in Europe's future. One reflected the demands of the vanquished Nazi generals, big business and their political spokesmen in shady organisations like the Bilderberg Group, founded in 1952 to campaign for a single European state with one currency. They sought this to counter the trade union movement's power and its achievements of public ownership and state-run welfare provision. The other vision, reflecting national and popular interests, was of a Europe of peacefully coexisting independent nations. Trade unionists have to decide whether to side with the vision of transnational firms, or with the more peaceful aspirations of national and democratic forces.

After the war, the governments of France, the Benelux countries, West Germany and Italy adopted the cause of European union. They used the word federalism to describe the aim of dissolving Europe's existing sovereign nations into a single European state. But the British political establishment had no wish, then, to join this union. Winston Churchill never believed that Britain should be part of the proposed European union. He told the House of Commons in 1950 that if he were asked, "'Would you agree to a supranational authority which has the power to tell Great Britain not to cut any more coal or make any more steel but to grow tomatoes instead?' I should say, without hesitation, the answer is 'No'."[3] He said in November 1951, "I never thought that Britain or the British Commonwealth should, either individually or collectively, become an integral part of a European Federation, and have never given the slightest support to the idea."[4]

Jacques Delors, the European Commission President from 1985 to 1994, admitted, "Even that great European, Winston Churchill, envisaged European integration only for the countries of the European continent, not for Britain."[5] Sir Con O'Neill, later the official in charge of Prime Minister Edward Heath's negotiations to enter the EEC, said, "I don't think Churchill thought for a moment that this country, that Britain would be part of his united Europe. It was for the French, it was for the Germans, for the Italians, for the Belgians, the Dutch; but not for us. Equally, I don't think he thought for a moment – whether we were in it or not – that it should be an organisation of constitutional, legal and treaty obligation. That is why what Churchill launched in 1946 led up not to the European Community. It led down quite a different road. It led to the Council of Europe – still in existence, still useful, but no longer since the foundation of the Community right back in 1950 and 1957, no longer enormously important."[6] Ernest Bevin, Labour's Foreign Secretary from 1945 to 1951, and Jean Monnet, the French businessman and bureaucrat who founded the European Movement, agreed that the Council was just 'a talking shop'.

Future Prime Ministers Harold Macmillan and Anthony Eden agreed with Churchill. Macmillan told the Strasburg Assembly in August

1950, "our people are not going to hand to any supranational authority the right to close down our pits or steel works. We will allow no supranational authority to put large masses of our people out of work." Eden said in 1951, "the experiment of the six cannot succeed without federation and I think it most probable that if we join the six we shall be faced with that decision in a few years' time ... I am sure that it must be federation in the sense of one parliament, one foreign policy, one currency etc. So far as I can judge events on the continent of Europe I do not want to become part of such a federation."[7]

Currency union was not a new idea. In the 1950s and 1960s, British governments were imposing federations based on single currencies on the West Indies, East Africa, Central Africa, Malaysia and southern Arabia. All collapsed in bitter disagreements.

The US state, although aware that it might be building a rival, sought to revive Europe as an anti-Soviet bloc, an economic and political prop for NATO. It pushed British governments to join a politically united Western Europe. Between 1947 and 1953, the CIA paid half the costs of the European Movement, which was one of those bodies that have "as their chief characteristic an anti-Bolshevik crusade"[8], as Gladwyn Jebb of the Foreign Office described it. US firms also aided the drive for a single European state: when Monnet started his Action Committee for a United States of Europe, the Ford Foundation funded it.[9]

From the beginning, the EU's founders' strategy was to deal first with economic targets, leaving the political targets till later. After each economic target was met, they lay low till the dust cleared, and then started for the next target. The aim was a steady leaching away of sovereignty in the basic economic arena. Meanwhile behind the scenes they carefully prepared for political union. At a certain point, when all the countries had been lured into the bag of economic union, they would tighten the drawstrings and declare full political union. As Monnet wrote, "Everyday realities will make it possible to form the political union which is the goal of our Community and to establish the United States of Europe."[10] He wanted to create this Europe on the model of the United States of America. However, according to Alexis de Tocqueville, four conditions had been needed to create the US state: the habit of local self-government, a common language, a coherent political class and a moral consensus.[11] None of these applied in Europe. Most importantly, Europe, unlike the USA, was already a group of historic sovereign nations each with its own national identity.

Robert Schuman, the French Foreign Minister (who had been a minister in the Vichy administration), spoke in 1950 of 'economic development as a first step in the federation of Europe'. The first supranationalist step was his proposed European Coal and Steel Community (ECSC), to which the French and German governments would give control over their coal and steel industries. Konrad Adenauer, the first Chancellor of the Federal Republic of Germany, said, "the significance of the Schuman proposal was first and foremost political, not economic. This plan was to be the beginning of a federal structure of Europe."[12] Monnet said, "Our Community is not a coal and steel producers' association: it is the beginning of Europe."[13] The British government had only recently put those industries under national control. On 1 June 1950, Schuman handed the British government an ultimatum: by 7 pm the next day, it had to say yes or no to the concept of the ECSC, even before entering the negotiations. Unsurprisingly, Britain was not keen to join, any more than France or Germany were keen that Britain should join.[14] The Treaty of Paris, signed in April 1951, established the ECSC, without Britain.

On 3 April 1952, Monnet said, "The fusion [of economic functions] would compel nations to fuse their sovereignty into a single European state." In 1957, he proposed a 'European stabilisation fund' claiming, "Via money, Europe could become political in five years." In 1958 he wrote, "the current Communities should be completed by a Finance Common Market which would lead us to European economic unity. Only then would the mutual commitments created by the Communities make it fairly easy to produce the political union which is the goal."

Between 1949 and 1960, the US government covertly spent $4 million on bodies promoting a single European state. In the 1950s, the CIA backed the campaign for Britain's entry into the European Economic Community (EEC).[15] It gave £1.3 million to the European Youth Campaign, a pro-EEC organisation, most to its British section. US Secretary of State Dean Acheson said that US covert actions "fostered the preparation and distribution of literature and even posters which attacked the principles of Communism and which centered attention upon the need for European economic unity."[16] It funded the Congress for Cultural Freedom and the Bilderberg Group, which both pushed for European integration. In 1955, US Secretary of State John Foster Dulles said that he wanted Europe to advance "beyond cooperative arrangements to Federal institutions, with necessary transfer of sovereign power." In 1957, President Dwight Eisenhower said that he hoped to "live long enough to see a United States of Europe come into existence." [17]

In March 1957, the two Treaties of Rome were signed, setting up the EEC and the European Atomic Energy Community (Euratom). Later, Edward Heath admitted that the aim behind the Treaty of Rome was the political union of Western Europe. "The aim was, and is ... ever closer political union. The means ... were and are economic."[18]

In 1955-58, when the six future EEC members were negotiating the Treaty of Rome, Britain's exports to Commonwealth countries were four times its exports to Europe. Britain had high tariffs in place and the government feared competition with German producers, so Churchill and Eden's policy of opposing Britain's joining a European Federation was a rational defense of British interests.[19] But as Britain's relative power declined and its economic prospects darkened, its rulers increasingly turned towards the EEC. By the 1960s, big business was starting to favour EEC entry as a way to control the trade unions and cut down the public sector.

Also, the US government continued to press Britain to join the EEC. President John Kennedy said, "we welcome the project of Britain's participation in the institutions of the Treaty of Rome." He also said, "It is best for the Atlantic Community if the United Kingdom joined the EEC on an unconditional basis." His Under-Secretary of State George Ball said that Britain should enter the EEC "only if they are prepared to accept the full implications of European unification – with the possible ultimate goal of some form of Federation." This constant US pressure helped to push the Macmillan government into applying to join.

In 1961, Macmillan came to an agreement with Kennedy. Macmillan promised that he would support the US 'limited intervention' in Laos, and keep quiet about the US government's responsibility for the illegal Bay of Pigs attack on Cuba. In return, he would be the US government's agent in the EEC. As Foreign Secretary Alec Douglas-Home pointed out, NATO would be 'underpinned' by the EEC. This renewed post-Suez alliance assisted Kennedy's planned aggressions against Laos and Vietnam. Parliament ratified Macmillan's approach to the EEC on 3 August 1961; only seven MPs voted against. The US-run International Monetary Fund rewarded the government the next day with a £714 million credit.

As the Bundesbank's first President, Karl Blessing, said in 1962, "The final goal of the Commission is a European monetary union ... As a European, I would be ready to approve of European monetary union and to accept a centrally directed federal central banking system; as a responsible central banking practitioner, and a realist, I cannot however avoid pointing out the difficulties which stand in the way. A common currency and a federal central banking system are only feasible if, apart from a common trade policy, there is also a common finance and budget policy, a common economic policy, a common social and wage policy - a common policy all around. In brief, this would only happen if there was a federal state with a European parliament with legislative powers in respect of all member states."[20]

In January 1963, General de Gaulle, rightly objecting to Britain's role as the US government's Trojan horse, delivered his famous 'Non', defeating British and US government policy. He explained, "England in effect is insular, she is maritime, she is linked through her exchanges, her markets, her supply lines, to the most diverse and often the most distant countries; she pursues essentially industrial and commercial activities, and only slightly agriculture ones. She has in all her doings very marked and very original habits and traditions. In short, the nature, the structure, the very situation that are England's differ profoundly from those of the Continentals."[21] A week later, France and Germany signed a Treaty of Friendship.

There was also a strong economic motive behind de Gaulle's vetoes of Britain's applications. France's farmers gained hugely from the Common Agricultural Policy, but the British government was not then prepared to pay vast sums into the CAP. De Gaulle vetoed British entry in 1963 and again in November 1967 because Britain was certain to block generous financing for the CAP.[22] In 1969, President Georges Pompidou lifted the veto; in exchange, the British government agreed to accept a permanent funding arrangement for the CAP.[23] It promised to accept the CAP as it was, so all the later promises to reform the CAP were just words to deceive the British public.[24]

From 1951 to 1965, the EEC, as was always intended, moved towards a single state by integrating its economic functions. This was the famous ratchet effect (a ratchet being a set of teeth on the edge of a bar or wheel with a catch allowing it to move in one direction only).[25] The EU has continuously both deepened and widened towards its 'ever closer union', so that member states have to adapt continuously to its pressure.[26] Every apparently separate change followed the deeper logic of unification.[27]

Walter Hallstein, the European Commission's first President (from 1958 to 1966), said that he could be considered as a kind of Prime Minister of Europe. Belgian Prime Minister Paul-Henri Spaak reminded the Council of Europe in 1964, "Those who drew up the Treaty of Rome ... thought of it as a stage on the way to political union."[28] In April 1965, EEC members signed the Treaty Establishing a Council and a Commission of the European Communities, creating the EEC's two most powerful supranational bodies, the Commission and the Council of Ministers. Yet from 1965 to 1984, the EEC stagnated, largely due to de Gaulle's successful assertion of French sovereignty against the EEC's efforts to form a single European state.

The US state continued to press Britain to join the EEC. In 1967, President Lyndon Johnson told Prime Minister Harold Wilson that Britain's entry would "certainly help to strengthen and unify the West." President Nixon's Secretary of State Henry Kissinger said in 1969 that the US government would "affirm our traditional support of European unity, including British entry into the Common Market."

In 1970, the Conservative Party under Heath won the election, promising, "Our sole commitment is to negotiate: no more, no less."[29] So he had no mandate to take us into the EEC. A Gallup poll in April 1970 showed that only 19% wanted us to enter the EEC. But on 28 October 1971, 69 Labour MPs, including Roy Jenkins, David Owen, Shirley Williams and John Smith, broke the Labour Party whip to vote with the Conservative Party for EEC entry. Later, pro-EEC Labour MPs secretly cooperated with Heath to get the legislation through the House of Commons.[30]

From the first, Britain's leaders knew that EEC entry would lead to a single currency and that a single currency was designed to lead to a single state. The influential Werner Report of 1970 said, "monetary union appears as a leaven for the development of political union, which in the long run it will be unable to do without." A Foreign Office document of 9 November 1970 stated, "The plan for economic and monetary union has revolutionary long-term political implications, both economic and political. It could imply the creation of a European federal state. With a single currency ... it will arouse strong feelings about sovereignty." But they also knew that they had to keep this quiet because they feared the impact on public opinion. Cabinet papers released in January 2001 under the 30-year rule showed that Heath's government suppressed the evidence that membership could lead to political and monetary union. Baroness Castle of Blackburn said of the revelations, "We always knew Heath had been dishonest. He kept patronising us by telling us our fears were misplaced. But now the truth is out. If the British people had known this they would never have voted yes."

In 1960, Britain's most senior legal officer, the Lord Chancellor, David Maxwell Fyfe, had written to Heath, "the Council of Ministers could eventually ... make regulations which would be binding on us even against our wishes ... It is the first step on the road which leads ... to the fully federal state. ... I must emphasise that in my view the surrenders of sovereignty involved are serious ones and I think that, as a matter of practical politics, it will not be easy to persuade Parliament or public to accept them. ... these objections ought to be brought out into the open."[31] Yet the Heath government's White Paper said, "The Community is no federation of provinces or countries. ... There is no question of any erosion of essential national sovereignty."[32] Heath told Parliament and the British people at the time, "there will be no blueprint for a federal Europe" and "joining the Community does not entail a loss of national identity or an erosion of essential national sovereignty."[33] He also said, "there are some in this country who fear that in going into Europe, we shall in some way sacrifice independence and sovereignty. These fears I need hardly say are completely unjustified." (It was not a matter of 'going into Europe', but of joining a specific body, the EEC - a typical Europhile confusion.) Yet when he was asked in 1990 whether he had in mind in 1972 'a United States of Europe' with a single currency, he replied, 'Of course, yes.'[34] A Chief Executive Officer who promoted a company merger based on such lies could be found guilty of fraud.[35]

In 1972, Heath, together with the Prime Ministers of France and Germany, Georges Pompidou and Willy Brandt, discreetly agreed to form a single market, a common currency, a European central bank, and a common defence and foreign policy. In 1973, Heath signed Britain into the EEC.

Two years later, in 1975, we were allowed a referendum on whether we should stay in. Wilson's Labour government spent £4.5 million on three leaflets for every household, two for entry and one against. The government's three-page document gave the British people clear assurances that have proven false: "There was a threat to employment in Britain from the movement in the Common Market towards an Economic and Monetary Union (EMU). This could have forced us to accept fixed exchange rates for the pound, restricting industrial growth and so putting jobs at risk. This threat has been removed. ... No important new policy can be decided in Brussels or anywhere else without the consent of a British Minister answerable to a British government and British Parliament ... the Minister representing Britain can veto any proposals for a new law or new tax if he considers it to be against British interest."[36] The referendum campaign was conducted on the basis of these pledges - no monetary union and a British veto over every proposal.

Yet the government had already secretly told the EEC, but not the British people, that it would commit Britain to monetary union: "We are prepared to envisage an orderly run-down of sterling after our accession. We shall be ready to discuss what measures might be appropriate to achieve a progressive alignment of the external characteristics and practices in relation to sterling with those of other currencies in the Community in the context of progress towards economic and monetary union in the enlarged Community, and we are confident that sterling can be handled in a way which will enable us to take our full part in that progress. In the meantime we shall manage our policies with a view to stabilising the sterling in a way which would be consistent with these longer term objectives."[37]

'Britain into Europe', backed by firms like IBM, Rank, ICI, Shell and Ford, spent £2.1 million on pro-EEC propaganda; the government's Central Office of Information spent £444,000 and the CBI £70,000. The CIA heavily funded the yes campaign.[38] The BBC was biased in favour of a yes vote before and during the campaign.[39] The Conservative Party, the Liberal Party and the Labour Committee for Europe (funded by the European Movement) all campaigned for a yes vote. The National Referendum Campaign had only £133,000 to campaign for a no vote. The press claimed, "Jobs will be safe in the Market." The Daily Express turned its coat and declared, "The Express is for the Market."[40]

The government's phrasing of the referendum question stressed its support for membership and exaggerated the importance of re-negotiation: "The Government have announced the results of the re-negotiation of the United Kingdom's terms of membership of the European Community. Do you think that the United Kingdom should stay in the European Community (the Common Market)?" The stress on the government's support for continued membership was a clear example of bias.[41] The question did not even mention the possibility of voting no: it could have asked, for instance, "Do you think that the United Kingdom should stay in the European Community (the Common Market) or not?" One poll estimated that the wording of the question could make a 20% difference.[42]

On 5 June, 17,378,581 people - 67.2% of those who voted - voted yes; 8,470,073 - 32.8% - voted no. The turnout was just 64.5%. So, a minority of the population, 43.3%, voted for the EEC. Bernard Donoughue, Wilson's press officer, commented years later, in a classic double entendre, "Mr Heath had taken the British Establishment into Europe. Harold Wilson took in the British people."[43]

The US state continued to back the EEC. In 1977, President Jimmy Carter said, "I strongly favour, perhaps more than my predecessors, a close interrelationship among the nations of Europe, the European Community in particular."

Yet the EEC became increasingly unpopular in Britain. In 1979, the turnout for the first Euro-election was only 31%. By 1982, polls showed that the "Majority would quit EEC."[44]

Successive governments took us further towards a single European state, none more so than Margaret Thatcher's. In 1979, she reduced our independent control over our economy by ending exchange controls. She crashed the economy, wrecking industry and creating unemployment to break the trade union movement. Her friend President Ronald Reagan backed her support for the EEC, saying in 1982, "We consider a strong and united Europe not a rival, but a partner." In 1983, Thatcher signed the Stuttgart 'Solemn Declaration on European Union', committing Britain to 'a united Europe', to 'convergence of economic development' and to 'progress towards Economic and Monetary Union'.

2: The Single European Market (1986)

The Treaty of Rome's Title III had promised the 'Free movement of persons, services and capital'. Its Articles 67 to 73 said its members must end all controls on the free movement of capital."[45] Thatcher, the Commission and the European Roundtable of Industrialists, employers from Europe's largest companies, now pushed for the Single European Act that set up the Single European Market programme, enforced between 1985 and 1992.[46]

In 1986, Thatcher signed us up to the Single European Act (SEA), one of the biggest strides towards a single European State. The Act introduced the Single European Market, adopted Thatcher's policy of scrapping exchange controls, made protectionism illegal, created the legal basis for a single EU foreign policy, greatly extended the practice of qualified majority voting (QMV) and included a commitment in principle to EMU.[47]

Significantly, the EU's leaders did not call it the Single European Market Act, but the Single European Act. The 'single' in the Single European Act has nothing to do with the single market.[48] It committed its signatories to the idea of a 'Single Europe,' obliging them "to transform relations ... among their states into a European Union." It was 'a giant stride along Europe's road to full union' as a leading member of the European Movement said. As the 1985 Commission White Paper on the SEA had pointed out, "Just as the Customs Union had to precede Economic Integration, so Economic Integration had to precede European Unity." More than any treaty since 1957, it speeded up the drive towards a single European state. EU-supporter

Michael Heseltine wrote that the Act "was as comprehensive a redefinition of national sovereignty as we have ever known."[49]

The Conservative Party's rhetoric about defending national sovereignty acted as a smokescreen for further steps towards European integration.[50] Thatcher, as a lawyer, of course read the small print and knew what she was signing. Nigel Lawson, her Chancellor of the Exchequer, pointed out, "She should have been clear at the time … there was not great scope for surprise. I think in signing that Act she should have known it was a very big step."[51] She could have stopped it by a veto, since unanimity was required for any modification of the EC's treaties, but instead she guillotined it through Parliament.[52]

As Lord Young, the Trade and Industry Minister, said, "The Single Market meant 'Thatcherism in Europe'.Thatcher and the European Roundtable of Industrialists wanted the SEM because it added to employers' powers. The head of the Bundesbank approved: "The single market means not stability but more flexibility in the labour market." It demolished job protections against globalisation, making the EU's labour markets more flexible, on the US model.[54]

A single EU-wide labour market made it easier for employers to reduce wages by playing workers off against each other. Deregulating the labour market raised, not lowered, unemployment. Britain had the least regulated labour market in the EU, so since it was easier, cheaper and quicker to dismiss British workers, international firms looking to 'downsize' often targeted British workers first, so unemployment, especially of manufacturing workers, remained unacceptably high. Big firms wanted lower wages, ever-larger and freer markets, and more sources of cheaper raw materials, which they wanted a single EU state to deliver. They saw the EU as a vast army of workers with a great array of skills, and at their backs a reserve of 30 million unemployed. Within the EU's territory, workers would be required to move to wherever work was available. Divided by culture, tradition, language, nationality and religion, they would offer tantalising opportunities to employers to 'divide and rule'.

The SEA's Article 13 read, "The internal market shall comprise an area without internal frontiers in which the free movement of goods, persons, services and capital is ensured." For businesses, getting rid of exchange controls, tariff barriers and barriers to migration between member countries were the EU's great advantages. Free movement of goods meant strike-breaking: in September 2000, when French workers blockaded Channel ports to cut fuel costs, the EU threatened to invoke the clause about the free movement of goods in order to justify efforts to break the blockade. Free movement of persons meant forced emigration and unemployment. Free movement of capital meant closures.

The EU ensured that the SEM also added to the EU's powers and removed democratic powers from EU states.[55] Peter Hain, later Labour's Minister for Europe, in 1995 denounced "an EU which puts the single market before democracy."[56] As he wrote, "the driving thrust of European integration was a capitalist one. Everything else - democratic structures and social policies - was subordinated to the Treaty of Rome's insistence on a free market for capital."[57]

The Commission saw the SEM as 'the most ambitious and comprehensive supply-side programme ever launched'.[58] The SEM pushed promoted liberalisation. So did the World Trade Organisation (WTO) and as Peter Sutherland, GATT's Director-General in the mid-1980s, said, "We wouldn't have a WTO if the European Union did not have a common commercial policy and did not negotiate with one voice."[59] The Single Market has helped to shape liberalisation on a world scale and in turn liberalisation has shaped the Single Market.[60] The SEM also increased EU interference in states' welfare, social and health programmes. The EU's drive towards market integration eroded national welfare state autonomy and sovereignty.[61] Its 'harmonisation' of social and labour market policies led to corporatism, cutting trade union powers and integrating workers into company structures in order to get them to accept job losses, worse conditions and wage cuts.[62]

What were the SEM's effects? Two years after the SEM ended exchange controls, the ERM, without their stabilising influence, effectively collapsed as a viable fixed exchange rate regime. Freeing the markets had destabilised the international economy.

The EU's 1988 Cecchini Report predicted that the SEM would raise the EU's gross domestic product by 7% and create five million new jobs. However, Cecchini's prediction was not based on good evidence, but on the assumption that governments would boost demand, a policy that EMU banned.[63] Far from producing the extra jobs predicted in the Cecchini report, the SEM speeded up decline. Mergers trebled between 1986 and 1996, resulting in savage job cuts.[64]

Nor did the SEM lead to increased exports, as the Commission had promised.[65] By enforcing competition and reducing states' powers to protect their industries, the SEM accelerated imports, which destroyed industries. The removal of restrictions on the movement of goods within the EU after 1992 undermined the informal agreements that protected national markets from imports.[66] The European Commission admitted in 1993, "The single market programme has done more for business than it has for workers."[67]

3: Inside the European Exchange Rate Mechanism (1990-92)

In 1989, Thatcher endorsed, with no debate in Parliament, the Delors Committee's recommendation of a single currency, when she could have vetoed that too.[68] In 1990, she endorsed the decision to hold the Inter Governmental Conference preparing the 1992 Maastricht Treaty on European Union, which took the EEC further towards becoming a single state. In 1990, the EU's leaders changed the EEC's name to the European Community: it was no longer just an economic community, but now a political one as well. As MEP Richard Corbett wrote, "the name of the EEC Treaty was changed to EC Treaty, to indicate its political, not just economic, finality."[69]

In the 1990s, British governments and some big firms became keener to merge Britain into a single European state. The City of London, the CBI, the Conservative Party, the Liberal Party, the Labour Party and the TUC all pushed for Britain to enter the European Exchange Rate Mechanism. A Gallup poll showed that 93% of the chief executives of large British firms and City institutions wanted us to join the ERM.[70] They told us it would bring prosperity, higher wages, more jobs, lower interest rates, lower prices and a stable currency. Instead we got the worst slump for 60 years. In October 1990, Thatcher, in her last act as Prime Minister, and John Major, in his only act as Chancellor of the Exchequer, took Britain into the ERM. The Sunday Telegraph wrote, 'Thank God'. Entry ruined

Thatcher; exit later ruined Major.

Under ERM, unemployment averaged 7% and inflation 7.8%. It cost France 700,000 jobs and Italy one million jobs. In Spain, 22% were unemployed. The ERM forced Denmark into slump: unemployment doubled to 12%, public spending was slashed, and investment, output and wages all fell. Ireland's unemployment soared from 11% to 23%. The EC's problems were not due to world conditions: during the ERM-induced 1990-92 slump, EC members did far worse than non-EC members. Across the EU, trade unions responded by taking action in defence of jobs and living standards, against wage freezes and cuts in public services.

ERM member governments spent billions defending their overvalued currencies, backing financial firms at the people's expense by cutting public spending and raising interest rates (in Sweden's case, to 500% for five days).[71] The Swedish government's three-month defence of the krone cost Sweden possibly 95 billion krone, three times its annual defence budget. But nonetheless, in late 1992, the pound, the Finnish mark, the Italian lira, the Swedish krone, the Spanish peseta, the Portuguese escudo and the Norwegian krone all had to be devalued. The narrow-band ERM eventually collapsed in 1993. Even the EU's monetary committee admitted that the ERM had not kept prices or money stable and had not cut inflation.

Britain's two-year ERM membership brought us the worst slump for 60 years, costing us £82.2 billion.[72] The ERM drove up real interest rates in all the member countries and was the main cause of a general recession.[73] Our economy shrank by 3.86%, costing £23.1 billion; it should have grown at its usual 2.5% rate, so the cost in lost growth was £30.3 billion; unemployment rose by 1.4 million, costing £10.8 billion; the government fruitlessly lost £18 billion of our currency reserves trying to stay in the ERM. Manufacturing output fell by 7% and manufacturing employment by 14%. Excessive interest rates made borrowing painful for firms, councils and homeowners, causing record numbers of bankruptcies and homes repossessed, and trapping 1.75 million homeowners into negative equity. Norman Lamont said that all this was 'a price worth paying'. Kenneth Clarke claimed, "The ERM had no effect on British business." Even as late as the 1992 general election, the Conservative, Liberal Democrat and Labour parties all stood on the same platform of keeping our ERM membership at the pound's overvalued rate and of keeping interest rates high to do this.

The government's policies made matters worse. Major wrote later, "to correct the economy, we would have to take decisions that were bound to hurt those I most wished to help."[74] Even after two disastrous years in the ERM, the Labour Party also continued to back staying in: Shadow Chancellor John Smith said, "The benefits of the Exchange Rate Mechanism in terms of stability far outweigh its disadvantages." The Treasury said that leaving the ERM would increase interest rates, and that lower interest rates were possible only in the ERM. When we left, we cut interest rates. An EC report of 1995 admitted that leaving had brought Britain real gains.[75]

4: What is Economic and Monetary Union?

Economic and Monetary Union means that all its members follow a single economic policy and a single monetary policy based on a single currency. A single, secretive institution, the European Central Bank, not the elected political bodies of the member countries, decides these policies. This Bank issues the euro. It decides how much money it wants to borrow, what rate of interest it pays on what it borrows and how the euro is valued against other currencies. This Bank is also responsible for all the members' financial assets. It does not answer to any elected bodies, not even to the European Parliament.

In Britain, the Bank of England issues our currency, and the Bank answers to the government, even if at arm's length, as the Labour government has ruled. The government decides what new coins and notes are issued, how much money it wants to borrow (that is, what government stock or National Savings bonds it wants to sell), what rate of interest it pays on what it borrows, and how the pound is valued against other currencies. The Bank is responsible for our gold reserves. All these powers would be handed over to the European Central Bank if we joined the euro.

Adjustment to exchange rates (the rates at which the pound sterling is sold overseas), particularly to interest rates (the cost of borrowing), is the government's standard tool to fine-tune the economy. The government can borrow money and set the interest rates it pays on what it borrows, which gives it flexibility in setting its budgets. A tax change takes a long time to come into effect, but a loan can be got overnight.

The government of Britain, whatever its complexion, must be able to have an economic policy. This is not to line up in favour of any particular past or present policy. If Britain entered the euro, economic policy for Britain would be made in Europe, not in Britain. The British government would have no more economic muscle than a borough council; it would be given a budget and a tightly defined area of policy to be carried out. To believe anything else was wishful thinking or daydreaming. British sovereignty over Britain would be finished. The euro is not an economic matter alone: it is the necessary base for political union, for a single European state. All its supporters in Europe know this and are quite open about it. It is only in Britain that politicians pretend that it is only an economic and not a constitutional matter.

Our years of membership of the EU have been a period of decline for Britain, a time of wasted money, wasted jobs, wasted communities and wasted people. To what extent this would have occurred if we had not been in the EU will never be known, but the EU was centrally involved throughout. If the £3.5 billion or so each year that we pay over net to the EU had been spent here, it would have made a big difference to our prosperity. Unfortunately, to date there has been an almost universal refusal to take the EU seriously as a threat. It seems to be boredom embodied, with its bureaucratic tedium, its directives and regulations, the impenetrable hedge of the Euro-institutions; the very vocabulary is off-putting. All the time, the pretence is that it doesn't really matter, because nothing is actually going on. But behind the smokescreen of verbiage, something has been happening; like a fire that smoulders quietly and then begins to shoot out tongues of flame, it is dangerous and must be stopped. EU strategists like to believe that people are stupid, unable to understand the difficult matters with which the EU is concerned. They present each new step as a fait accompli, but also as a springboard for the next step.

But we are not stupid, and where we are ignorant it is because we want to be, because we want to ignore the EU. But unfortunately, ignoring it will not make it go away. We need to know it, in order to see why it poses such a threat to us.

The word 'sovereignty' has not always been appreciated in the British trade union movement as something that applies to us. We have supported many trade union movements in their struggles for national liberation and sovereignty, but somehow if we apply the word to Britain it has connotations of the terrible British Empire. We reject that connotation and assert the true meaning of the word - it expresses a nation's democratic right to self-determination and to look after its own population without interference from those whom it does not elect.

Some academics have tried to reduce the importance of nation. The historian Linda Colley suggested that Britain's rulers created the nation in the 18th century.[76] Sociologist Benedict Anderson claimed that nations were just 'imagined communities'.[77] Historians Terence Ranger and Eric Hobsbawm asserted that national traditions were just artificial inventions.[78] Previously, postmodernists and post-structuralists attacked the concept of class.[79] Now they turn their destructive critiques onto the concept of nation.

Sovereignty is double-edged. If we demand, as we must, the final say in our country's affairs, then, when things go wrong we must accept the responsibility. There has been a lack of resolve in recent years, a tendency to stand in the wings and watch rather than get involved in the fray, particularly while Thatcher strutted the stage in the 1980s. There is now a growing sense that the EU must be stopped, and we hear some surprising voices saying so. Even some businessmen are not as keen on the EU as they were: with the Soviet Union gone, there is no need for a buffer against it, and the big firms increasingly have global, not just continental, ambitions.

We have to use our labour movement organisations to insist that Britain rules itself, that we keep our ability to decide our own economic and monetary policy, that we keep our independent currency and refuse to enter the euro. As the Community and Youth Workers' Union General Secretary Doug Nicholls said at the 1999 TUC, "It is beyond belief that at this time in our history as a Trade Union movement we could on the one hand correctly condemn the Bank of England for its anti growth obsession with fighting inflation by means of high interest rates and a high pound, while suggesting incorrectly on the other hand as the General Secretary and General Council Statement are doing, that we may be prepared to ultimately give these fundamental levers of our economy over to a European Central Bank run by 21 unelected bankers who will meet under the terms of the Amsterdam Treaty 'in secret' and who will be specifically forbidden from heeding any influence from their national Parliaments. This would be a hostile take-over indeed. If Eddie George is difficult to persuade beyond his one line job description now, how much more difficult to influence the ECB as a trade union movement in the future."

In the euro, we would no longer be able to run our own affairs. Sovereignty and democracy are indivisible: if we give away our sovereignty we would be throwing away the rights of every future generation to decide their own futures and the right of every future government to govern Britain in Britain's interests. The trade union movement seems sometimes to forget that its main contribution to Britain has not been just a sequence of struggles for improved terms and conditions and progressive labour laws. The trade union movement's main and distinctive contribution has been to instil within our culture a sense of democracy, a well-justified feeling that what we did and said mattered in our society. This was expressed in the key ideas of no taxation without representation, universal suffrage, accountability, collective discipline, freedom of association, the power of the debate and the vote, and agreement to adhere to a majority position. These all stemmed from the struggles and organisation of the trade union movement. They have influenced not just parliament and local councils but the controlling bodies of many civil bodies, from the smallest community association to the largest nationalised industry. All the EU's politics and structures conflicted with this history and culture of democracy. The trade unions above all other organisations should oppose the attempt to repeal our democratic heritage.

5: The Maastricht Treaty (1992) and the political motive behind Economic and Monetary Union

The Treaty on European Union, also known as the Maastricht Treaty, signed on 7 February 1992, was a huge step towards a single European state. It incorporated Economic and Monetary Union and European Political

Union, the single currency and political unity. It set up a three-pillared structure for the EU. Pillar one covered the EU's economics, centrally the Single European Market, and Economic and Monetary Union: this was the most supranational pillar, and was the model for the other two, the Common Foreign and Security Policy, and cooperation on Justice and Home Affairs. EMU fulfilled Delors' Three-Stage Plan for a single currency and a single economic and financial policy for all EU member countries.

The Treaty extended the Commission's powers from 11 to 20 areas of government, and provided for 111 new kinds of occasions when decisions could be made by QMV. The Major government opted out of two Treaty provisions, but signed up to the rest. By the Treaty, the EU could impose an economic policy even if we voted against it, and it could make us apply VAT at a given high rate to products previously immune from it.

A consistent policy ran through the Treaty: free movement of capital. It put no restraints on complete foreign ownership of any public or private institutions, for instance the defence industry, the media, or energy resources. The Treaty said that governments had to privatise coal, the railways and the post. EMU would prevent any country's governments and local authorities from setting up new industries or firms, and would forbid them to support existing ones. It would prevent them from increasing public spending or levying taxes to invest in domestic industry.

It outlawed full employment policies, effective welfare policies and intervention to promote leading national industries. The Central Bank was not allowed to lend money to national, state or regional governments for any reason.

Its Article B laid down that the EU would have "a Common Foreign and Security Policy including the eventual framing of a common defence policy, which might in time lead to a common defence." This replaced the previous intergovernmental objective of European Political Cooperation by the supranational aim of common foreign and defence policies. It also established citizenship of the EU. This Treaty was "concluded for an indefinite period."

Article 43 stated that all the EU's existing Treaties were sacrosanct and could not be renegotiated. So the Conservative Party policy of seeking to renegotiate those Treaties that it did not like was pointless. There was no room for flexibility or revision: the EU train can only move one way.

The Treaty laid down EMU's form. Article 3a1 said that members must adopt "an economic policy ... conducted in accordance with the principle of an open market economy with free competition." Article 99 gave the Council of Ministers the power to harmonise all indirect taxation. (Indirect taxation, as part of the Single European Market, was decided at EU, not at national, level.[80]) By Article 100 it could issue directives on all laws relating to the single market. Article 103 empowered it to draft by qualified majority voting "the broad guidelines of the economic policy of the Member states". By Article 104c it could fine states for "excessive government deficits".

Article 3b Title II of the Treaty defined subsidiarity (a term borrowed from the Roman Catholic Church - where it had not stopped the Church centralising all authority in the Pope![81]) "In areas which do not fall within its exclusive competence, the Community shall take action, in accordance with the principle of subsidiarity, only if and in so far as the objectives of the proposed action cannot be sufficiently achieved by the Member States and can therefore, by reason of the scale or effects of the proposed action, be better achieved by the Community."[82] Firstly, this asserted that certain areas were the EU's 'exclusive competence': member states would no longer have any powers in those areas. Secondly, it extended the EU's powers, legitimising EU action in those areas that did not already fall within its competence. Thirdly, the EU itself would decide whether member states had achieved 'the objectives of the proposed action', and whenever and wherever it wanted to act, the EU would surely find that the states had not 'sufficiently achieved' these objectives.[83] Even when he was Minister for Europe, Peter Hain noticed that subsidiarity did not prevent what he called the EU's 'creeping federalism', saying, "The powers have all been going towards Brussels and away from nation states. We have no means of enforcing subsidiarity."[84] Some said that because of subsidiarity, Britain would not lose its sovereignty at all, or at least not much. According to this, member countries would keep sovereignty over all matters with just one exception – any matter that was so important that it must be decided centrally. And who decided which these matters were? The EU's central decision-making bodies!

The Treaty's most important creation was the European Central Bank. As the Bank's historian, Matt Marshall, wrote, "That bank would be the most powerful institution in Europe, having the power to set interest rates, and with it, the power to move trillions of dollars of capital, and speed up or slow down the economy – in short, have more direct impact on the fortunes of more citizens around the world that any other institution apart from the US Federal Reserve. Unlike the European Commission, the ECB would not be a mere puppet institution, making proposals subject to government veto. The ECB would be fiercely independent, set the agenda and be accountable to no one. It would be supranational. It would enjoy raw power at its best. As members of the ECB's council, the central bankers would be masters of Europe's financial world."[85]

By Article 23 of the Protocol setting up the Bank, it "may ... acquire ... all types of foreign security exchange assets, securities and all other assets in the currency of any country or units of account in whatever form held; hold and manage the assets referred to in this Article." It could take our reserves and financial assets. Article 105 empowered the Bank to "supervise credit institutions and other financial institutions". Article 106 empowered it to fine states that did not do as it ordered. The European Council appointed the members of the Bank's executive board.[86] Their actions were to be secret and unaccountable.[87] MEPs could quiz the Bank, but they could not alter its policies, or hold it to account, any more than you or I could change our bank manager's policies, or hold him to account. The difference, of course, was that at least you or I could change our bank. With the European Central Bank, there was no alternative!

Under Article 108, the Governors were forbidden to speak for or represent their countries. The Bank's members, the 'independent' central banks and their Governors, were not accountable to national governments or parliaments. The Bank was bound by treaty not to take instructions from elected national governments, or from any EU body. The ideal of an integrated fiscal and monetary policy is made impossible by the fact that Article 7 of the Treaty specifically forbids the Council from influencing the Bank in any way.[88] When the newly elected German finance minister Oscar Lafontaine called for lower interest rates across Europe, Wim Duisenberg, the ECB's first President, responded, "It is normal for politicians to give their views, but it would be very abnormal if those suggestions are listened to."[89] Duisenberg accurately summed up his approach, "You might say, I hear but I don't listen." This would not be a listening bank! It was illegal for governments to try to influence the Bank: we could be fined for trying. This confirms that the Bank did not represent the sum of its members' national interests, but the single interest of the eurozone considered as a whole.

Article 109h empowered the Commission to decide what measures a member state could take in a balance of payments crisis. Article 109j made binding on members all the Bank's decisions on prices, tax levels, public spending, the single interest rate for all member nations, the single exchange rate against other currencies, and they were enforceable by penalty interest charges and sanctions. If we wanted to spend money investing in industry, the EU could fine us. Article 109j also obliged every country that joined the euro to join the ERM for two years: "Any member State wishing to join but not participating in the Single Currency would have to be a member of the new ERM ..."[90] (A new ERM was formed on 1 January 1999, based around the euro.) Joining the euro would force Britain to repeat our ERM experience, the 1990-92 slump. By Article 123 the Commission and the Bank would decide at what rate Britain would be told to join the euro. This meant that there was no point in any debates about the right rate for Britain: we would have no say. The Bank would not let us enter the euro at a lower rate because this would disadvantage the other countries, to our relative benefit.

The government opted out of Articles 104c, 107 and 109j. However, if Britain entered the euro, we would suffer the whole package. But even the Articles into which we were opted meant an unacceptable loss of sovereignty.

The EU laid down the law, "All Member States must pursue disciplined and responsible monetary policies directed towards price stability." The Treaty bound the Bank to make price stability its only goal, allowing the Bank's directors no flexibility at all. It bound them not to take into account, nor to aim for, economic growth, prosperity, higher wages or full employment. The Bank's single remit was low inflation, even if this meant higher unemployment or no growth. As Horst Welteke, President of the Bundesbank and ECB council member, said on 29 August 2001, "The ECB council does not have the mandate to steer growth but to keep the value of money stable."[91] Duisenberg argued that slower growth in the eurozone was a good thing, because it damped down inflationary pressures. If Britain joined the euro, the ECB's bias to low inflation rather than to low unemployment would force our unemployment levels up towards those in France and Germany.[92]

The EU's Ecofin Council said, "Monetary policy cannot, without adequate support from fiscal and other policies, achieve its objective of price stability ... a Stability and Growth Pact to ensure strict budgetary discipline on an enduring basis is therefore essential." In addition, "There is a system of penalties in place to prevent a Member State, which did not join the Single Currency, from devaluing its currency and gaining a competitive advantage against the euro."[93] So when the British government refused to devalue the pound, it was not acting on its own judgement of what would benefit our economy, but in obedience to EU dictates.

The EU's rulers expressly wanted EMU as the base of a single European state, a United States of Europe.[94] As Jean-Luc Dehaene, a former Prime Minister of Belgium, said, "Monetary union is the motor of European integration."[95] Dr Otmar Issing, Chief Economist of the European Central Bank, observed, "There is no example in history of a lasting monetary union that was not linked to one state." In 1991, the EC's six Christian Democrat leaders asserted 'the irreversibility of the democratic and federal developments of the future union'.[96]

Jacques Delors said, "Yes, we have to have transfers of sovereignty to achieve economic and monetary union. Why deny it?" Delors wrote of the 'Community's spiderlike strategy to organise the architecture of a Greater Europe'.[97] In July 1988, he told the European Parliament, "In ten years, 80% of economic legislation – and perhaps tax and social legislation – will be directed from the Community."[98] His forecast was right: 80% of Britain's administrative law comes from the EU - more than 30,000 Regulations and Directives, and another 50,000 Decisions, guidelines and other instructions.

The EU's leaders designed EMU as a way of locking in the political union that they desired. EMU was supposed to make political union irreversible.[99] Joining the euro, like joining the EU, was supposed to be forever.[100]

EMU was not about economic and monetary cooperation; it was about merging economies as a way of merging states.[101] It threatened sovereignty more than any other EU ploy. As a change in the centre of the economic and social system, it involved the very core of sovereignty, unlike a foreign policy change.[102] EMU decisively shifted power from national authorities to the ECB and the money markets.[103] As Peter Hain observed, "In today's Europe bankers and the money markets rule the roost."[104] Further, the euro would need centralised policing, which would strengthen the drive towards an EU state.

Control of the currency is not a neutral, technical, economic matter; it is at the heart of a country's ability to rule itself. As the great economist John Maynard Keynes said, "Whoever controls the currency, controls the Government." Under EMU, the European Central Bank would control the euro, so it would control the government. Entering the euro would transfer power from national governments to bankers.[105]

The Bank's control of the government would mean that the British people did not and could not control it. Inside the euro, we could vote in a British general election (as we did in 1997) for high growth, thriving industry and good public services, but we would find that our vote made no difference. As the Campaign against Euro-federalism summed it up, "Voters cannot change anything regarding the European single currency by changing the majority in their national parliaments or national governments, or the majority in the European Parliament. The undemocratic nature of EMU and the ECB is written in the detail of the Maastricht Treaty. It cannot be changed without all 15 EU States agreeing in a new Treaty."[106]

Peter Hain, before he became Minister for Europe, wrote that the Bank's "independence to which the EU is now legally committed amounts to the privatisation of monetary policy." He asserted that the Maastricht Treaty "is about as uncompromising as it could be in shielding the bankers from democratic accountability. For socialists such a transfer of power to unelected bankers is completely unacceptable." He warned, "if the monetarist regime of Maastricht were to be implemented in line with the Treaty's legal obligations, democracy would be consigned to the scrapheap. For not only would control of monetary policy be handed over to unelected bankers, control over fiscal policy would be subject to the strict limits prescribed in the Treaty and control over currency levels would be relinquished. What scope would remain for national governments to shape policy in line with their electoral mandates? Virtually none." And he summed up, "The policy, legally enshrined in the Maastricht Treaty, of a European Bank independent of democratic control and dedicated almost exclusively to price stability must be reversed. It is economically disastrous and politically dangerous."[107]

Central banks obey the dictates of the financial markets, which decree an all-out fight against inflation at any cost, so the banks become the deadly enemy of those who earn their living from work.[108] When the ECB's Chief Economist, Otmar Issing, wrote a book on the Bank's monetary policy, he did not mention its impact on jobs or industry.[109] He larded the book with praise for the monetarist Milton Friedman, ignoring his disastrous impact on Chile's economy. Monetarists wrongly claimed that the battle against inflation was the overriding economic aim, because low or zero inflation would produce higher growth.[110] But in the real world, other things being equal, low inflation did not cause high growth but resulted from low growth, and high inflation did not cause low growth but resulted from high growth.[111] Monetarism was a policy of deflation, producing unemployment and low wages. As Keynes said, "Deflation does not reduce wages 'automatically'. It reduces them by causing unemployment." As Bill Morris, General Secretary of the Transport and General Workers' Union, judged, the euro would "enthrone the dogma of laissez-faire economics ever more securely in Europe. If the experience of the last 15 to 20 years world-wide has proved anything, it is that the free market is not the road to full employment." In sum, joining the euro would increase unemployment and lower our wages.

When Major was Chancellor of the Exchequer, he explained to the Treasury and Civil Service Committee on 25 July 1990, "the Delors package for Stage Three would involve transfer of sovereignty from the United Kingdom and from Parliament of a sort that neither the Government nor Parliament would find themselves able to accept." He had warned, "A single currency is about the politics of Europe, it is about a federal Europe by the back door."[112] As he wrote later, "And yet Maastricht had been a fork in the road. Our partners wanted a single currency. We did not. They wanted a Social Chapter. We did not. They wanted more harmonisation of policy. We did not. They wanted more Community control of defence. We did not. Increasingly, they talked in private of a federal destination, even though in public they were reassuring about a Europe of nation states."[113] But instead of vetoing the Maastricht Treaty, he just got an opt-out from EMU's Stage Three.

Only one member country, Denmark, asked its people what they thought of the Maastricht Treaty. In June 1992, they voted 51/49 against it. (In international law, if any of the partners to a treaty fails to ratify it, it has no validity.) Instead of accepting this, the EU's leaders decided to defy democracy. The Danes would be asked again, until they got the answer right. The EU then removed four key matters from the version of the treaty on which the Danes were to vote: defence, EMU, EU citizenship and cooperation on legal and internal affairs. The Danes voted for this unique rump treaty on 18 May 1993. No EU member people has ever voted for the full Maastricht Treaty.

Yet every parliamentary party in Britain backed the Treaty. Since 1992, all the Conservative MEPs have been 'allied members' of the European People's Party (EPP), which wants 'a Federal Union', a single currency and a European Constitution. The EPP aims to assist "the process of unification and federal integration in Europe and contribute to the creation of the United States of Europe." The Socialist Group, including the Labour MEPs, also wants a single EU state and constitution.

For the Conservatives, Kenneth Clarke, Major's Chancellor, boasted, "I have not read the Maastricht Treaty but it doesn't matter because I know what it says." He got the gist of it: "I look forward to the day when the Westminster Parliament is just a Council Chamber in Europe."[114] In 1995, three years after the government of which he was a member had signed the Maastricht Treaty pledging Britain to join EMU and abolish the pound, Clarke wrote, "I can assure you that I am totally unaware of anyone considering the 'abolition of national currencies'." He admitted, "if you go so far as to transfer tax and public spending you are moving near a superstate."[115] Clarke's support for the EEC had a long pedigree: in

1961 he had invited the pro-EEC fascist leader Oswald Mosley to address Cambridge University's Conservative Association.

The US government backed EMU, even though this was not in US interests. Similarly, between the wars, the USA had pressed Britain to return to the gold standard, causing huge damage.[116] At the EU-US Presidential Summit on 7 May 1993, President Bill Clinton said, "We fully support Europe's efforts towards further integration." He said that political and economic union was 'a goal which the United States strongly supports'. Secretary of State Warren Christopher said in 1996 that President Clinton "has been a strong supporter of deeper European integration, reaffirming the commitment made, in earlier years, by President John Kennedy." Clinton said in 1997, "There are a lot of very brilliant people who believe that the nation-state is fast becoming a relic of the past."[117] (This did not apply to the USA.)

6: What is the political aim behind the euro?

We have seen that the EU's leaders intended EMU to lead to PU, political union, a single EU state.[118] They wanted to merge currencies in order to merge states.[119] The euro was about ending national sovereignty and democracy. Some argued that globalisation had already ended national sovereignty. But it made a huge difference whether a country's own government or a supranational body ran its economic and monetary policy. A state that gives up control over its national currency is giving up control over all its significant domestic economic policy choices.[120]

The euro's attack on sovereignty was at the same time an attack on democracy.[121] Entering the euro would take away the democratic control within our trade unions' reach, control over monetary policies through interest and exchange rates, and control over fiscal policies through levying and spending taxes. As the TUC General Council stated, "It is a matter of democracy that citizens should be able to elect governments that raise taxes and are accountable for the delivery of public services. If the public are dissatisfied then they can remove those responsible at a subsequent election."[122] But in the euro, we could neither choose nor remove those who raised taxes, the EU's bodies, primarily the Commission and the

European Central Bank. We would be no more able to choose or remove them than Catholics can choose or remove the Pope.

Endnotes

[1]. Guardian, 9 September 2002.

[2]. See Mark Mazower, Dark continent: Europe's twentieth century, Penguin, 1999, page 205.

[3]. Cited page 136, Cris Shore, Building Europe: the cultural politics of European integration, Routledge, 2000.

[4]. CAB 129/48, C(51)32, cited page 292, David Dutton, Anthony Eden: a life and reputation, Arnold, 1997.

[5]. Cited page 24, Adrian Hilton, The principality and power of Europe: Britain and the emerging Holy European Empire, Dorchester House, 2nd edition, 2000.

[6]. Cited page 40, Michael Charlton, The price of victory, BBC, 1983.

[7]. Cited page 50, John Turner, The Tories and Europe, Manchester University Press, 2000.

[8]. Cited page 392, Kenneth O. Morgan, Labour in power 1945-51, Oxford: Oxford University Press, 1984.

[9]. For details of Monnet's lifelong collaboration with the leaders of the US establishment, see Clifford P. Hackett, Monnet and the Americans: the father of a united Europe and his U.S. supporters, Washington D.C.: Jean Monnet Council, 1995.

[10]. Cited page 147, Cris Shore, Building Europe: the cultural politics of European integration, Routledge, 2000.

[11]. See Larry Siedentop, Democracy in Europe, Allen Lane, 2000, pages 10 and 15.

[12]. Cited page 16, Cris Shore, Building Europe: the cultural politics of European integration, Routledge, 2000.

[13]. Cited page 235, Martin Holland, 'The Common Foreign and Security Policy', Chapter 12, pages 230-46, in Laura Cram, Desmond Dinan and

Neill Nugent, editors, Developments in the European Union, Macmillan, 1999.

[14]. See Michael Charlton, 'The Schuman Plan – losing the initiative', Chapter 4, pages 89-123, in The price of victory, BBC, 1983.

[15]. See Peter Shore, Separate ways: the heart of Europe, Duckworth, 2000, page 11.

[16]. Cited pages 97-8, Scott Lucas, Freedom's war: the US crusade against the Soviet Union 1945-56, Manchester University Press, 1999.

[17]. Cited page 7, Geir Lundestad, 'Empire' by integration: the United States and European integration, 1945-1997, Oxford University Press, 1998.

[18]. Cited page 767, John Campbell, Edward Heath: a biography, Cape, 1993.

[19]. See Andrew Moravcsik, The choice for Europe: social purpose and state power from Messina to Maastricht, UCL Press, 1999, pages 123, 131-2, 134-5 and 164-5.

[20]. Cited page 85, Matt Marshall, The Bank: the birth of Europe's Central Bank and the rebirth of Europe's power, Random House Business Books, 1999.

[21]. Cited page 65, Peter Shore, Separate ways: the heart of Europe, Duckworth, 2000.

[22]. Andrew Moravcsik, The choice for Europe: social purpose and state power from Messina to Maastricht, UCL Press, 1999, page 189.

[23]. See Andrew Moravcsik, The choice for Europe: social purpose and state power from Messina to Maastricht, UCL Press, 1999, pages 193, 224, 265, 282, 292, 303, 308 and 309.

[24]. Andrew Moravcsik, The choice for Europe: social purpose and state power from Messina to Maastricht, UCL Press, 1999, page 282.

[25]. See Richard Corbett, The European Parliament's role in closer EU integration, Macmillan, 1998, pages 40-5.

[26]. See Trevor Hartley, Constitutional problems of the European Union, Oxford: Hart Publishing, 1999, page 12.

[27]. See Christopher Hill, 'United Kingdom: sharpening contradictions', Chapter 3, pages 68-89, in Christopher Hill, editor, The actors in Europe's foreign policy, Routledge, 1996, page 76.

[28]. Cited page 11, Colin Pilkington, Britain in the European Union today, Manchester University Press, 2nd edition, 2001.

[29]. Cited page 248, John Campbell, Edward Heath: a biography, Cape, 1993.

[30]. See David Gowland and Arthur Turner, Reluctant Europeans: Britain and European integration, 1945-1998, Longman, 2000, page 182.

[31]. The National Archive: FO371/150369, 14 December 1960.

[32]. The UK and the European Communities, Cmnd 4715, 7 July 1971.

[33]. Cited page 360, John Campbell, Edward Heath: a biography, Cape, 1993.

[34]. Cited page 82, Adrian Hilton, The principality and power of Europe: Britain and the emerging Holy European Empire, Dorchester House, 2nd edition, 2000.

[35]. See Richard Weight, Patriots: national identity in Britain 1940-2000, Macmillan, 2002, page 482. See also Anthony Sampson, The essential anatomy of Britain: democracy in crisis, Hodder & Stoughton, 1992, page 157; and Desmond Dinan, Ever closer union: an introduction to European integration, Macmillan, 2nd edition, 1999, page 65.

[36]. Cited page 13, Peter Shore, Separate ways: the heart of Europe, Duckworth, 2000.

[37]. Exchange of letters attached to the Treaty of Accession of the United Kingdom, 22 January 1972, cited page 35, Anthony Cowgill and Andrew Cowgill, The Treaty of Nice in Perspective: Volume One - Analysis, British Management Data Foundation, 2001.

[38]. Radio 4, 3 February 2000 at 8 pm, Document: A letter to The Times.

[39]. Radio 4, 3 February 2000 at 8 pm, Document: A letter to The Times.

[40]. Daily Express, 27 May 1975.

[41]. See Anthony Forster, Euroscepticism in contemporary British politics: opposition to Europe in the British Conservative and Labour parties since 1945, Routledge, 2002, page 59. See also Colin Pilkington, Britain in the European Union today, Manchester University Press, 2nd edition, 2001, page 181.

[42]. See David Butler and Uwe Kitzinger, The 1975 referendum, Macmillan, 2nd edition, 1976, page 248.

[43]. Bernard Donoughue, page 205, in 'Harold Wilson and the renegotiation of the EEC terms of membership, 1974-75: a witness account', pages 191-206, in Brian Brivati and Harriet Jones, editors, From reconstruction to integration: Britain and Europe since 1945, Leicester University Press, 1993.

[44]. Daily Telegraph, 27 November 1982.

[45]. See Kenneth Dyson and Kevin Featherstone, The road to Maastricht: negotiating Economic and Monetary Union, Oxford University Press, 1999, page 710.

[46]. See Justin Greenwood, Representing interests in the European Union, New York: St Martin's Press, 1997, pages 1 and 13; Volker Bornschier, page xii, 'Preface', pages xi-xiv, in Volker Bornschier, editor, State-building in Europe: the revitalization of Western European integration, Cambridge University Press, 2000; Colin Pilkington, Britain in the European Union today, Manchester University Press, 2nd edition, 2001, page 199; and Vivien Schmidt, page 177, in 'Convergent pressures, divergent responses: France, Great Britain, and Germany between globalization and Europeanization', Chapter 9, pages 172-92, in David Smith, Dorothy Solinger and Steven Topik, editors, States and sovereignty in the global economy, Routledge, 1999, page 7.

[47]. See Kenneth Dyson and Kevin Featherstone, The road to Maastricht: negotiating Economic and Monetary Union, Oxford University Press, 1999, page 710.

[48]. See Christopher Piening, Global Europe: the European Union in world affairs, Lynne Rienner, 1997, page 36.

[49]. Michael Heseltine, The challenge of Europe: can Britain win? Weidenfeld and Nicolson, 1989, page 23, in his chapter 2, accurately titled, 'Creeping federalism', pages 15-37.

[50]. See John Turner, The Tories and Europe, Manchester University Press, 2000, pages 99 and 108.

[51]. Cited page 108, John Turner, The Tories and Europe, Manchester University Press, 2000.

[52]. See Renaud Dehousse, The European Court of Justice: the politics of judicial integration, Macmillan, 1998, page 162.

[53]. Cited page 96, John Turner, The Tories and Europe, Manchester University Press, 2000.

[54]. See Stephen George and Ian Bache, Politics in the European Union, Oxford University Press, 2001, pages 337-8.

[55]. See George Ross, page 177, in 'European integration and globalization', Chapter 10, pages 164-83, in Roland Axtmann, editor, Globalization and Europe: theoretical and empirical investigations, Pinter, 1998.

[56]. Peter Hain, Ayes to the left: a future for socialism, Lawrence & Wishart, 1995, page 39.

[57]. Peter Hain, Ayes to the left: a future for socialism, Lawrence & Wishart, 1995, page 158.

[58]. Cited page 302, Kenneth Armstrong and Simon Bulmer, The governance of the Single European Market, Manchester University Press, 1998.

[59]. Cited page 78, Charlotte Bretherton and John Vogler, The European Union as a global actor, Routledge, 1999.

[60]. See Charlotte Bretherton and John Vogler, The European Union as a global actor, Routledge, 1999, page 58.

[61]. See Stephan Leibfried and Paul Pierson, page 268, in 'Social policy: left to courts and markets?' Chapter 10, pages 267-92, in Helen Wallace and William Wallace, editors, Policy-making in the European Union, Oxford University Press, 4th edition, 2000.

[62]. See John Turner, The Tories and Europe, Manchester University Press, 2000, page 151.

[63]. See Jeffrey Harrop, The political economy of integration in the European Union, Edward Elgar, 3rd edition, 2000, pages 73-81, especially page 78. See also David Mayes, page 3, 'Introduction', pages 1-27, in David Mayes, editor, The European challenge: industry's response to the 1992 programme, Harvester Wheatsheaf, 1991.

[64]. See Stephen George and Ian Bache, Politics in the European Union, Oxford University Press, 2001, page 336.

[65]. See Lynden Moore, Britain's trade and economic structure: the impact of the European Union, Routledge, 1999, pages 256-7 and 57.

[66]. See Andrew McLaughlin and William Maloney, The European automobile industry: multi-level governance, policy and politics, Routledge, 1999, page 160.

[67]. On the SEM's effects, see Nicholas Costello, Jonathan Michie and Seumas Milne, Beyond the casino economy: planning for the 1990s, Verso, 1989, pages 28, 31, 36 and 44-5.

[68]. See Ken Endo, The Presidency of the European Commission under Jacques Delors: the politics of shared leadership, Macmillan, 1999, page 146, and Margaret Thatcher, The Downing Street years, HarperCollins, 1993, pages 555 and 741.

[69]. Richard Corbett, The European Parliament's role in closer EU integration, Macmillan, 1998, page 316.

[70]. Financial Times, 16 June 1989.

[71]. See Eric Stern and Bengt Sundelius, 'In defence of the Swedish crown: from triumph to tragedy and back?' Chapter 8, pages 135-51, in Pat Gray and Paul 't Hart, editors, Public policy disasters in Western Europe, Routledge, 1998.

[72]. See Brian Burkitt, Mark Baimbridge and Philip Whyman, There is an alternative: Britain and its relationship with the EU, Campaign for an Independent Britain, 1996, pages 23-5. See also John Grahl, After Maastricht: a guide to European Monetary Union, Lawrence & Wishart, 1997, pages 78, 82-102, 104 and 184-5.

[73]. John Grahl, After Maastricht: a guide to European Monetary Union, Lawrence & Wishart, 1997, page 185.

[74]. John Major: the autobiography, HarperCollins, 1999, page 312.

[75]. See David Gowland and Arthur Turner, Reluctant Europeans: Britain and European integration, 1945-1998, Longman, 2000, page 300.

[76]. Linda Colley, Britons: forging the nation, 1707-1837, Yale University Press, 1992. Note the ambiguity of her chosen word 'forging', which can mean both faking and making.

[77]. Benedict Anderson, Imagined communities: reflections on the origin and spread of nations, Verso, 1991.

[78]. See Terence Ranger and Eric Hobsbawm, editors, The invention of tradition, Cambridge University Press, 1992.

[79]. See for example David Cannadine, Class in Britain, Yale University Press, 1998, Ornamentalism: how the British saw their empire, Penguin, 2002, and his article in the Financial Times, 31 October 1998.

[80]. See George Ross, page 172, 'European integration and globalization', Chapter 10, pages 164-83, in Roland Axtmann, editor, Globalization and Europe: theoretical and empirical investigations, Pinter, 1998.

[81]. See the discussion in Larry Siedentop, Democracy in Europe, Allen Lane, 2000, pages 31-2.

[82]. Cited page 157, Renaud Dehousse, The European Court of Justice: the politics of judicial integration, Macmillan, 1998.

[83]. For a useful discussion, see David McKay, Federalism and European Union: a political economy perspective, Oxford University Press, 1999, pages 20-1.

[84]. Andrew Grice, Hain warns of 'creeping federalism' in EU, Independent, 22 July 2002, page 1.

[85]. Matt Marshall, The Bank: the birth of Europe's Central Bank and the rebirth of Europe's power, Random House Business Books, 1999, page 3.

[86]. On the board, see Kenneth Dyson, The politics of the Euro-zone: stability or breakdown? Oxford University Press, 2000, pages 71-2.

[87]. See Kenneth Dyson and Kevin Featherstone, The road to Maastricht: negotiating Economic and Monetary Union, Oxford University Press, 1999, page 791. For more detail on the Bank's modus operandi, see Neill Nugent, The government and politics of the European Union, Macmillan, 4th edition, 1999, pages 293-7.

[88]. John Grieve Smith, There is a better way: a new economic agenda, Anthem Press, 2001.

[89]. Matt Marshall, The Bank: the birth of Europe's Central Bank and the rebirth of Europe's power, Random House Business Books, 1999, page 14.

[90]. Anthony Cowgill and Andrew Cowgill, The Treaty of Nice in Perspective: Volume One - Analysis, British Management Data Foundation, 2001, page 38.

[91]. Cited, Mark Tran, Growing pains for European bank, Guardian, 30 August 2001.

[92]. See Jeffrey Harrop, The political economy of integration in the European Union, Elgar, 3rd edition, 2000, page 322.

[93]. Anthony Cowgill and Andrew Cowgill, The Treaty of Nice in Perspective: Volume One - Analysis, British Management Data Foundation, 2001, page

38.

[94]. See Sidney Pollard, The development of the British economy 1914-1990, Arnold, 4th edition, 1992, pages 429-32.

[95]. See Kenneth Dyson and Kevin Featherstone, The road to Maastricht: negotiating Economic and Monetary Union, Oxford University Press, 1999, pages 273-4.

[96]. Cited page 264, John Major: the autobiography, HarperCollins, 1999.

[97]. Cited page 208, Cris Shore, Building Europe: the cultural politics of European integration, Routledge, 2000.

[98]. Cited page 120, John Turner, The Tories and Europe, Manchester University Press, 2000.

[99]. Kenneth Dyson and Kevin Featherstone, The road to Maastricht: negotiating Economic and Monetary Union, Oxford University Press, 1999, page 273.

[100]. Christian Chabot, Understanding the euro: the clear and concise guide to the new trans-European economy, McGraw-Hill, 1999, page 36.

[101]. On EMU, see Desmond Dinan, Ever closer union: an introduction to European integration, Macmillan, 2nd edition, 1999, Chapter 16, pages 453-81.

[102]. See Kenneth Dyson and Kevin Featherstone, The road to Maastricht: negotiating Economic and Monetary Union, Oxford University Press, 1999, page 194.

[103]. See Kevin Featherstone, page 325, 'The political dynamics of Economic and Monetary Union', Chapter 16, pages 311-29, in Laura Cram, Desmond Dinan and Neill Nugent, editors, Developments in the European Union, Macmillan, 1999.

[104]. Peter Hain, Ayes to the left: a future for socialism, Lawrence & Wishart, 1995, page 155.

[105]. See Kenneth Dyson and Kevin Featherstone, The road to Maastricht:

negotiating Economic and Monetary Union, Oxford University Press, 1999, page 747.

[106]. Single currency is an assault on democracy and sovereignty, Democrat Broadsheet Number 10, Campaign against Euro-federalism, 2001.

[107] Peter Hain, Ayes to the left: a future for socialism, Lawrence & Wishart, 1995, pages 174, 173, 168 and 165-6.

[108]. See William Wolman and Anne Colamosca, The Judas economy: the triumph of capital and the betrayal of work, Addison-Wesley, 1997, pages 141 and 143.

[109]. Otmar Issing et al, Monetary policy in the euro area: strategy and decision-making at the ECB, Cambridge University Press, 2001.

[110]. See John Mills, Managing the world economy, Macmillan, 2000, pages 23 and 127.

[111]. See John Mills, Managing the world economy, Macmillan, 2000, pages 199-203.

[112]. Cited page 145, Adrian Hilton, The principality and power of Europe: Britain and the emerging Holy European Empire, Dorchester House, 2nd edition, 2000.

[113]. John Major: the autobiography, HarperCollins, 1999, page 579.

[114]. Cited page 112, Adrian Hilton, The principality and power of Europe: Britain and the emerging Holy European Empire, Dorchester House, 2nd edition, 2000.

[115]. On Jonathan Dimbleby, BBC, 1999.

[116]. Frank Costigliola, Awkward dominion: American political, economic, and cultural relations with Europe, 1919-1933, Cornell University Press, 1984, page 112.

[117]. Cited New York Times, 25 November 1997.

[118]. See Cris Shore, Building Europe: the cultural politics of European

integration, Routledge, 2000, page 17. See also Stephen Cope, page 47, 'The Europeanisation of British policy-making', Chapter 3, pages 34-48, in Stephen Savage and Rob Atkinson, editors, Public policy under Blair, Palgrave, 2001; Edward Nevin, The economics of Europe, Macmillan, 1990, page 284; Martin Feldstein, page 60, EMU and international conflict, Foreign Affairs, November/December 1997, Volume 76, Number 6, pages 60-73; Ali El-Agraa, The European Union: history, institutions, economics, politics, Prentice Hall Europe, 5th edition, 1998, page 563; and Laura Cram, Desmond Dinan and Neill Nugent, page 355, in 'The evolving European Union', Chapter 18, pages 353-65, in Laura Cram, Desmond Dinan and Neill Nugent, editors, Developments in the European Union, Macmillan, 1999.

[119]. See Paul de Grauwe, Economics of monetary integration, Oxford University Press, 4th edition, 2000, page 215. See also Jeffrey Harrop, The political economy of integration in the European Union, Edward Elgar, 3rd edition, 2000, page 1; Ali El-Agraa, The European Union: history, institutions, economics, politics, Prentice Hall Europe, 5th edition, 1998, page 15; Christian Chabot, Understanding the euro: the clear and concise guide to the new trans-European economy, McGraw-Hill, 1999, pages 37-8; Kenneth Dyson and Kevin Featherstone, The road to Maastricht: negotiating Economic and Monetary Union, Oxford University Press, 1999, page 1; Martin Feldstein, page 60, EMU and international conflict, Foreign Affairs, November/December 1997, Volume 76, Number 6, pages 60-73; and Clive Archer, The European Union: structure and process, Continuum, 3rd edition, 2000, page 95.

[120]. See John McCormick, Understanding Europe: a concise introduction, Macmillan, 1999, page 195. See also Martin Holland, European integration: from Community to Union, Pinter, 1994, page 198; Amy Verdun, European responses to globalization and financial market integration: perceptions of Economic and Monetary Union in Britain, France and Germany, Macmillan Press, 2000, pages 1 and 212; George Ross, page 171, 'European integration and globalization', Chapter 10, pages 164-83, in Roland Axtmann, editor, Globalization and Europe: theoretical and empirical investigations, Pinter, 1998; Richard Corbett, The European Parliament's

role in closer EU integration, Macmillan, 1998, page 327; Paul Teague, Economic citizenship in the European Union: employment relations in the new Europe, Routledge, 1999, page 165; Anthony Giddens, Runaway world: how globalisation is reshaping our lives, Profile Books, 1999, page 80; and John Turner, The Tories and Europe, Manchester University Press, 2000, page 3.

[121]. See Richard Cooper, page 70, 'Yes to European monetary union, but no to the Maastricht Treaty', Chapter 5, pages 69-71, in Alfred Steinherr, editor, 30 years of European monetary integration from the Werner Plan to EMU, Longman, 1994. See also Cris Shore, Building Europe: the cultural politics of European integration, Routledge, 2000, page 94.

[122]. TUC General Council statement, 25 July 2001.

Chapter 2: European Union 1992-2002

1: Our unique trade unions

2: The trade unions and the employers

3: Towards the single EU state (1992-97)

4: The Labour government promotes the euro

5: The Nice Treaty (2000) and federalism

6: We win the referendum on the euro

*	The former Prime Minister of Spain, Felipe Gonzalez, wrote, "The single currency is the greatest abandonment of sovereignty since the foundation of the European Community ... It is a decision of an essentially political nature ... We need this united Europe ... we must never forget that the euro is an instrument for this project."[1]

*	"Joining the euro in the foreseeable future would therefore increase unemployment in Britain substantially." Business for Sterling Memorandum to the Treasury Select Committee, 26 July 2000.

*	In October 2000, in Denmark, the only country where the people had ever been asked their opinion about the euro, they voted for the second time against joining. Before the referendum, supporters of the euro had threatened that if Denmark did not join, interest rates and unemployment would soar, and wages and the krone would plummet. What happened? Interest rates fell, no jobs were lost, wages rose and the krone was stable.

*	On 14 September 2003, Sweden held a referendum on whether to join. On an 81% turnout, the Swedish people voted against by 56% to 42%. Interestingly, the polling companies had predicted a Yes win, Gallup by 1%, Ruab by 0.2%, predictions that Yes supporters publicised widely just before the real poll. However, no European nation has yet voted for the euro.

1: Our unique trade unions

Our trade union concept in Britain is that you are a trade union member first and foremost. Where you work is secondary and incidental: our skill defines us, not our employer. Our trade unions are based on the workplace. This tradition of workplace trade union organisation is unique to Britain.[2] The state, in the form of the law, had no place in setting the rules at work: workers decided the rules in daily workplace struggle with the employer.[3] This continual decision-making at work is an essential component of democracy.

The trade union movement succeeded in defeating successive British governments' efforts to end this voluntarism. Labour's 'In Place of Strife' in 1969, the Conservatives' 1971 Industrial Relations Act and Labour's Social Contract of 1974-76 had all imposed state controls on trade unions. Barbara Castle made explicit the underlying anti-democratic aim of these efforts at state control - to make workplace struggles unnecessary: "I believe the Social Contract drawn up by the Labour government of 1970 is still the key. It is designed to persuade wage-earners that their government, given its chance, can do more to improve their standard of living than any wage negotiation can do."[4] The effect, as we have seen, was to worsen, not improve, peoples' standards of living.

By contrast, the EU concept was that you worked for a company first, belonged to its works council second and possibly to a company union third. This model grew up in countries that had to cope with fascist regimes, had lower levels of trade union membership than in Britain and often had trade union centers split on sectarian lines. In France, for instance, only 10% of workers are in unions and too many of them rely on the law, not on their organisations. EU law increasingly intervened in workplaces, not to extend rights but to prevent trade unionism.[5] Adopting this European model in Britain would take us back nearly 200 years.

We can send representatives to Brussels when we need to find out about, say, proposed anti-union laws or industrial closures. We welcomed the benefits that we gained from the EU, like paternity rights, parity in rights for part-time workers, the working time directive, health and safety directives, consultation for redundancy. The question remains, why don't we make the gains ourselves? For what has been conceded can all too easily be taken back. The test is whether the roles, actions and decisions benefit the members. We need to keep an independent mind and always ask what strings are attached.

Trade unions are entitled to use every avenue to defend their members' interests, and trade union members are entitled to act as necessary to advance their interests. Different levels of engagement have different purposes: trade unions know the difference between pragmatic decisions and becoming incorporated, between using EU bodies and being used by them. Britain's trade unions had opposed Thatcher's privatisations and deregulation, but this opposition was compromised by their support for EU integration.[6]

Some said that the Social Charter can help our struggle for wages and jobs.[7] But it does not cover small and medium-sized businesses; it does not protect pay or the right to strike or most other forms of industrial action or the right to belong to trade unions. It does nothing for the unemployed. Its protection of economic and social rights is a charade, because there is no mechanism for enforcing it.[8] The Dutch president of the Personal Representatives' Group in charge of negotiating the Amsterdam Treaty said of its clauses on workers' rights, "We have to find some nice words, provided they will have absolutely no effect."[9]

The EU tries to use the European Trades Union Congress as a top level of trade unionism to give direction to national trade unions just as the Commission does to national civil services. The Commission gives the ETUC four million ECUs a year enabling it to employ 49 staff.[10] The Commission also helps the ETUC with translation costs and spent 31 million ECUs in 1992-93 to support pilot works councils. However, the ETUC is a wholly artificial construction created by EU bureaucrats, completely divorced from workers and their workplaces. It is a lobby dependent on the EU structures that are implementing the EU regime of deregulation and privatisation.

The ETUC's major goal for the past twenty years was the European Works Council Directive, designed to create European-wide works councils that could take part in Europe-level collective bargaining to drive up wages and conditions across the EU. The Directive passed in September 1994 achieved neither aim: it said that the councils' consultations with the employer "shall not affect the prerogatives of the central management."[11]

The EU has a common trade union policy, to destroy our trade unions and replace them by toothless works councils. Germany's works councils are forbidden by law to strike or engage in collective bargaining.[12] Across the EU, many works councils meet only once a year.[13] EU employers did not want to negotiate with trade unions. Jacques Delors may have promoted social dialogue – but the difficulty was finding employers willing to talk or negotiate.[14] The EU's 2001 publication Employment in Europe never mentioned unions once in 142 pages.

General Motors' director for European industrial relations said that the sole purpose of its works council was "to contain the influence of the German unions."[15] The TGWU gave another example: "Pepsi-Cola went even further and tried to by-pass the unions in its voluntarily negotiated agreement. This American-owned TNC took the initiative in setting up its EWC by calling 'snap elections' and putting forward its own candidates. Thus, fifteen of the twenty-one employee representatives attending the first meeting, at which its structure would be determined, were pro-company, non-union people. Even these were put in hotel rooms with no phone and a personnel manager as room mate. The IUF [International Union of Food, Agricultural, Hotel, Restaurant, Catering, Tobacco, and Allied Workers' Associations] representative was barred from the meeting. The structure that was negotiated gives the company the initiative and the right to set the agenda at all future meetings and explicitly excludes the IUF."[16]

Some writers about society, Will Hutton and Anthony Giddens for example, claimed that we were all stakeholders in a community, a civil society with a common interest. This 'Third Way' reconciled - but only in theory - capital and labour, dismissing class conflict as reactionary and out of date. But in the real world, the two opposing classes have conflicting interests: higher wages/lower wages, full employment/mass unemployment, rebuilding the economy/freeing capital. And the British people know this: polls show that larger and larger majorities accept that there is class conflict. The problem with all these 'Third way' alternatives to struggle is that the capitalist class is clearly waging class war to raise profits and cut wages and that governments are doing their bidding. An atomised 'civil society' is no counterweight to capital. The only opposition is the organised working class.

Our trade union struggles are basically national, where we live, work and fight. The working class can mount opposition to capitalism and its governments at the national level.[17] This is where capitalism has to win. So our class has to wage the basic economic struggle to preserve or improve living standards and working conditions through direct conflict with the employers. Attempts to leap over our trade unions and their struggle or to ignore them in favour of civil society or the 'community' are recipes for permanent subjection.[18]

For trade unions to focus on Brussels is a diversion from the necessary work of recruiting to and rebuilding our trade unions in the workplace. Growing strength at the workplace leads to growing national influence, not vice versa.[19] We may have the right to recognition but all too often did not use it. We have the minimum wage, and mass unemployment. We should not belittle our gains, but we need to see them in the perspective of our long-term aims of a full-employment, high-growth economy.

On 12 May 1999, the TUC held a conference in London on 'Trade unions and the euro', intended to promote early entry into the euro. Eight of the nine platform speakers spoke for it. However, the Community and Youth Workers' Union published that morning the results of an ICM poll that it had commissioned. The poll showed that 61% of trade unionists opposed entry and only 15% supported the call for early entry. 79% said that they had received no information, despite the call from the 1998 TUC for debate throughout the trade union movement. The debate at the conference also showed that the call for early entry did not reflect the membership's wishes. Trade unionists maintain this high level of opposition.

Opposing EMU is neither 'left wing' nor 'right wing', as the divisions within Labour, Liberal Democrat and Tory ranks show. Some said that they supported entering the euro because the Conservative Party opposed it. Did they oppose it when the Conservative Party supported it? And, if the Tories changed back to supporting the euro, would they then change to opposing it? Some claimed that they supported the euro because the Conservative Party's right wing opposed joining the euro and its left wing supported joining the euro. Would they have backed those left wing Tories like R. A. Butler who appeased Hitler and opposed those right wing

Tories who opposed Hitler? Some seem to want to fight Thatcher decades too late – a mirror image of those Tories who still worship at her shrine.

Within the trade union movement there is fierce debate. Some, notably TUC general secretary John Monks, whom employers saw as compliant to their interests - an article in Business Week described him as willing to 'deliver on needed cuts in pay and benefits' - cheer on the euro crusade.[20] Some union leaders try to persuade us that 'EMU is inevitable'. But it is no more inevitable, and no less absurd, for a union to join an employers' organisation than for an independent country to join the euro. It is only inevitable in the sense that if you choose to step off a cliff, you inevitably fall. But we do not have to step off! Some claim that there is no alternative, echoing Thatcher's justification in the 1980s of her discredited policies. 'Inevitably' and 'no alternative' are not words and phrases suited to democracy.

Bill Morris of the TGWU warned that the labour movement faced the danger of 'a headlong rush into the single currency, bringing huge cuts in public spending and public service at a time of slowing economic growth'.[21] On 3 July 2001, he said that joining the euro should not depend just on passing the five tests, but also on the EU's achieving more transparency and democracy in its institutions, including the European Central Bank and the European Parliament - two tests even more difficult to pass![22]

In September 2002, the TUC changed its policy. It passed a motion on the euro stating, "Congress does not believe that the interests of manufacturing industry, public services and the trade union movement will be best served by a referendum on the European Single Currency unless a sustainable exchange rate between the pound and the euro is achieved; greater government support for the consolidation and expansion of the European Social Model is demonstrated; and assurances regarding any repercussions of entry on public expenditure are received.

Congress supports the policy of the Government that the five tests set by the Chancellor of the Exchequer will define whether a clear and unambiguous case for joining the euro can be made. The high pound is damaging British industry. Congress calls on the Government to give priority attention to bolstering British manufacturing, and to ensuring that our public service provision and workers' rights are enhanced to the level of our EU partners. Congress therefore calls on the Government to bring forward its assessment of the five economic tests.

In preparation for a referendum Congress calls on the General Council to place before each Congress prior to any such referendum factual information concerning prices, unemployment, growth, public expenditure, the Stability and Growth Pact and industrial relations in each of the eurozone countries."

The absence of such objective information-gathering by the General Council in 2001-02 nearly led to the reference back of its report on its work over the year. Only 52% of the delegates voted for the report, which was just a mask to enable Monks to campaign for the euro regardless. Reports wrongly said that a General Council statement on the euro had been passed. Not so – although Council statements take precedence over motions, on this occasion there was no statement, so the motion alone was to guide the Council's work over the coming year.

The rush for the euro that Monks and a few other Council members wanted was stopped. The TUC adopted a more critical negotiating position. In effect the British trade union movement added a new test for the nation that must be passed before a referendum could be held: are we as a trade union movement sure that the euro would be in our best interests?

2: The trade unions and the employers

The European Commission, the employers and their agents promoted the myths that every country consisted of a happy middle class majority, with an inevitable backward underclass of losers. Their proposed remedy was a condescending social policy of partnership and inclusion. But as long ago as 1936, David Lloyd George wrote, "In a modern industrial state, the vast bulk of the population consists of wage-earners and those dependent on them."[23] The word worker refers to any person who earns his or her living from going to work, whether in factory or office, school or hospital. The need to work for a living distinguishes workers from capitalists, those who get their money mainly from owning assets.[24] All of us who depend on our work to make our living have to organise in our workplaces and unions to improve our wages and conditions.

The EU's overriding goal was doing what European businesses wanted.[25] The Commission openly promoted the EU as a free enterprise role model for the Eastern European countries.[26] Big firms controlled the EU to such an extent that many thought that EU stood for Employers' Union.[27] Michael Heseltine stated, "we are creating a capitalist Europe."[28]

Those who looked to the EU for protection against further privatisations should note that the Commission's White Paper Growth, Competitiveness, Employment of June 1993, proposed, "certain services for which the State has been responsible hitherto and which are subject to increasingly tight budget restrictions could be transferred permanently to the market. There are many examples of such new services related to communication and social relations: education and training, culture, security, etc."[29] They should also note that the previous President of the Commission, Romano Prodi, as Italy's Minister for Industry, and Prime Minister from May 1996 to October 1998, was largely responsible for driving through Europe's biggest-ever privatisation programme.[30] Jose Manuel Barroso, the current President, did the same to Portugal.

The EU was an agent of, not a barrier to, globalising capital. Its deregulatory agenda strengthened the effects of globalisation and financial liberalisation.[31] EU unification was not a defensive response to global capital; it oiled the 'globalising' process.[32]

The EU promoted global deregulation and privatisation, earlier through the failed Multilateral Agreement on Investment, after 1995 through the newly formed World Trade Organization (WTO). In December 1998, the European Council stated "its commitment to the WTO as the basis for the EU's commercial policy and the main framework for further trade liberalisation. It reaffirms its support for comprehensive, wide-ranging WTO negotiations."[33] The European Commission resurrected the MAI's basic ideas in its action plan on the Transatlantic Economic Partnership. The WTO, like the IMF and the World Bank, was designed to assist the giant firms in the dominant countries to exploit the world's resources.[34]

The EU was allied to other key agents of globalisation like the International Chamber of Commerce, the World Business Council for Sustainable Development, the Bilderberg Group, the Trilateral Commission and the World Economic Forum. These aimed to run the United Nations; for instance, they used the UN Development Programme to set up their Global Sustainable Development Facility.

Some now write of the 'globalisation' promoted by the EU and the US government as a new, irreversible and beneficent process. But what did 'globalisation' really do to nations' economies? The US and European ruling classes demanded liberalisation, deregulation and indebtedness, fuelling the crises in Asia, Latin America, the former USSR, etc. US and EU companies gain from cheap buyouts of banks and corporations, exploit low-wage labour and exercise greater control over trade and economic policies. Huge amounts of profits and interest accrue to companies headquartered in the USA and Europe. Globalisation as a concept expresses an idea of an irreversible uniform spread of benefits across the world. But what we experience is rather a concentration of wealth and power from which a tiny minority gains at the expense of the vast majority.[35]

The financial liberalisation of recent decades put a brake on output, investment and productivity.[36] Mexico, for instance, grew by 6% a year between 1951 and 1981 when it pursued industrialisation and protectionist policies. But when it joined the North American Free Trade Agreement in 1994, the economy, jobs and wages all collapsed.[37] Between 1980 and 1999, labour's share of Mexico's national income was cut from 38% to 27%.

Business leaders used the regional groupings - the EU, NAFTA, the Association of South East Asian Nations and Mercosur, the Southern Cone Common Market of Latin America - to get together to impose lower wages and worse conditions.[38] All these continental groupings are created in order to add to the powers of billionaire investors and exporters.[39]

Jose Lutzenberger, former Brazilian Minister of the Environment, pointed out, "We must realise that all these new free-trade arrangements, NAFTA, GATT and so on, were not made to benefit ordinary people. They were conceived by the powerful for the powerful. Transnational corporations need global markets not only to get cheap resources from the Third World, but also to destroy within their own countries the social conquests of their workers."[40] The EU's Treaties belonged with the other capitalist agreements; the EU clearly belonged with openly capitalist organisations, exploiting its own workers and the workers of the other continents.[41]

What did globalisation do politically? It used the links between capitals based in different countries to make decisions behind people's backs. It tried to impose its own priority of profit against people's demands for control over their lives and work. It subordinates nations to capital.[42] It undercut democracy and national sovereignty. Global capital was, for now, out of democratic control, but it did not have to be. Capital, not people's needs or demands, drives capitalist societies. Globalisation was supposed to strengthen the employer's hand, by adding weight to their threats to move abroad. The threat to enlarge the EU to include states from Eastern Europe played a similar role.

But globalisation's effects on political and economic independence were overstated.[43] Nations could, when they wished, control capital, shape their economic lives and assert their political power. But one could not expect bankers, either in the ECB or in national banks, to control capital! Trade unions had a far stronger bargaining position than employers made out.[44] Employers often threatened to move, but rarely did so because moving had huge costs. During the 1990s, US foreign direct investment in manufacturing in Asia, Africa and Latin America was only 1% of gross private investment. Capital did not just rush to the cheapest labour: if it did, Africa would have more than 1.5% of global investment. Capital has followed sales opportunities and other locational advantages rather than just cheap labour.[45] Employers' physical capital made them far less mobile than all the talk about footloose capital implied. They had high sunk costs in plant, infrastructure, subcontracted production and supply networks and services, skilled workers and local knowledge.

Global capital, to expand, still depended on having workers to exploit. The more skilled the workers, the greater the profits, so the greater the employer's dependence on them. But the more skilled the workers, the more organised they were. And organised workers could pin back and defeat the employer. An individual worker was no match for an employer, but the history of the 20th century showed again and again that organised workers could defeat not just a single employer but all of them.

Like the EU, the British Empire was a form of globalisation that denied self-rule to its member nations. It too was based on exploitation and ruled by force and fraud. Trade unions traditionally opposed this form of forced unity, so why should they back the new EU form?

The EU was designed by business for business. Our trade unions should retrieve and reassert national sovereignty, taking their place in the worldwide struggle against the transnational companies.

3: Towards the single EU state 1992-97

All the EU's leaders, except the British ones, make no secret of their aim to create a single European state based on a single currency, the euro, with a single system of tax and spending, a single government, a single citizenship, a single frontier, a single army, a single flag, and a single system of criminal law. Every EU initiative follows a single agenda, dissolving Europe's independent states into a single state. The EU's own publication, The ABC of Community Law, stated, "The EC has areas of responsibilities which together constitute essential attributes of statehood." It said that the EU is "in the process of acquiring a status similar to that of an individual state."[46]

Walter Hallstein, the first Commission President, set out the agenda - 'Customs union, economic union, political union'. The EU's direction was clear, witness the shift from the earlier 'common' market to the more recent 'single' market. 'Common' meant a voluntary sharing in a community of individual member states, but 'single' implied a union into a single state.

The EU's rulers used the Maastricht Treaty as a stepping stone towards full political union in a single EU state. Chancellor Helmut Kohl told the Council of Europe in 1995, "We want the political unification of Europe. If there is no monetary union, then there cannot be political union, and vice versa."[47] He also said, "In Maastricht we laid the foundation stone for the completion of the European Union. The European Union Treaty introduces a new and decisive stage in the process of European Union which within a few years will lead to the creation of what the founding fathers of modern Europe dreamed after the last war: the United States of Europe."[48]

The former Prime Minister of Spain, Felipe Gonzalez, wrote, "The single currency is the greatest abandonment of sovereignty since the foundation of the European Community ... It is a decision of an essentially political nature ... We need this united Europe ... we must never forget that the euro is an instrument for this project."[49]

Bundesbank President Hans Tietmeyer said, "A country that merges its currency with that of another cannot be politically independent." He also said, "A European currency will lead to member nations transferring their sovereignty over financial and wage policy as well as in monetary affairs. It is an illusion to think that states can hold on to their autonomy over taxation policy."[50] In March 1995 he said, "It is more than a union of central banks - a system which decides monetary policy. Every politician, and I think every voter in the country, should be aware that monetary union is more. It has a political dimension." He also pointed out, "Monetary union is a path of no return. No subsequent revision or withdrawal of any kind is either legally or politically provided for."

The Bundesbank's Annual Report of 1995 said, "As a monetary union represents a lasting commitment to integration which encroaches in the core area of national sovereignty, the EMU participants must also be prepared to take further steps towards a more comprehensive political union." The German Christian Democratic Union consistently called for a single state in which the European Commission would "take on the features of a European Government." The SDP-Green coalition government that succeeded Kohl in 1998 followed the same policy. Oskar Lafontaine, its first Finance Minister, said, "the United States of Europe has been the aim of the [German] Social Democratic Party all along."[51] As ex-President of Germany Herzog said, "Our aim is the end of the nation state." Helmut Schlesinger, former Bundesbank President, said, "The primary target of a monetary union - as well as the whole history of the European Community - is a political one." Karl Lamers, the foreign policy spokesman for Germany's Christian Democratic Union, said, "monetary union is the cornerstone of political union", "economic and monetary union is the central part of the project for European unification" and "the Commission will take on the features of a European Government."

Irish Foreign Minister Ruairi Quinn agreed that the euro was political not economic in aim, saying, "EMU is undoubtedly and fundamentally a political project." John Bruton, former Prime Minister of Ireland, said,

"Economic and Monetary Union is, in the final analysis, a political project." Charlie McCreevy, Irish Finance Minister, said, "Economic and Monetary Union is one of the most far-reaching and momentous steps of the European Union exercise."

The French Foreign Minister Herve de Charette said in June 1996, "The Franco-German axis must continue to fulfill its federating function ... The single currency project is the principal and ... only European federating project ... the powerfully federalist character of this project has yet to be appreciated."[52] Jean-Claude Trichet, Governor of the Bank of France, said, "The Council of Ministers will have far more power over the budgets of member states than the federal government in the United States has over the budget of Texas." Former French Premier Rocard said in September 1996, "The euro will lead inevitably to the formation of a single government to control the European Central Bank. Once we have a single currency, we will immediately have a single foreign policy." Dominique Strauss-Kahn, a French Finance Minister, said, "The euro will lead to an economic government of Europe." He also said, "The Euro is a conquest of sovereignty."

In June 1997, the Treaty of Amsterdam took us further towards a single EU state. It brought both the Common Foreign and Security Policy, and Justice and Home Affairs, within the EU's Treaties, putting them under the Commission's control and under the European Court of Justice's jurisdiction. It aimed at 'bringing about the legal termination of the independence, sovereignty and right to self-government for all time'. It also included the Stability and Growth Pact, designed to enforce the economic policies decided by the EU. Again, the new Labour government could have vetoed the treaty, but did not.

After the euro's launch on 1 January 1999, German Foreign Minister Joschka Fischer told the European Parliament, "For the first time in the history of the European integration process ... an important part of national sovereignty, to wit monetary sovereignty, has passed over to a European institution ... the introduction of a common currency is not primarily an economic, but rather a sovereign and thus eminently political act."[53] He pointed out, "The federation exists already in Frankfurt, in the European Central Bank. The euro is a first step towards the final objective." He said,

"Transforming the EU into a single state, with one army, one constitution and one foreign policy is the critical challenge of the age."[54] And, "The top priority is to turn the EU into a single political state."[55] In May 2000, he said, "At Maastricht, one of the three essential sovereign rights of the modern nation-state - currency, internal security and external security - was for the first time transferred to the sole responsibility of a European institution. The introduction of the euro was not only the crowning-point of economic integration, it was also a profoundly political act, because a currency is not just another economic factor but also symbolises the power of the sovereign who guarantees it." Fischer said, "Currency, security and constitution, those are the three essential components of the sovereignty of modern nation states, and the introduction of the euro constituted the first move towards their communitarisation in the EU." He called for "a transition from a union of states to full parliamentarization as a European Federation ... And that means nothing less than a European Parliament and a European Government which really do exercise legislative and executive power within the Federation. This Federation will have to be based in a constituent Treaty."[56]

The Berliner Zeitung wrote approvingly that Fischer "presented a vision which goes much further than that of Kohl: a federation which is hardly in any way different from a federal state like the United States of America." Fischer also said, "Let us be clear – the eleven countries in the euro have already given up part of their sovereignty. They have transferred it to the EU. Adopting the euro was a step towards a certain objective. We try to avoid the word federation, but how else can it be described? It is a democratic federation. We have a federation already."[57] Fischer said at Humboldt University, Berlin, on 12 May 2000, "If we are to meet this historic challenge, and integrate the new member states without substantially denting the EU's capacity for action, we must put into place the last brick in the building of European integration, namely political integration ... This last step will then be the completion of integration in a European Federation. ... Such a group of states would conclude a new European framework treaty, the nucleus of the constitution of the Federation. On the basis of this treaty, the Federation would develop its own institutions, establish a government which, within the EU, would speak with one voice

... a strong parliament and a directly elected president. Such a driving force would have to be the avant-garde, the driving force for the completion of political integration."

Italy's Treasury Minister, Carlo Ciampi, said, "The euro is a decisive step towards the ever closer political union of Europe." He also said, "Common responsibility for the European currency will also engender a common decision-making instance for the European economy. It is unthinkable to have a European Central Bank but not a common leadership for the European economy. If there is no counterweight to the ECB in European economic policy, then we will be left with the incomplete construction which we have today ... However, even if the building is not finished it is still true that monetary union is part of a supranational constitution ... It is our task for the future to work with the appropriate means for the transfer of traditional elements of national sovereignty to the European level." Ciampi went on, "It is therefore the duty of those countries which already belong to the EU to encourage the concept of supranationalism."

Wim Duisenberg, the monetarist President of the European Central Bank, said, "the process of monetary union goes hand in hand, must go hand in hand, with political integration and ultimately political union. EMU is, and was always meant to be, a stepping stone on the way to a united Europe."[58]

Jacques Santer, Delors' successor as Commission President, said, "The realisation of the Economic and Currency Union is not possible without a political union."[59] He described finalising the euro's original membership as, 'a landmark date on which European integration took on a new momentum'. He also said, "It is now up to us to see that we embark on the next stage leading to political unity, which I think is the consequence of economic unity, so that Europe can in the future also play a political role on the international stage, leading even as far as a common defence policy." The Commissioner for Monetary Union, Yves-Thibault de Silguy, said in November 1998, "The debate in the UK has always underestimated the momentum behind Economic and Monetary Union."

Laurent Fabius, French Foreign Minister, said on 9 May 2000, "Yes, it is an economic government, if you like, that is what we are going to do."

Pierre Moscovici, France's Minister for Europe, proposed in June 2000 that the Commission should stay the same size, or even reduce its size, after new members join the EU: "there should still be twenty – or fewer than twenty – even if there are thirty members because a government needs to be a close knit group."[60] He also said, "We are saying that together we can build a new superpower, and its name will be Europe."[61]

Romano Prodi told the European Parliament on 13 October 1999, "The single market was the theme of the Eighties; the single currency was the theme of the Nineties; we must now face the difficult task of moving towards a single economy, a single political entity. For the first time since the fall of the Roman Empire we have the opportunity to unite Europe." He said, "The euro can only lead to closer and closer integration of countries' economic policies ... This demands that member states give up more sovereignty." And, "The euro was not just a banker's decision or a technical decision. It was a decision that completely changed the nature of the nation state. The pillars of the nation state are the sword and the currency and we changed that. The euro decision changed the concept of the nation state and we have to go beyond that... The real goal is to draw on the consequences of the single currency and create a political Europe." He wrote, "the renunciation of one's right to coin money is a huge political decision. The state is, in fact, giving up one of its most cherished instruments of sovereignty."[62] In November 1999 he said, "Here in Brussels, a true European government has been born." He went on, "I have governmental powers, I have executive powers for which there is no other name in the world, whether you like it or not, than 'government'." He constantly referred to his European Commission as the 'government of Europe'. In February 2000, he said, "European government is a clear expression I still use. You need time, but step by step the European Commission takes a political decision and behaves like a growing government."[63]

On 9 February 2000, Prodi launched a five-year plan for the EU, 'Shaping the New Europe: Strategic Objectives 2000-2005'. It showed the EU's leaders' clear intent to create a single European state. It admitted, "there is hardly any sector of social and economic activity not affected by European Union policy and legislation, and where authorities in the Member States are not part and parcel of European governance." It hailed the Common Agricultural Policy as a model for 'the establishment of a mechanism for collective governance'. The document went on, "Over the next decade we will complete our economic integration and, even more importantly, give shape to a new political Europe. The next five years will be decisive ... The Commission has a pivotal role to play. It is Europe's executive arm, the initiator of ideas and proposals and the guardian of the Treaties. The Commission has always been the driving force for European integration, and it will provide strong leadership in years to come."[64] Prodi wanted to abolish every veto: as he said, "After 2006 no more decisions can be taken by unanimity."[65] He told the European Parliament on 13 February 2001, "Are we all clear that we want to build something that can aspire to be a world power? In other words, not just a trading bloc but a political entity. Do we realise that our nation states, taken individually, would find it far more difficult to assert their existence and their identity on the world stage?" He said on 29 May 2001, "The genius of the founding fathers lay in translating extremely high political ambitions, which were present from the beginning, into a series of more specific, almost technical decisions. This indirect approach made further action possible."

Gerhard Schroeder, Germany's Chancellor, said at The Hague on 19 January 1999, "The introduction of the euro is probably the most important integrating step since the beginning of the unification process. It will have consequences that nobody can fully assess at present. It is certain that the times of individual national efforts regarding employment policies, social and tax policies are definitely over. The internal market and the common currency demand joint co-coordinating action. This will require us to bury finally some erroneous ideas of national sovereignty." He said, "The introduction of the common European currency was ultimately by no means only an economic decision. It was an original political act to hand over sovereignty over one of the most important areas of national authority to a European authority ... For this reason alone, monetary union requires of us Europeans decisive advances in the field of political integration. ... Of course the risks will remain, especially if we don't follow up the bold step that led to a single currency with further bold steps towards political integration." At a Brussels press conference on 29 May 1999, he said, "It will be necessary to encourage those member states in this direction who perhaps have not yet gone as far, or do not wish to go so far on the subject of integration." On 19 January 2001, he told the Bundestag, "Only ever further integration will be capable of counteracting the centrifugal forces in an enlarged EU. We are ready for that. So is France."

Fischer told the European Parliament's Constitutional Affairs Committee in June 2000 that 'the European federation' increasingly resembled 'a United States of Europe'. In October 2000, he forecast that the EU would be a federation by 2010, and that Britain would be part of it. In November, he said that the EU would become a 'fully sovereign' state that would be completed by 2005. He called for "the development of a European federation which would develop its own institutions, especially a government which within the European Union should speak with one voice on behalf of the members of the Group on as many issues as possible with a strong parliament and a directly elected President. The last step will then be the completion of integration in a European federation."[66]

In July 2000, the European Parliament proclaimed that the euro was 'an essential identity-building factor in the process of European integration'.[67] It had passed a Resolution, on 22 October 1998, saying, "In order to ensure its political future the European Union must go beyond the completion of the internal market and the introduction of the single currency and move towards a real political union." Its President said, "The Parliament and the Commission are allies against the member states. Together we have to prevent the member states from taking back power."[68]

The President of the European Parliament, Nicole Fontaine, said on 13 October 2000, "With regard to closer cooperation, Parliament is open to making it more flexible and extending it, given that 'closer integration' is in the natural order of things. But we have always said that we want to avoid any risk of closer cooperation fragmenting Community powers, causing legal confusion and blurring the Union's image when what is actually needed is a far more high profile and intelligible Union, both domestically and internationally, so that the Union can finally start playing its proper role on the world scene." She also said, "What is at stake is the long term survival and credibility of the Union's institutions. The first priority is of course extending qualified-majority voting, with its natural corollary, codecision. I know that, yes, progress has been made in some forty areas. This is hardly negligible, what counts is not the number forty. What counts is how we envisage the enlarged European Union of tomorrow. What are its long-term prospects? In this connection, the combined effect of the two fundamental principles which govern the single market, namely freedom of movement and fair competition, mean that sooner or later all issues linked to economic activity will, in one way or another, become essential to the smooth operation of the internal market. This includes issues which currently appear to be blocked, such as social and cohesion policy, taxation, external trade, justice and home affairs. Let us not kid ourselves. These four areas are essential."

4: The Labour government promotes the euro

In the 1970s, the Labour Party had opposed EMU. In 1975, it said, "there was a threat to employment in Britain from the movement in the Common Market towards an Economic and Monetary Union. This could have forced us to accept fixed exchange rates for the pound restricting industrial growth and so putting jobs at risk." In 1978, the Callaghan government rejected entering the Exchange Rate Mechanism, warning that it "would place obligations on us that might result in unnecessary deflation and unemployment." A 1978 Treasury Green Paper said that joining a European Monetary System would be against Britain's interests: it would work against higher employment and economic growth; it would aid the stronger economies in the EMS at the expense of the weaker ones; and it would prevent exchange rates being realigned when necessary.

But in the 1980s the Labour Party changed to supporting EMU, although they tended to present this support in the most low-key way possible, knowing that the change was not popular. (Although London's Mayor, Ken Livingstone, let the cat out of the bag and revealed what being 'pro-Europe' meant when he said, "I've always been pro-Europe. I want to see the end of the nation state, and a United States of Europe.")

So, while the euro's supporters across the Continent all openly accepted and supported the policy of forming an EU state, the Labour

The EU Bad for Britain

Party's leaders limited themselves, in public, to supporting EMU. In 1994, the Labour Party said that it "supports progress towards economic and monetary union." Tony Blair, its new leader, increasingly promoted EMU and the EU. In January 1995, he said, "The agenda set by Jacques Delors on economic development must be pushed." In April 1995, he said, "We should consider extending Qualified Majority Voting in certain areas such as social, environmental, industrial and regional policy." He backed a single currency and a common foreign and defence policy, saying, "If we want to maintain our global role now, we must be a leading player in Europe." And, "The real patriotic case, therefore, for those who want Britain to maintain its traditional global role, is for leadership in Europe." In December 1996, he said that Britain's interests in areas like the single market and reforming the Common Agricultural Policy could best be served by giving up the veto.

But before the 1997 election, Blair recognised that the euro, along with the whole 'euro-project', was becoming more and more unpopular, jeopardising his chances of winning the election. So he accepted the idea of a referendum on the euro, distancing Labour from its least popular policy. By accepting that a referendum on this matter was needed, he acknowledged that it was a political and constitutional issue. He also talked of sovereignty, "Of course there are emotional issues involved in the single currency. It's not just a question of economics. It's about the sovereignty of Britain and constitutional issues too." (It is noteworthy that these were acknowledgements, not commitments, though they did contradict his ally Kenneth Clarke's assertion that, "A single European currency would not be a major constitutional issue.") Also, Blair wrote in the Sun, "New Labour will have no truck with a European superstate. We will fight for Britain's interests and to keep our independence every inch of the way ... the single currency cannot be judged purely on economic terms ... our sovereignty, heritage and way of life matter too." Again, his high-sounding declarations carefully made no solid pledges.

Labour's manifesto stated, "Our vision of Europe is of an alliance of independent nations choosing to cooperate to achieve goals they cannot achieve alone." It promised, "Retention of the national veto over key matters of national interest such as taxation, defence and security, immigration, decisions over the budget and treaty changes." Blair, Brown and company knew that if they admitted the truth, even more of us would oppose the EU. They played 'softly, softly, catchee monkey' and claimed that the decision on joining the euro was a technical, economic matter. They tried to play down the euro's political significance.[69]

After the election, Gordon Brown boasted, "We are the first British government to declare for the principle of monetary union, the first to state that there is no overriding constitutional bar to membership." As the late Lord Shore observed, "Gordon Brown is the most ardent Europhile in the Government."[70] Brown liked to let people think that he was the most euro-sceptic Cabinet minister, but this was just part of his effort to position himself as a 'left' alternative Prime Minister. The record showed his true colours.

On 23 February 1999, the government introduced the National Changeover Plan, to prepare for entering the euro. The Prime Minister said, "In order to give ourselves a genuine choice in the future, it is essential that the Government and business prepare intensively during this Parliament, so that Britain will be in a position to join the single currency early in the next Parliament." Blair secretly prepared Michael Heseltine and Kenneth Clarke to welcome what Heseltine called a 'step forward'.[71]

The Plan listed the 'EMU Phases':

1. Decision (i.e. to join the euro 'in principle', but it did not say that).
2. Four months later, Referendum.
3. 12 to 15 months later, Britain joined the euro. Note that the government assumed the referendum produced the result that it wanted. Transition phase started.
4. 24 to 30 months after the referendum, euro coins were in circulation. Transition phase ended.
5. Six months later the process was complete, and sterling was abolished.

Even before the British people voted on the euro, it cost us millions of pounds as computers, printers, financial forms, stationery, and new machinery for car parks, cashiers and vending machines were made ready for a changeover that might never happen.

But the British people made clear their opposition to becoming part of a single EU state. In the June 1999 euro-elections, 77% abstained, and of those who voted, most voted for parties that opposed entering the euro.

The government set up 'Britain in Europe' on 14 October 1999 'in order to campaign in favour of UK membership of the single currency'. The government also said that it might give up our veto over more areas of transport, the environment and the workings of the Luxembourg Court.[72]

Blair tried to win people round to his pro-euro policy by talking both sides of the debate. He told the House of Commons, "The euro project is ... of course, an intensely political act ... the euro cannot be conceived of except politically."[73] He said that the decision on entering the euro was 'the most important question facing Britain today'. Privately, he wrote, "We cannot avoid this debate on Europe. ... On the euro, we need to be firmer, more certain, clearer. The truth is the politics is [sic] overwhelmingly in favour: but the economics has to be right; and at present it is not."[74] He said on 6 October 2000, "the political case for Britain being part of the single currency is strong. I don't say political or constitutional issues aren't important. They are. But to my mind, they aren't an insuperable barrier. What does have to be overcome is the economic issue."[75] He acknowledged that the debate was political – but then said that the politics of joining were so right that they needed no debate. Blair's ally John Monks, the TUC General Secretary, told the Liberal Democrat Party Conference in September 2000, the euro was a 'political as well as an economic issue'.[76]

On 8 November 2000, the government published the Fourth Report on Euro Preparations. This revealed that, despite government efforts, only 7.5% of small and medium sized firms had made any preparations for the euro. Over 80% said that they would not make any significant preparations before a referendum. Even the Treasury's own figures showed only a tiny increase in preparations from 13% of small and medium enterprises in 1998 to 17% in 2000, despite broadening the question's wording from 'preparations' to 'preparations or general strategy'. Polls by ICM and MORI showed that only about a third of firms supported the government's commitment to the euro.

In 2000, the government spent at least £16.2 million promoting the euro to firms, under the guise of 'information'. It admitted to spending another £40 million on preparing for converting to the euro all the government and public bodies' accounts and payment systems. Paddy Ashdown described this expenditure as 'a crossing of the Rubicon': it made clear to everyone the government's intent to hold and win a referendum as early as possible.

5: The Nice Treaty (2000) and federalism

A new European treaty was signed in Nice in December 2000. It was a massive assault on EU member nations' powers. It cut back sovereignty in key policy areas; in particular, it robbed nations of control over introducing the euro. The agreed reductions in member states' powers meant a huge step towards a centralised European state.

Under Section 5.2 of the Treaty, political parties whose programmes or members' attitude violate democratic principles and basic rights may be suspended by the European Court of Justice at the request of the Commission, after consulting Parliament and the Council; the suspension measures shall be adopted, on the Commission's proposal, by a decision of Parliament and the Council adopted by qualified majority voting. This would mean that parties opposing Britain's membership of the EU such as the United Kingdom Independence Party, the Socialist Labour Party, or even a Conservative Party that had adopted an anti-EU stance, could be banned. How soon before parties find themselves brought up before a Committee for Un-European Activities?

Under its Section 19.1, the co-decision procedure and qualified majority voting in the Council of Ministers become the general rule for legislative decision-making. It abolished the co-operation procedure, i.e. the unanimity requirement, which gave each nation a right of veto and which used to apply within the framework of Title VII of the EC Treaty, covering economic and monetary policy. 90% of all EU laws would be passed by QMV. The Commission's view was that the Treaty should remove national vetoes on taxes that affect the Single Market.[77] The German and French governments supported this proposal.

Under Section 19.2, the co-decision procedure was extended to

39 new legislative areas, including some environmental measures, the appointments of the EU President and the Common Foreign and Security Policy representatives, international agreements, self-employment, geographical mobility, border controls, intellectual property, World Trade Organization proceedings, workers' rights, culture, the cohesion and structural funds, cooperation with overseas countries, measures for introducing the euro, industrial policy, agreements on foreign, justice and home affairs, rules governing the European Central Bank's Council, emergency financial aid to member states (possibly those having trouble funding their pensions), freer trade in financial services, European Court of Justice procedures, regional subsidies, implementing rules governing asylum, immigration and refugee policies (where Britain kept its opt-out), agriculture and fisheries policy, budgetary, fiscal, economic and monetary policy, competition, and harmonisation measures.

Under Section 19.3, unanimity in the Council was confined to decisions of a fundamental and constitutional nature (treaty amendments, accessions, own-resources decisions, electoral procedure, application of article 308 of the EC Treaty). So the EU, having removed our vetoes on economic and monetary policy, could force the euro on Britain, without a referendum, and against the opposition of the majority of the British people.

Under Section 35.2, no restrictions at all would be placed on the ECJ's jurisdiction. This would enable the EU's rulers to suppress all opposition through 'legal' means. The Treaty provided for even more Commissioners, up from 20 to 26 as new members join, and for even more MEPs, up from 626 to 738. It also gave more powers to the Commission's President.

Article 137, on Social Provisions, allowed QMV to be introduced on decisions about the representation and collective defence of workers' interests. The Council of Ministers could decide how workers were to be represented. This interference in trade union organisations was especially dangerous, since member governments, the European Central Bank and the money markets all wanted to reduce trade union rights.

Article 157, on Industry, stated, "The Community and the Member States shall ensure that the conditions necessary for the competitiveness of the Community's industry exist. For that purpose, in accordance with a system of open and competitive markets, their action shall be aimed at: speeding up the adjustment of industry to structural changes; ..." The Treaty introduced QMV to decide the measures it wanted. As we have seen, when they say competitiveness, they mean more unemployment and worse wages and conditions.

The Treaty meant that if a majority of the EU's members decided to make us abolish the pound, the government would have no veto and we would be supposed to do what they tell us. If a majority of the EU's members decided to run down what is left of British industry, the government would have no veto and we would be supposed to do what they tell us. If a majority of the EU's members decided that we should have a European system of justice, ending the right to jury trial and habeas corpus, the government would have no veto and we would be supposed to do what they tell us.

Lord David Owen commented on the Treaty, "We now know that the British government intends to give up the veto in Article 43 on closer cooperation and replace this single nation veto with a new provision for two countries to veto. President Chirac briefing the press after Biarritz said, "It is out of the question that one single country may block a desire for enhanced cooperation". The only defence of this as yet formally unannounced lifting of the veto by our Prime Minister was that otherwise "the UK would be completely sidelined". But when as night follows day in the next IGC in 2004 the call comes to convert other vetoes in other parts of the Treaties to two instead of one country will the UK again concede for fear of being sidelined? Will there be a new qualified majority vote for matters of vital national interest, namely two votes to block instead of one?

"Germany and Italy tabled a paper to the IGC which is very important for several reasons. It was at the centre of the negotiations at Biarritz and it was privately agreed with the French beforehand. The paper proposes "an open, functional avant-garde which serves the process of integration". It goes on to say "the goal is not so much enhanced cooperation but 'enhanced integration'. The use of enhanced cooperation must serve the common good of more rapid and increased integration". This is an area where it is folly to reduce the single nation veto agreed by Tony Blair only three years ago in negotiations at Amsterdam and ratified in Treaty form only last year. This constitutional slide is becoming an avalanche."

Lord Owen said, "My fundamental purpose in raising these constitutional questions is that I, as a lifelong European supporter, see a real threat of us sliding into a form of European integration where we wake up to find we have ceased to be a self-governing nation. The Prime Minister in a sound bite described the EU as developing into a 'superpower not superstate'. I believe that to be a profoundly misguided direction for the EU to embark on, for almost by definition were the EU to become a superpower it would have become a superstate. The EU is a unique mixture of intergovernmentalism and supranationalism. It is a multi-powered organisation deriving its power from multiple sources. Superpowers exercise their power from the single source of their nation state. There is now only one superpower, the United States of America.

"We could only aspire within the EU to exercise such unified power were we to merge into a United States of Europe, with a directly elected President answerable to a European Parliament, with a European Finance Minister with a European Central Bank, a European Foreign Minister, a European Army with a European Defence Minister and the nuclear forces of France and the UK under the command of the European President. A fantasy some might say - would that that were true. It is not a present reality, but it is a present danger. It will happen over the next two or more decades unless there is a popular resistance across the EU led by the UK. We have seen enough of the politics and the politicians at the start of the 21st Century to know that to an extent unparalleled in our history it is likely to be dominated by a strange combination of an elite embracing centralised globalism, contained by popular demand for identifiable units of decision making with which they can relate. How those two forces interact over the first quarter of this century will probably determine the shape of the whole century. My message is very simple to this country. "Stay awake", watch your politicians with a forensic attention to the detail of European legislation. Listen less to their words, watch their action."

The member governments all prepared to ratify the Nice Treaty without asking the peoples what they thought. Unfortunately for the EU's leaders, the Irish Constitution obliged the Irish government to consult the people. In the referendum of 7 June 2001 on whether to ratify the Treaty, the Irish people voted against by 54% to 46% on a poll of 34.8%. The political establishment and the Roman Catholic Church campaigned for it. So did the Irish Confederation of Trade Unions, yet the strongest votes against the Treaty were in Dublin's working class areas - maybe the trade unions should listen to and respect their members' views in future. Many took the No campaign's sensible advice, 'if in doubt, vote No'. So the only people in the EU allowed a say on the Nice Treaty rejected it, just as the Danes, the only people in the EU allowed a say on EMU, had rejected it.

On 11 June 2001, the 15 EU Foreign Ministers, including Foreign Secretary Jack Straw, issued a statement rejecting the Irish people's vote: "While respecting the will of the Irish people, the foreign ministers expressed their regrets at the outcome of the Irish referendum on the Nice Treaty. They rule out any re-opening of the text signed at Nice. The process of ratification will be continued on the basis of this text and in accordance with the planned timetable." The EU leaders, including Blair, stated that enlargement was irreversible, and that the governments would ratify the treaty by the end of 2002. They carried on regardless, treating the No vote as if it was a Yes vote; in effect, they overruled the people. On 11 July 2001, the Belgian government warned Austria against holding a referendum on the Nice Treaty. Louis Michel, the Belgian Foreign Minister, said, "it is very dangerous to organize referendums when you're not sure to win them." And he asked, "Has a country the right to prevent the progress of Europe?" So they pressed the Irish people to vote again, on exactly the same treaty, within eighteen months, although Irish law forbade two votes in quick succession on the same subject. The Yes camp won the second referendum, held on 19 October 2002.

The EU's leaders pressed on for a single EU state. On 30 April 2001, the German Social Democratic Party stated, "We want the commission from now to be strengthened to become a government – a real European government beside the national governments. ... There is no alternative to further integration and Europeanisation. ... In ten years we shall live in a Europe with a constitution. In ten years we shall live in a Europe with a [single] currency. ... An internal market and a common currency demand more energetic harmonisation of fiscal policy, especially with regard to taxes on business, the taxation of capital gains, the taxation of investment in energy and the organisation of value added and corporation tax."[78]

In May 2001, the French Socialist Party put forward its own proposals for European integration, including an 'economic government' that could levy taxes from Brussels. The plans were revealed in a leaked party document entitled 'The European Project of Socialists', marked 'internal working paper: not for circulation'. The paper called for the EU defence force to intervene around the world, and urged uniform policies on immigration and asylum. It called for the EU's charter of rights to be made legally binding, and proposed a European police force, an environment authority and an elected EU president. It advocated that the European parliament should set corporation taxes and that EU governments should harmonise their spending, even sharing a common budget day.

In February 2002, Chancellor Schroeder stressed that euro membership meant signing up for political union. "European monetary union has to be complemented by a political union; that was always the presumption of Europeans including those who made active politics before us." He also said, "What we need to Europeanise is everything to do with economic and financial policy."[79]

Guy Verhofstadt, the Belgian Prime Minister, said that some countries "want an inter-governmental Europe; others, like us, want a federal Europe. We have to choose, once and for all." He called for closer European integration and for stronger EU institutions to prepare for this.

The Party of European Socialists, whose President was the late Robin Cook, said in its manifesto of May 2001 that it sought "a European government to promote the European social model." It wanted an EU President and Prime Minister, and wanted the Commissioners to become 'European ministers'. It called for a "federation of states and people that will participate in the construction of a European Political Union."

All these statements give the lie to claims that, "Other European countries are not pushing for strides towards federalism" (Blair in 1995), "Nobody is talking about federalism in Europe" (Commissioner Leon Brittan), 'out-of-context quotations from European politicians about "federalism"'[80] (Simon Buckby of the pressure group Britain in Europe) and "The truth is that the Union is not going to be a State of any kind."[81]

(Commissioner Neil Kinnock). A diplomat was once defined as somebody sent abroad to lie for his country: a Commissioner is somebody sent abroad to lie against his country.

British public figures agreed that EMU was a political project aimed at the political union of Europe. Sir Roy Denman, a former EC representative to the USA, wrote, "By that time [2002] a new entrant will be required to accept not just a single currency but a degree of harmonisation of fiscal and economic policy toward political union that the British electorate might not stomach."[82] He later wrote, "Adopting the euro would be a leap into the unknown. Many suspect that the Government has been less than frank about the political integration that will follow economic union. A referendum would be a very considerable risk."[83] Roger Liddle, Blair's special advisor on Europe for seven years, said, "We have to be more honest and open with people that Europe has always been a political project."

William Buiter, a member of the Bank of England Monetary Policy Committee, said, "First and foremost, however, EMU is a major step on the road to 'ever closer union' in Europe. It represents the opening of a new chapter in the European federalists' agenda, a significant transfer of national sovereignty to a supra-national institution." The Bank of England's Chairman Sir Eddie George said on 12 September 2000, "Monetary union is fundamentally a political rather than an economic issue. It necessarily involves the deliberate pooling of national sovereignty over important aspects of public policy, in the interests of not just a collective economic advantage but of a perceived wider political harmony within Europe."[84] The late Hugo Young, the Guardian's euro-enthusiast, wrote, "Integration is, of course, political" and "The euro is a massive shift to further integration."[85]

6: We win the referendum on the euro

In May 1998, the leaders of eleven member states committed their countries to joining the euro: not one government put the issue to the people in a referendum or election. Similarly, the leaders of three member states committed their countries to staying out of the euro: again, not one put the issue to the people. The 1992 referendum in Denmark had put the

EU's leaders on their guard. Supporters of the EU liked to claim that "elite opinion was getting too far in advance of public opinion."[86] This assumed a single possible line of progress, with the clever elite far ahead of the dim masses. A more democratic explanation was that the majority of people in every country resolutely opposed the loss of national sovereignty.

Even the calling of a referendum depended on the people's efforts, not on the government's wishes: referendums were forced on reluctant governments. As Lord Owen pointed out in his speech to the Cardiff Business Club on 23 October 2000, "We would never have had the referendum of 1975 on EC Accession or been promised a referendum on the Euro in the 1997 Election unless there had been a popular demand for the people to set their judgement on these two questions above that of their Parliamentarians." But how could we ensure that the campaign was fair when the government so clearly wanted to enter the euro? As Robin Cook said about the referendum, "It's not just difficult to frame the question. The difficulty, of course, is getting the correct answer."[87]

The proposed referendum on the euro would be the first consultative, as opposed to endorsing, referendum ever held in Britain. The government set up the Neill Commission to advise it on how to ensure that the referendum would be fair, and then in November 2000 it passed the Political Parties, Elections and Referendums Act, which rejected the Commission's key recommendations. The Election Commission Committee, charged with overseeing the referendum, comprised the Home Secretary, a Minister, the Chair of one Select Committee, two Labour MPs and four others, so the government had a built-in majority. The government would still be able to fix the referendum in five different ways.

1. The government would not be neutral; it would make every effort to get the result it wanted. It rejected an amendment in line with Lord Neill's recommendation that all government information on the euro should be impartial. As Home Secretary Jack Straw told the Home Affairs Select Committee in October 1998, 'it seems unrealistic to expect the government to be neutral on an issue to which ministers have devoted substantial energy and resources.'"[88] Lord Bassam, the government's Home Affairs spokesperson, stated, "Amendment 203 would additionally require that material circulated by the government during the referendum period

as a whole must be factual and impartial ... In other words, it is proposed that ... it should be incumbent upon the government to prepare neutral material during the ... referendum period. This would not work."[89]

In 1975 the Heath government managed to reframe the debate by 'renegotiating' the terms of Britain's EU membership. They might well play this card again, in the form of pledges to reform EU institutions or improve our rebates, or by claiming that the five tests have all been passed. They would word the question to get the answer they wanted, as Heath did.

2. Funding. There are two sides to the question, so each side should be treated as a single unified campaign. But Neill instead recommended that each part of each campaign be treated as separate, entitled to a separate, capped fund. It set a £5 million limit on spending by any political party. Labour and the Conservatives could spend £5 million each, and the pro-euro parties, the Liberal Democrats, Plaid Cymru and the Scottish National Party £4 million each. So the pro-euro parties could spend £17 million and the antis just £5 million!

The government set no limits for itself: except for the last 28 days before the referendum, it could spend as much as it wanted. It was estimated that by July 2002 the government had already spent £65 million promoting the euro. Some people and organisations from other countries would interfere in any future referendum on euro entry, as the CIA did in the 1975 referendum, and as President Mitterrand did when he interfered in the German and Italian elections and illegally funded his allies Kohl and Craxi. Again, just before the 1997 election, Santer made a speech attacking Britain's Eurosceptics: this was an unprecedented intrusion into the domestic affairs of a member state.[90] But it set a precedent that the EU could follow in any future referendum campaign.

The government rejected an amendment to the Act that would have prohibited the European Commission from campaigning during a referendum, stating that under EU law it had no power to do so. Lord Bassam again: "There is a need for some realism about the intentions of the Commission. That needs to go hand in hand with some realism about what such a prohibition could achieve. An explicit ban on referendum expenditure or the publication of referendum material by the institutions of the EU would beg (sic) the question of how such a ban could be enforced

... Given the immunities for which the protocol on the privileges and immunities of the European Communities provide, the jurisdiction of our courts in relation to a breach of the provisions of this part by an institution of the Community would be extremely doubtful."[91] This clears the way for all the EU's bodies to intervene in all future British elections and referendum campaigns with no limits on their spending.[92] Also, the European Court of Justice has ruled that European companies are not foreign, so they could put money into a British referendum campaign.

3. The media. There is a need to oversee public service broadcasting, especially the BBC and local radio stations. The BBC has shown bias, both in its treatment of the matters of the euro and the EU, and in its choice of speakers: it has a selection policy that implies that only right-wing Tories oppose the euro; it never invites anti-euro speakers from the trade unions, and only rarely from the Parliamentary Labour Party. Minotaur Media Tracking's first report, on the BBC's coverage from 9 May to 6 June 1999 of the elections to the European Parliament, showed how biased it was. It gave the 'Pro-Euro Conservative Party', which won 1.2% of the votes and no seats, as much prominence as the Conservative Party. By contrast, it only allowed the UK Independence Party one, negative, interview, although UKIP won 7% of the votes and three seats. Not a single Labour Euro-sceptic went on air for a single minute in the 400 hours of coverage monitored; the BBC hardly ever noticed the existence of the Labour Euro-Safeguards Campaign. Another report found that from 21 May to 21 July 2000, the BBC's 'Today' programme put on air two-and-a-half times more people for the euro than against it, and not a single Labour Euro-sceptic. Recently the BBC appointed Andrew Marr, one of the most pro-euro figures in public life, as its political correspondent.

4. The civil service. Limits need to be set to the involvement of civil servants, particularly to the government's legion of political advisers.

5. The timetable of the campaign. Neill recommended that the government should be impartial for the last 28 days of the campaign, but it should be impartial for longer than this. The Congress for Democracy suggested 100 days.

Robert Worcester of the opinion-polling firm MORI cynically outlined the government's strategy for the referendum: tell the punters that 'the men with staring eyes' are for the pound, and that sober sensible citizens like Gordon Brown are for the euro. The government pretended that only the Tories and the far right opposed the euro, which was, for many people, the kiss of death. The euro lobby never mentioned that UNISON and other trade unions opposed the euro. This lobby would do anything to win the referendum: euro-enthusiast Hugo Young wrote, "a referendum that has to be held must also, at all costs, be won."[93] Tribune columnist Paul Anderson showed the level of debate when he wrote an article, 'Idiots against the single currency'.[94] Sir Peter Marshall, KCMG, told the Royal Commonwealth Society, "Hence if the EU has to be sold to the British public, the economic arguments have to be very delicately balanced. It is necessary to be 'economical with the truth'."

In October 2000, Worcester said, "It is absolutely impossible for them to win a referendum. I think it is off the agenda both for this Parliament and the next."[95] This judgement was particularly striking because in the summer Worcester had produced a pamphlet for the Foreign Policy Centre, 'How the Euro Referendum will be won: lessons from the 1975 Referendum'.

As people perceived the euro's many drawbacks, it became increasingly unpopular. David Clark, Robin Cook's former adviser, pointed out, "Labour's timidity has been rewarded with opinion polls which show majorities against entry so large and persistent that many now doubt whether a referendum is winnable."[96] Polls ever since 1992 have shown that on average we have been 60% against, and 27% for. In April 2000, less than a third of British people thought that being an EU member was 'a good thing', or that Britain gained from membership. In an ICM poll of 4 November 2000, 71% of British people opposed euro entry, 2% more than in October. In contrast only 18% of people thought that Britain should join. The 53% majority against entry was the largest since ICM started regular polling on the issue in February 1995. Jeremy Heywood, Blair's Principal Private Secretary, told EU leaders that the Prime Minister "intends to call a referendum within two years of the election and he is very confident of winning it". But the British people's resistance forced changes in the government's timetable.

In a Mori poll in March 2001, 52% said they would vote to leave the EU in a referendum held on that question. The European Commission's July 2001 Eurobarometer report on British attitudes to the EU showed that that almost two-thirds of us believed that joining the euro would end our national independence, and 60% did not trust the EU to protect Britain's interests.[97] The Guardian report was entitled, 'Britain's euro ignorance', although we would say that these conclusions showed understanding of the euro, not ignorance. The report's author, Dr Denis Balsom, concluded that people's opinions about the euro were based on 'prejudice and the innate conservatism of British public opinion', an opinion based on his prejudice, not on the evidence.

In August 2002, an ICM poll showed that those who said that they would vote against the euro in a referendum rose by three points to 59%. Those who said that they would vote to join also rose, by one point to 28%. The Guardian's home affairs editor, Alan Travis, managed to sum this up as, "This month's figures show some movement in favour of those who support the euro."[98] The article's headline 'Voters attack Labour's green record' did not exactly bring out the finding that a growing number opposed the euro.

The Liberal Democrats wanted Britain to enter the euro at the earliest possible moment. So did Plaid Cymru and the Scottish National Party. Plaid Cymru resolved in 2000, "Conference therefore supports the adoption of the euro by the United Kingdom at the earliest opportunity once sterling has again reached a competitive level." The Scottish National Party declared, "We therefore conclude that: Scotland's best interests would be served through normal membership of the European Single Currency area as soon as it is practically possible and under conditions which secure Scotland's optimal competitive position."

To win the June 2001 general election, Blair had to dissociate himself from his most unpopular policy, support for the euro. Promising a referendum on the euro allowed him to separate Labour's prospects from the euro's prospects: Labour's pro-euro policy was not an issue in the elections. The election was explicitly not a referendum on the euro. Labour has never asked us what we think of the euro, so Jack Straw spoke less than the truth when he said in August 2002, "We believe in principle the euro benefits people in Britain and we have had that endorsed in successive elections." As in the 1997 election, Labour promised a referendum on the euro and as in 1997 it then broke the promise, cheating its way to electoral success.

The Times backed Labour as the best option for 'consolidating the core aspects of Thatcherism and extending them to fresh areas of policy'.

The election result was no mandate for euro entry. Labour got just 24.2% of the electorate's votes, in the lowest peacetime turnout since 1874: only 59.4% voted. The other pro-euro parties got 12.4% between them: Liberal Democrats 10.9%, SNP 1.1%, and Plaid Cymru 0.4%. So just 36.6% of the electorate voted for parties backing the euro. Some who had voted for any of these parties would have done so in spite of its policy on the euro. Tactical voting, with large numbers of Labour voters switching to the LibDems to defeat the Conservative candidate, showed that the election saw not so much a pro-Labour as an anti-Tory vote, not a mandate for Labour's policies but a rejection of the Conservatives. There was an unusually small swing since the 1997 election; four weeks (or was it four years?) of intense campaigning had changed hardly anybody's mind, which should be a warning to the euro-enthusiasts.

Blair told the October 2001 Labour Party conference that the economic tests were fundamental and not just window dressing. He said, "But if they are met, we should join; and if met in this Parliament, we should have the courage of our argument, to ask the people for their consent in this Parliament." The government said that sometime before June 2003 they would assess whether Britain had met the conditions.[99]

On 1 December 2001, Charles Clarke, Chairman of the Labour Party, said that the government should push ahead with plans to take Britain into the euro even if it brought no positive economic benefits. This showed that the prime motivation for entry was not economic but political. On 11 March 2002, Michael Jacobs, general secretary of the Fabian Society, said, "It is not just a question of economics. Adoption of a single currency is a constitutional change: it relocates sovereignty over monetary policy, and therefore over economic policy more widely. The acts both of joining and of not joining would significantly alter our relations with the rest of the European Union. The Government has to go out and win the argument and the sooner the better."

Whichever way the British people voted in elections, we opposed entering the euro and becoming part of the EU state. Those who voted Labour in 1997 and 2001 did so despite Labour's pro-EU policy, not because of it: there was no mandate for entering the euro. The British people, not the government, made Britain's policy on the euro: we stopped it being introduced here. In effect, we had held our own referendum on the euro and we had won it.

Endnotes

[1]. Cited page 17, News in brief, European Journal, June 1998, Volume 5, Number 8.

[2]. See Paul Edwards et al, pages 3-5, 'Great Britain: still muddling through', Chapter 1, pages 1-68, in Anthony Ferner and Richard Hyman, editors, Industrial relations in the new Europe, Blackwell, 1992.

[3]. See Paul Edwards et al, page 3, 'Great Britain: from partial collectivism to neo-liberalism to where?' Chapter 1, pages 1-54, in Anthony Ferner and Richard Hyman, editors, Changing industrial relations in Europe, Blackwell, 1998.

[4]. Barbara Castle, Fighting all the way, Macmillan, 1993, page 606.

[5]. See Paul Teague, Economic citizenship in the European Union: employment relations in the new Europe, Routledge, 1999, page 20.

[6]. See Lowell Turner, page 55, 'Prospects for worker participation in management in the single market', Chapter 3, pages 45-79, in Lloyd Ulman, Barry Eichengreen and William Dickens, editors, Labor and an integrated Europe, The Brookings Institution, 1993.

[7]. On the Charter, see Desmond Dinan, Ever closer union: an introduction to European integration, Macmillan, 2nd edition, 1999, pages 423-6; on the EU's social policy generally, see his pages 420-9.

[8]. Cited page 252, Kim Moody, Workers in a lean world: unions in the international economy, Verso, 1997.

[9]. Cited page 18, Franklin Dehousse, Amsterdam: the making of a treaty, Kogan Page, 1999.

[10]. On the ETUC, see Justin Greenwood, Representing interests in the European Union, New York: St Martin's Press, 1997, 'Labour interests', Chapter 7, pages 155-76. See also Kim Moody, Workers in a lean world: unions in the international economy, Verso, 1997, pages 242-7, and Wolfgang Lecher, editor, Trade unions in the European Union: a handbook, Lawrence & Wishart, 1994, pages 247-55.

[11]. See Kim Moody, Workers in a lean world: unions in the international economy, Verso, 1997, pages 243-4; directive cited page 244.

[12]. See Lloyd Ulman, Barry Eichengreen and William Dickens, page 8, 'Labor and an integrated Europe', Chapter 1, pages 1-12, in Lloyd Ulman, Barry Eichengreen and William Dickens, editors, Labor and an integrated Europe, The Brookings Institution, 1993.

[13]. See Paul Teague, Economic citizenship in the European Union: employment relations in the new Europe, Routledge, 1999, page 197.

[14]. See Wolfgang Lecher, Trade unions in the European Union: a handbook, Lawrence & Wishart, 1994, page 272.

[15]. Cited page 245, Kim Moody, Workers in a lean world: unions in the international economy, Verso, 1997.

[16]. Transport and General Workers' Union, T & G Record, October 1996.

[17]. See Kim Moody, Workers in a lean world: unions in the international economy, Verso, 1997, page 274.

[18]. See Kim Moody, Workers in a lean world: unions in the international economy, Verso, 1997, pages 287, 290, 299 and 305.

[19]. See Justin Greenwood, Representing interests in the European Union, New York: St Martin's Press, 1997, pages 173 and 260.

[20]. Business Week, 16 December 1996, pages 61-5.

[21]. Observer, 10 June 2001.

[22]. See Christine Buckley, Union to urge tougher test for the euro, The Times, 3 July 2001, page 24.

[23]. David Lloyd George, War memoirs, Volume 2, Odhams, 1936, page 1141.

[24]. See William Wolman and Anne Colamosca, The Judas economy: the triumph of capital and the betrayal of work, Addison-Wesley, 1997, page x.

[25]. See Justin Greenwood, Representing interests in the European Union, New York: St Martin's Press, 1997, page 10.

[26]. See the European Commission, The European Community and its eastern neighbours, Luxembourg: Office for Official Publications of the European Communities, 1990, page 10. See also Charlotte Bretherton and John Vogler, The European Union as a global actor, Routledge, 1999, page 139.

[27]. See Michael Mann, page 196, 'Is there a society called Euro?' Chapter 11, pages 184-207, in Roland Axtmann, editor, Globalization and Europe: theoretical and empirical investigations, Pinter, 1998.

[28]. Michael Heseltine, The challenge of Europe: can Britain win? Weidenfeld and Nicolson, 1989, page 88.

[29]. White Paper, Part B, Chapter 5.

[30]. See Romano Prodi, Europe as I see it, Polity, 2000, page 54. In this book, he constantly peddled the virtues of privatisation; see his pages 51, 54, 107 and 112.

[31]. See Kenneth Dyson and Kevin Featherstone, The road to Maastricht: negotiating Economic and Monetary Union, Oxford University Press, 1999, page 792. See also Helen Wallace, page 3, 'The institutional setting: five variations on a theme', Chapter 1, pages 3-37, in Helen Wallace and William Wallace, editors, Policy-making in the European Union, Oxford University Press, 4th edition, 2000.

[32]. See George Ross, 'European integration and globalization', Chapter 10, pages 164-83, in Roland Axtmann, editor, Globalization and Europe: theoretical and empirical investigations, Pinter, 1998, page 179. See also Wyn Grant, The Common Agricultural Policy, Macmillan, 1997, page 228.

[33]. Cited page 193, Neill Nugent, The government and politics of the European Union, Macmillan, 4th edition, 1999.

[34]. See Guglielmo Carchedi, For another Europe: a class analysis of European economic integration, Verso, 2001, pages 171-8.

[35]. See James Petras and Henry Veltmeyer, Globalization unmasked: imperialism in the 21st century, Zed Books, 2001, page 66.

[36]. See David Felix, 'Asia and the crisis of financial globalization', Chapter 7, pages 163-91, in Dean Baker, Gerald Epstein and Robert Pollin, editors, Globalization and progressive economic policy, Cambridge University Press, 1998. See also Arthur McEwan, page 66, 'Comment', pages 64-6, on Ute Pieper and Lance Taylor's paper, 'The revival of the liberal creed: the IMF, the World Bank, and inequality in a globalized economy', Chapter 2, pages 37-63, in Dean Baker, Gerald Epstein and Robert Pollin, editors, Globalization and progressive economic policy, Cambridge University Press, 1998.

[37]. See Mehrene Larudee, 'Integration and income distribution under the North American Free Trade Agreement: the experience of Mexico', Chapter 11, pages 273-95, in Dean Baker, Gerald Epstein and Robert Pollin, editors, Globalization and progressive economic policy, Cambridge University Press, 1998.

[38]. See Kim Moody, Workers in a lean world: unions in the international economy, Verso, 1997, page 18.

[39]. James Petras and Henry Veltmeyer, Globalization unmasked: imperialism in the 21st century, Zed Books, 2001, page 154.

[40]. Cited page 132, Philip Resnick, 'Global democracy: ideals and reality', Chapter 8, pages 116-43, in Roland Axtmann, editor, Globalization and Europe: theoretical and empirical investigations, Pinter, 1998. See also Kim Moody, Workers in a lean world: unions in the international economy, Verso, 1997, page 43.

[41]. Michael Mann, pages 205-6, 'Is there a society called Euro?' Chapter 11, pages 83-89, in Roland Axtmann, editor, Globalization and Europe: theoretical and empirical investigations, Pinter, 1998.

[42]. See George Ross, pages 177-8, 'European integration and globalization', Chapter 10, pages 164-83, in Roland Axtmann, editor, Globalization and Europe: theoretical and empirical investigations, Pinter, 1998. See his

discussion on pages 175-81, especially pages 180-1.

[43]. See Eric Helleiner, pages 145-9 in 'Sovereignty, territoriality and the globalization of finance', Chapter 7, pages 138-57, in David Smith, Dorothy Solinger and Steven Topik, editors, States and sovereignty in the global economy, Routledge, 1999.

[44]. See Ha-joon Chang, 'Globalization, transnational corporations, and economic development: can the developing countries pursue strategic industrial policy in a globalizing world economy?' Chapter 4, pages 97-116, in Dean Baker, Gerald Epstein and Robert Pollin, editors, Globalization and progressive economic policy, Cambridge University Press, 1998. See also Kim Moody, Workers in a lean world: unions in the international economy, Verso, 1997, pages 79-83.

[45]. See Ali El-Agraa, The European Union: history, institutions, economics, politics, Prentice Hall Europe, 5th edition, 1998, page 472.

[46]. Klaus-Dieter Borchardt, The ABC of Community Law, Office for Official Publications, the European Communities, cited page 30, Is Europe becoming a superstate? Keith Marsden, European Journal, January/February 2001, Volume 8, Number 3, pages 30-2.

[47]. Cited page 29, Jeremy Nieboer, The pros and cons of Economic and Monetary Union, European Journal, June 1998, Volume 5, Number 8, pages 28-34.

[48]. Cited page 211, Cris Shore, Building Europe: the cultural politics of European integration, Routledge, 2000.

[49]. Cited page 17, News in brief, European Journal, June 1998, Volume 5, Number 8.

[50]. Cited page 94, Cris Shore, Building Europe: the cultural politics of European integration, Routledge, 2000.

[51]. Cited page 23, Peter Shore, Separate ways: the heart of Europe, Duckworth, 2000.

[52]. Cited page 174, Adrian Hilton, The principality and power of Europe:

Britain and the emerging Holy European Empire, Dorchester House, 2nd edition, 2000.

[53]. Cited pages 23-4, Peter Shore, Separate ways: the heart of Europe, Duckworth, 2000.

[54]. Cited page 24, Peter Shore, Separate ways: the heart of Europe, Duckworth, 2000.

[55]. The Times, 26 November 1999.

[56]. Cited page 34, Brian Denny, Politics of the euro: economics of the madhouse, Campaign Against Euro-Federalism, 2001.

[57]. Cited page 13, Laurence Robertson, It's time for honesty, European Journal, Summer 2000, Volume 7, Number 9, pages 12-3.

[58]. Cited page 94, Cris Shore, Building Europe: the cultural politics of European integration, Routledge, 2000.

[59]. Cited page 29, Jeremy Nieboer, The pros and cons of Economic and Monetary Union, European Journal, June 1998, Volume 5, Number 8.

[60]. Cited page 24, Richard Sage, The dangers of 'flexibility', European Journal, Summer 2000, Volume 7, Number 9, pages 24-6.

[61]. Cited page 3, David Liebler, European defence: an American perspective, European Journal, Summer 2000, Volume 7, Number 9, pages 3-4.

[62]. Romano Prodi, Europe as I see it, Polity, 2000, page 17.

[63]. Cited page 82, Adrian Hilton, The principality and power of Europe: Britain and the emerging Holy European Empire, Dorchester House, 2nd edition, 2000.

[64]. Shaping the new Europe: strategic objectives 2000-2005, European Commission, 2000.

[65]. Cited in La Stampa, 1 November 2000.

[66]. Cited pages 6-7, Lord Chalfont, NATO on the brink, European Journal, November/December 2000, Volume 8, Number 2, pages 5-7.

[67]. Cited page 12, Sunday Telegraph, 9 July 2000.

[68]. BBC, Radio 4, 20 July 1999.

[69]. Joel Krieger, British politics in the global age: can social democracy survive? Polity, 1999, page 165.

[70]. See David Gowland and Arthur Turner, Reluctant Europeans: Britain and European integration, 1945-1998, Longman, 2000, page 330.

[71]. See Andrew Rawnsley, Servants of the people: the inside story of New Labour, Hamish Hamilton, 2000, page 236.

[72]. Government White Paper, IGC: Reform for Enlargement, HMSO, February 2000.

[73]. Hansard, 23 February 1999, column 181.

[74]. Tony Blair's leaked memo, Standing up for Britain, December 1999, cited page 8, Guardian, 27 July 2000.

[75]. Cited page 12, Daily Telegraph, 7 October 2000.

[76]. Cited page 2, Press Release, Lord Shore, House of Lords, 24 September 2000.

[77]. See 26 January 2000, COM (2000) 34.

[78]. See John Hooper and Kate Connolly, Germany wants EU integrated in 10 years, Guardian, 1 May 2001, page 15.

[79]. See interview in The Times, 22 February 2002.

[80]. Roger Beetham, editor, The euro debate: persuading the people, Federal Trust, 2001, page 191.

[81]. Roger Beetham, editor, The euro debate: persuading the people, Federal Trust, 2001, page 205.

[82]. International Herald Tribune, 14 October 1998.

[83]. Financial Times, 11 July 2000.

[84]. Cited page 2, Press Release, Lord Shore, House of Lords, 24 September 2000.

[85]. Hugo Young, Guardian, 4 July 2000 (ironically, the USA's Independence Day).

[86]. Neill Nugent, The European Commission, Palgrave, 2001, page 230.

[87]. LWT, Jonathan Dimbleby, 6 April 1997, cited page 144, Adrian Hilton, The principality and power of Europe: Britain and the Holy European Empire, Dorchester House, 2nd edition, 2000.

[88]. Andy Mullen and Brian Burkitt, The euro: the battle for British hearts and minds, Congress for Democracy, 2002, page 15.

[89]. Cited page 17, Andy Mullen and Brian Burkitt, The euro: the battle for British hearts and minds, Congress for Democracy, 2002.

[90]. John Turner, The Tories and Europe, Manchester University Press, 2000, page 207.

[91]. Cited page 17, Andy Mullen and Brian Burkitt, The euro: the battle for British hearts and minds, Congress for Democracy, 2002.

[92]. See Paving the way for that euro referendum, Daily Telegraph, 29 November 2000, page 33.

[93]. After the election it's full steam ahead for the euro, Hugo Young, Guardian, 1 May 2001, page 18.

[94]. Paul Anderson, Idiots against the single currency, Tribune, 12 July 2002, page 13.

[95]. Daily Telegraph, 19 October 2000.

[96]. David Clark, Tell Gordon to stop playing games, Guardian, 12 June 2001, page 18.

[97]. Andrew Osborn, Britain's euro ignorance, Guardian, 3 July 2001, page 1.

[98]. Alan Travis, Voters attack Labour's green record, Guardian, 29 August

2002, page 1.

[99]. See George Jones, New currency for a new world, Daily Telegraph, 3 October 2001, page 1.

Chapter 3: The drive towards a single EU state

1: Corpus Juris and ID cards

2: The police

3: Foreign policy

4: Defence policy

5: Aid and development

6: Borders, immigration, race and asylum

7: Religion

8: Devolution and regionalisation

9: London: Britain's capital city

*   Prime Minister Tony Blair said in January 2000, "Europe today is no longer just about peace. It is about projecting collective power."

We saw in earlier chapters how Britain is being shoved towards a complete change of sovereignty, merging Britain into a new overarching state called Europe, with a single government, a single currency, a single economic policy and a single tax system. In this chapter, we will examine the EU's plans to impose on us a single legal code, a single European police force, a single foreign policy, a single defence policy, a single immigration and asylum policy and a single religion. It would dissolve Britain into regions of a single EU state with a single border and a single capital.

1: Corpus Juris

The European Commission wants to put all EU members under a single legal system. The Commission first proposed Corpus Juris, meaning 'Body of Law', at a very discreet seminar of jurists that Directorate General XX held in April 1997 in San Sebastian, Spain. Its programme stated, "The objectives of the seminar were twofold: to seek to call the attention of jurists in general to the need for effective protection of the Community budget, particularly in connection with fraud against subsidies: and to make known the contents of the Corpus Juris for protection of these financial interests, which has been conceived as the embryo of a future European Criminal Code."

In February 1998, the European Parliament passed a resolution calling for 'the proposals on setting up a European judicial network' to be pursued. Conservative MEPs voted unanimously for Corpus Juris. The Parliament's president, Jose-Maria Gil-Robles, called it 'an important model for the realisation of a common juridical and judicial space'. The Commission published it under the imprint of the Director-General for Financial Control, so that they could then introduce it under the Amsterdam Treaty's Article 280.4, where no nation could veto it.

In November 2000, the European Parliament voted for a judicial cooperation unit, Eurojust, and for measures to create a 'genuine European Area of Justice' leading to 'the emergence of a European criminal law'. This allowed Eurojust to bring together Public Prosecutors from member states into a single Public Prosecution Service to deal with crimes like terrorism, drugs trafficking, counterfeiting, and trafficking in human beings. The EU wants to give that Service its own jurisdiction, its own law.

What would Corpus Juris involve? It would be a single Criminal Code, overriding national laws throughout the member states and covering all areas of criminal activity. It would use the continental inquisitorial model. A single Public Prosecutor based in Brussels would run it, combining police and prosecution powers. He would be accountable to nobody. He would be able to 'instruct' national judges to issue a 'European arrest warrant' against suspects. He could jail citizens without charge and without anyone having to produce evidence against them for periods of six months, renewable then for three months at a time, with no fixed time limit and no limit to the number of renewals. Suspects would have no right to a public hearing. The sequence of events would be: suspicion, arrest, imprisonment, investigation, charge.

Clearly, this would end the historic British right of habeas corpus whereby the accused must be taken to a public court within a very short period of time, usually 24 hours, and the authorities must conduct their investigations, assemble at least a prima facie case and produce their evidence before they can order an arrest. Habeas corpus protects us all from being jailed without trial. As Lord Scott of Foscote, a Law Lord, suggested, "people arrested under the catch-all warrant might not receive a fair trial in the country to which they were sent."[1] Given that no EU country has habeas corpus, it is doubtful whether any trials in any continental country are fair by British standards.

Corpus Juris would also allow extradition and permanent imprisonment anywhere within the EU for offences committed or those that the authorities suspected might be committed. It would set up a 'Judge of Freedoms', whose only duty would be to check that arrest warrants had been made out according to the correct procedure, not to check whether there were any grounds for the arrest. Further, an accused could be retried on the same charge even if found not guilty - double jeopardy. (Not surprisingly, in 2001 the Blair government started pushing for this.) A career judiciary would make the judgements; they would be the judges and prosecutors. Defence lawyers would be a separate, lower, caste.

Corpus Juris would end our right to trial by an independent jury of one's peers. It states, "Courts must consist of professional judges ... and not simply jurors or lay magistrates", a clear dismissal of our system. In trial by jury, the jurors are sovereign over the law: they can disregard the law if they think that it would give an unjust verdict. As Oliver Wendell Holmes put it, "The jury has the power to bring in a verdict in the teeth of both law and facts."[2] The jurors, representing the people, are sovereign over the judge, representing the state, since the people give the government its authority and they have the right to assert that authority over the state. The jury possesses "the undisputed power to acquit, even if its verdict is contrary to the law as given by the judge and contrary to the evidence."[3] The jury has an "unreviewable and irreversible power ... to acquit in disregard of the instruction on the law given by the trial judge."[4]

The government and the EU both insisted that the Corpus Juris proposal was only a discussion paper - the euro began as a discussion paper - although one Home Office Minister admitted that it 'would have implications for national sovereignty'.[5] The Lord Chancellor, Lord Irvine of Lairg, wrote to the Magistrates Association about Corpus Juris, "Many of the recommendations, if adopted, would conflict with the legal traditions of many member states, including the United Kingdom."[6] Corpus Juris was another part of the EU's attack on the national sovereignty of all its member states. As Verhofstadt said, "The EU arrest warrant is as important as the single currency." Labour's 'red lines' promising that it would never accept criminal and civil law harmonisation have vanished.

Compulsory identity cards are another EU idea. A Home Office representative told a 'faith group' meeting, "ID cards are the result of an EU decision and all member states are going to adopt them."[7] The Labour government accepted the idea in 2000, well before 9/11 gave it the excuse that the scheme was to do with fighting terrorism. However, the only research ever conducted into ID cards' effect on terrorism concluded, "The detailed analysis of information in the public domain in this study has produced no evidence to establish a connection between identity cards and successful anti-terrorism measures. Terrorists have traditionally moved across borders using tourist visas (such as those who were involved in the US terrorist attacks), or they are domiciled and are equipped with legitimate identification cards (such as those who carried out the Madrid bombings).

"Of the 25 countries that have been most adversely affected by terrorism since 1986, eighty per cent have national identity cards, one third of which incorporate biometrics. This research was unable to uncover any instance where the presence of an identity card system in those countries was seen as a significant deterrent to terrorist activity."

Governments have traditionally claimed that ID cards would reduce benefit fraud. But this is not true either. The Parliamentary Under-Secretary at the Department of Work and Pensions, Chris Pond, revealed that people not being who they said they were when making a claim causes only a tiny fraction of the benefit fraud problem. The Department found that of the estimated £2 billion total annual benefit fraud, only £50 million, 2.5%, came from claiming a false identity. Almost all benefit fraud was based on people lying about their circumstances, not about their identity.

The government says that a new ID infrastructure for benefits could cost £5.5 billion. This is 110 times the annual loss through false identity. The likely price to each of us is £35 to £40 for a card without a passport, £85 for an 'enhanced' biometric passport. A recent poll said that only 18% of us would be happy to pay even £30 for a card.

Nor is there evidence that ID cards would reduce illegal immigration or any other crimes. Police need evidence linking individuals to crimes, not evidence linking people to cards. Giving police the power to stop people who are going about their lawful business is an unnecessary and unacceptable extension of the state's powers. It is part of Labour's corporatist agenda.

The government may try to introduce ID cards under the Royal Prerogative, by-passing Parliament, as the previous government did with the new plastic ID card-style driving licence with photographs, which it introduced from July 1996, to comply with an EC directive. The Home Office has confirmed that the ID card scheme comes from the EU: "The European standard to which the driving licence/identity card would need to conform does not allow for national symbols, only the European 'Circle of Stars'."

We don't have to accept these cards. The Australians defeated the idea in 1987, after massive public protests split the government. New Zealanders also defeated the idea. Canada abandoned the idea last year after public protests.

This government overrules the rule of law, suspends habeas corpus and defends those who close down theatres. Its acts, particularly the Racism and Xenophobia Directive and a new offence of 'religiously aggravated threatening behaviour', threaten our freedom of thought and speech: behaviour is either threatening or it isn't – the law should deal with actions, not with thoughts.

We have already lost habeas corpus, due to the EU's 'anti-terrorist' laws. The EU defines terrorism far too widely, as 'intentional acts destabilising the fundamental political, constitutional, economic and social structures'. By this definition, the EU could call terrorist any opposition to the Constitution, even voting against it in a referendum!

ID cards, like Corpus Juris, are just another part of the EU's attack on the national sovereignty of all its member states. Both are attacks on Britain's sovereignty, our hard-won freedoms and our common law, which is unique in Europe. The British mixture of the law of statute and common law has become a barrier to the EU's legislative onslaught. In particular, Blair sees common law, with its basis of evolving legal precedent through the courts by way of plaintiff and defendant, as far too independent of the state. The history and development of common law, that is, equity, tort, contract and trust, are unique to Britain, and throughout our history they have acted as a dynamic. This contrasts with other countries that place greater emphasis on statute law through parliamentary lawmaking.

As Frederick Engels wrote, "English law is the only one which has preserved through ages, and transmitted to America and the Colonies, the best part of that old Germanic personal freedom, local self-government and independence from all interference but that of the law courts which on the Continent has been lost during the period of absolute monarchy, and has nowhere been as yet fully recovered."[8]

2: Police

Kohl said in 1992, "A European Army and a European police-force lie at the end of the road to European Union."[9] Corpus Juris needs a police force to enforce it, so the EU is setting up the 5,000-strong Europol force. This would be a new top layer of police, just as the European Commission is a new top layer of government. In November 2000, the European Parliament voted for a European Police College, whose remit was 'developing a European approach in the field of crime-fighting, border surveillance, protecting internal security and maintaining law and order.'[10]

Under the Europol Convention, article 41, paragraph 1, "The officers of the new EU police force, Europol, are immune from criminal prosecution should they break the law while carrying out their activities." The Amsterdam Treaty's Article 8 reiterates that members of Europol are 'immune from legal process of any kind for acts performed ... in the exercise of their official functions'. Traditionally, in Britain, no one, including the police, was above the law (with certain exceptions for foreign diplomats). Europol is not accountable for its actions to the European Parliament or to MPs from EU member countries. Elected representatives are not even allowed to see its annual report, which is subject to the EU's strict secrecy laws.

Europol is to have the right to engage in national policing operations. So Europol officers could arrest British citizens, arraign us before European courts, and try us and sentence us under EU jurisdiction.

In recent years British governments set up a national detective group and a national intelligence unit. In 2000, Blair started putting local police forces under central government control.

The Council of the European Union planned to give the EU's law enforcement agencies access to all communications data, archiving all phone-calls, e-mails and faxes for up to seven years. ENFOPOL 98 went through the EU Justice and Home Affairs Council in May 2001, extending this surveillance to mobile phones, Internet usage and websites. Typically, the public was refused access to relevant documents because disclosure "could impede the efficiency of ongoing deliberations." This swept away all the protections for personal freedom and privacy set up by international data protection and privacy rules. According to the Sunday Times, "The EU is setting up a paramilitary police force to intervene in conflict areas across the world to protect the EU's political and economic interests. Brussels has drawn up plans for a 5,000-strong armed police capability able to carry out 'preventative and repressive' actions in support of global peacekeeping missions. The new body, which may be given the name European Security and Intelligence Force (Esif), would work alongside a 60,000-strong EU defence force that is also being set up. The security force - likened to France's gendarmerie or the Royal Ulster Constabulary and made up of policemen from Britain and other EU members - would be intended primarily for use in trouble spots such as Kosovo. Although it is not clear when recruitment to the force will begin, it is expected to be fully operational by 2003. The French Government wanted to have it ready by the end of 2001.

"Critics fear, however, that its units, armed with light machine-guns and trained to operate alongside EU ground troops, may eventually be used to suppress disorder within member states. No restrictions on its sphere of operations have been placed in the regulations so far agreed by EU governments, and detailed 'rules of engagement' have not yet been drawn up. "This is an appalling development," said Timothy Kirkhope, the former Home Office minister and now Conservative chief whip in the European Parliament. "Although they say this police force would be used only in places like Kosovo, once the structure is in place there is an implied threat to deploy it anywhere, including on home soil." Tony Bunyan, the director of Statewatch, said the creation of the force was part of a broader drive by the EU to enhance its powers: "The European Union is working hard to become a player alongside the United States in policing the world."

"It was of particular concern, Bunyan added, that details of the new structure would be kept secret, under regulations quietly agreed by EU governments during the summer that end the right of public access to information about both military and civilian crisis management. A Foreign Office spokesman said the need for an international policing ability had been revealed in Kosovo when British troops found themselves engaged in police work to 'restore and maintain law and order'. The new police units, like the EU's defence arm, will be under the control of a political and security committee, composed of ambassadors from each EU country.

"Effective operational command, however, will be in the hands of Javier Solana, the Spanish former Secretary-General of NATO who is now Secretary-General of the Council of Ministers. A spokesman for Solana said last week that the police units would be modelled on such paramilitary forces as Spain's guardia civil, the Italian carabinieri, and the French gendarmerie. There were already more than 3,000 policemen from EU countries deployed abroad, in the Balkans, Guatemala and East Timor, making the target of 5,000 a modest one. The big change was to organise things collectively, the spokesman said. "We cannot tell where a crisis may occur and EU assistance is requested, so there is no geographic limitation being placed at all."

"Experts believe deploying a police force of 5,000 would require more than 15,000 men committed and trained for service with the EU. The impetus for the creation of the force has been the perception of Britain, France and Germany that the UN failed to act effectively in preventing bloodshed in the Balkans. But the present plan is considerably more ambitious, calling on the EU to intervene on the world stage either in co-operation with or instead of the UN."[11]

3: Foreign policy

As befits a would-be state, the EU sought to create and impose a single foreign policy.[12] President Chirac said, "developing a European Union foreign and defence policy is a fundamentally political project." Hans van den Broek, the Commissioner for external political relations, said, "the voice of Europe will only be heard in world affairs if there is a single voice."[13] Gerhard Schroeder said on 19 January 1999, "But the European Union is insufficiently prepared for its international role in a foreign and security political sense. I only expect limited improvements from the changes to the Amsterdam Treaty. Our standing in the world regarding foreign trade and international finance policies will sooner or later force a Common Foreign and Security Policy worthy of its name. National sovereignty in foreign and security policy will soon prove itself to be a product of the imagination."

The Common Foreign and Security Policy threatened Britain's independent control of its nuclear weapons. Kohl said, "the German government is well disposed to discuss the composition of the nuclear defence of Europe."

The EU wanted a single EU seat on the UN Security Council, ending Britain and France's memberships. By 2000, the EU maintained 127 overseas delegates, and 164 states had permanent diplomatic missions to the EU. It had its own embassies, flag and anthem. The WTO recognised the EU as a government: the WTO Secretariat described the EC response to the WTO Trade Policy Review as the 'Report by the Government'.[14] EU member states, though still members of the WTO, could no longer speak or negotiate there in their own right.

EU supporters maintained that Britain should abandon its independence forever on the off chance that a single EU state would prevent wars. But the main forms of war are world war between rival empires and war against nations, opposed by national liberation wars. The 20th century's world wars began as conflicts between empires such as the EU wants to be, and nations fought liberation wars to escape such empires. EU apologists claimed that nationalism caused wars. For example, Valerio Lintner referred to 'the spiral of decline into nationalism that resulted in the Second World War'.[15] But this would make Indian nationalists, for instance, as guilty of World War Two as the Nazis.

In 2005, Margot Wallstrom, vice-president of the European Commission, used VE Day to blame the Second World War on 'nationalistic pride and greed and international rivalry for wealth and power'. This denigrates the nations who successfully fought for their independence against the aggressive force of Nazism, which was a counter-revolutionary assault on national sovereignty, not an assertion of national sovereignty. She accused those who oppose the EU Constitution of risking a return to the holocaust, saying, "Yet there are those today who want to scrap the supranational idea. They want the European Union to go back to the old purely inter-governmental way of doing things. I say those people should come to Terezin [a camp for Jews] and see where that road leads."

The EU aimed to form a single state able to expand eastwards and southwards and to resist the North American Free Trade Area (NAFTA) and the Association of South East Asian Nations (ASEAN). An EU Common Foreign and Security Policy with huge spending on military hardware and a centrally controlled army were signs of gathering war clouds, not of universal peace breaking out. We do not want Britain to be lined up in an EU state against a US-led bloc.[16] A single EU state increased the dangers of conflict with the USA and Japan.[17]

It was not the EU that prevented war in Europe between 1945 and 1992. The Allies' defeat of Hitler Germany deterred the German ruling class from going to war again and the Allies' agreements at Yalta and Potsdam established peaceful coexistence between Europe's nations. It was not NATO that kept the peace. Peaceful coexistence in Europe lasted only until the Soviet Union's demise in 1991. Almost at once war broke out again in Europe, in Yugoslavia in 1992.

After the Soviet demise, the EU, far from preventing wars, waged wars against nations in Eastern Europe, aiding Germany's traditional 'drive to the East'. For Germany, now much the largest member country, the EU was the way to become a major force in the world again. As the CDU Parliamentary Committee on European Affairs said, "Never again must there be a destabilising vacuum of power in central Europe. If European integration were not to progress, Germany might be called upon, or tempted by its own security constraints, to try to effect the stabilisation on its own and in the traditional way." In 1993, with EU and NATO backing, Germany achieved its long-term aim of splitting Czechoslovakia, which became 'a German peninsula'.[18] Germany saw itself as leading the EU: Theo Waigel, former German Finance Minister, said in 1997, "Germany as the biggest and most powerful economic member state will be the leader whether you like it or not." Helmut Kohl, unaware that reporters were present, said in East Germany, "When we build the house of Europe the future will belong to Germany."

The EU, led by Germany, was responsible for splitting Yugoslavia, for the resulting civil wars and NATO's aggression in 1999.[19] As a senior British diplomat said, the EU's decision to recognise Croatia and Slovenia early in 1992 was "disastrous ... it made the war in Bosnia inevitable."[20] The day before President Clinton launched the 1999 air attack on Yugoslavia, he said that a strong U.S.-European partnership "is what this Kosovo thing is all about." The EU backed the US-British attack.[21] Later, the House of Commons Foreign Affairs Committee concluded that the attack was anillegal aggression: "Operation Allied Force was contrary to the specific terms of...the basic law of the international community." NATO created puppet states like Kazakhstan, Kosovo and Bosnia to assist EU and US exploitation and transport of oil. Germany funded and organised the terrorist 'Kosovo Liberation Army'. EU enlargement takes the borders of this huge new state up to the Russian border, greatly increasing the danger of war.[22]

In a speech in April 1999, Blair explained, "Globalisation is not just economic. It is also a political and security phenomenon" demanding an "important qualification" to the principle of "non-interference in the internal affairs of other countries." This avowal of the 'right' to interfere opened the way to wars. Blair told the Polish Stock Exchange in Warsaw on 6 October 2000, "Whatever its origin, Europe today is no longer just about peace. It is about projecting collective power. ... Such a Europe can, in its economic and political strength, be a superpower - a superpower, but not a superstate."[23] So the EU, far from being a peaceful association of nations, was an aggressive power.[24]

The EU backed the 'sharp shock' approach to the countries of the former Soviet bloc. Between 1991 and 1994, Russia's GDP fell by 35% and its industrial production by 50%. The number of cows fell by 40%, of pigs by 68%, of sheep and goats by 37%. Its debt soared to $130 billion by 1997, and an estimated $30-40 billion a year fled the country, a third of it illegally. In 1992, wages were cut by 40%, and were halved again in 1993-95. The Russian people called its effects 'catastroika'.[25] The EU's policy of prioritising capitalism there meant cutting down democracy.[26] The European Commission's Forward Studies Unit proposed a 'benign' Pinochet-style dictatorship for Russia.[27] The EU particularly sought to interfere in the energy-rich region of the Caucasus, assisting European companies to exploit its oil and gas.[28]

The EU backed the US and British governments' sanctions on Iraq that killed one million Iraqi people, including 500,000 children. Richard Butler, former head of the UN's weapons inspection team in Iraq, said that the sanctions "simply aren't working other than to harm the ordinary Iraqi people." Kofi Annan, the UN Secretary-General, wrote, "The potential long-term benefits of sanctions (!) should be weighed against the immediate and long-term costs to children, including the collapse of health and education infrastructures, reduced economic opportunities, increased child labour in informal sectors and increased infant morbidity and mortality. The suffering of Iraqi children, as reported by the UNICEF, and of children in the Balkans are troubling cases in point." (The EC had imposed sanctions on Serbia and Montenegro from 1991 to 2000.)

The EU has consistently assumed a right to intervene in African countries' internal affairs. Far from expressing peaceful cooperation between nations, the EU banded together ex-imperial powers that want to re-establish control over Africa's resource-rich countries.[29] As Ghana's leader Kwame Nkrumah said in 1968, "Europe as a whole, and West Germany in particular, find profitable outlets for big business in Africa through agencies of such organisations as the EEC." Belgium, France and

Britain use the EU as cover for their attempts to impose economic control of central Africa, just as Germany is doing in the Balkans and Spain in Latin America. They use a Euro-chauvinism, a puffing of 'European civilisation', as against a presumed lack of civilisation in the other continents, to camouflage their neo-colonialism.[30]

The French state went as far as complicity in the genocide carried out by its client Rwandan dictatorship in 1994, training and arming those who killed an estimated 800,000 people.[31] In 1994, France sent forces into the Congo to protect its Rwanda clients. Since the 1997 nationalist revolution there, the USA, Britain, France and Belgium have all intervened, using Ugandan forces and the Rwandan Patriotic Front as proxy armies. A British-run firm of mercenaries, Arient, has fought there and the EU backs mercenaries from Uganda and Rwanda. In July 2001, Belgian Prime Minister Guy Verhofstadt visited the Congo. He demanded a 'multi-dimensional' role for Belgium, including 'reform' of the state's security services, a clear interference in Congo's internal affairs.[32] Belgium is still the centre for the world's trade in diamonds, most of which come from Congo, Angola, Botswana, Tanzania, Namibia and Sierra Leone. The war and the occupation of the East of the country have led to the deaths of three million people, virtually ignored by Western media.

The EU was also ready to bully its own members. In 2000, it cut links with Austria because it objected to the Austrian government's composition. This was ostensibly because of remarks made years ago by Jorg Haider, the Chairman of Austria's Freedom Party. But Robin Cook let slip the real reason when he said that it was because of Haider's policies of opposing EU enlargement and opposing illegal immigration into Austria. This intervention in Austria's internal affairs was illegal by the EU's own laws. Why should the EU decide who should be in the Austrian government? Its composition did not affect any other country and until it did, it was a matter for the Austrians alone.

In 2004, at the Commission on Human Rights, the EU refused to co-sponsor and vote in favour of the draft resolution that proposed to investigate the massive, flagrant and systematic human rights violations being committed against more than 500 prisoners at the naval base that the US government is keeping, against the will of the Cuban people, in the Harbour of Guantánamo. The EU, which always objects to no-motion actions, this time presented such an action in order to prevent any investigation against its ally.

As we have seen, the EU increasingly imposed its own foreign policy and there was even less democracy in foreign policy than in domestic policy.[33] Some supported this, claiming that it would end the British state's pursuit of imperial interests, but instead the EU backed these interests, as it backed those of other ex-imperial European powers. In particular, Britain's rulers aimed to use their links with the EU (as with the USA) to increase their power to interfere in other countries' internal affairs. But the British people did not need these links, because we did not need to intervene abroad. By getting rid of these links, we would be starting to deal with the out-dated institutions and approaches that disrupted our relations with other countries.

The EU wants a centralised foreign policy to destroy nations' sovereignty and national foreign policies. The EU's whole point is the destruction of the working classes of Europe. Blair aims to smash the remnants of nation in Europe, in France and Germany.

The basis of our foreign policy should be the equal sovereignty of every nation. Respect for the sovereignty, economic independence and territorial integrity of other nations means non-interference in other nations' internal affairs, establishing economic relations of equality and mutual benefit, and striving for peaceful negotiated settlements of disputes. We have moved beyond empire, beyond the freezing concept of the 'Soviet threat', beyond Thatcherism, beyond the notion of Economic and Monetary Union. We should move forward, making our own way, untrammelled, not entangled.

4: Defence policy

The EU consistently sought to create a single defence policy, enforced by a single army.[34] According to Joschka Fischer, this force would be 'another pillar in the process of European unification'. French Prime Minister Lionel Jospin said, "By pooling its armies, Europe will be able to maintain internal security and to help prevent conflicts throughout the world. The successful deployment of the Eurocorps was a step in the right direction. But we need to go further. If we manage to achieve this in the second half of 2000, we will have passed a milestone towards the creation of a united political Europe." Jospin said that bringing together its armed forces would be 'a decisive step towards building a political Europe'. He said the EU must have its own 'autonomous military capabilities'. President Chirac said that an integrated European defence and foreign policy was 'a fundamentally political process' and, "The European Union will affirm itself on the international stage when its inhabitants manifest with force this sense of European belonging." He called for a European Army 'able to put 60,000 into combat in out-of-area operations' independentt of SHAPE' (NATO's Supreme Headquarters Allied Powers, Europe).

Hans Eichel, German Finance Minister, said, "Why does Europe need 15 Foreign Ministers when one is enough? Why do member states still need national armies? One European Army is enough."[35] Verhofstadt said, "the Eurocorps is an instrument for converting the rapid reaction force into the nucleus of what is to be the future European defence system."

Prodi said that the EU must be able 'to launch and conduct military operations under EU command'. In February 2000, Prodi announced in Latvia, "Any attack or aggression against an EU member nation would be an attack or aggression against the whole EU; this is the highest guarantee."[36] This statement transformed the EU from a socio-economic union into a military alliance. He said, "When I was talking about the European army, I was not joking. If you don't want to call it a European army, don't call it a European army. You can call it 'Margaret', you can call it 'Mary Ann', you can call it any name."[37]

In 1995, the Labour Party said that it opposed the EU's aim of setting up a common European defence. Yet once in power, it did all it could to create a European military force. In December 1998, Blair and Chirac issued a Joint Declaration after their meeting in St Malo: "The European Union needs to be in a position to play its full role on the international stage ... to this end, the Union must have the capacity for autonomous action, backed up by credible military force, the means to decide to use them and a readiness to do so. ... The European Union will also need to have recourse to suitable military means. (European capabilities predesignated within NATO's European pillar or national or multinational European means outside the NATO framework.)"[38]

In June 1999, the European Council decided to set up the EU's own permanent, single command structure independent of NATO. This comprised the European Political and Security Committee to control defence policy, the European Military Staff Committee to plan strategy, the European Military Committee to draw up military advice, a headquarters, logistics and intelligence supports, and an EU 'high representative', Javier Solana. In June 2000, the French and German governments agreed to create a joint satellite reconnaissance system, outside NATO, designed to make the EU independent of US intelligence. Elmar Brok, chairman of the European Parliament Committee on common security and defence policy, said, "The EU can take over the responsibility for European-led operations."

Lord Owen warned on 23 October 2000, "We must wake up to what is happening in our name. How many people know, for instance, that for the first time in our history a British Prime Minister is allowing the European Commission to involve themselves in questions of defence and military policy? We now know the government is proposing to put European defence and military questions under the Common Foreign and Security Policy (CFSP) without proposing any amendments at Nice to Title V of the Treaty on European Union which would prevent a European Commissioner consulting the European Parliament on defence and military matters. The European Parliament for the first time will be able to ask questions, make recommendations and debate progress on military matters. Also the Commission will by Treaty wording be fully associated with such defence and military matters. Yet the Prime Minister has told the British people that defence and military matters in the EU will be purely intergovernmental. From now on that particular line deserves a hollow laugh. Defence and military matters are being brought into the ambit of the European Commission and the European Parliament by deliberate design and it is not honourable to pretend otherwise. I know of no other Prime Minister in my lifetime, other than Edward Heath, who would have contemplated such a change and the Conservative Cabinet, let alone party, would never have tolerated him doing it."

The EU wound up the West European Union in November 2000, and in December, at the Helsinki European Council, agreed to form a European Rapid Reaction Force, ending NATO's decision-making monopoly on military matters in Europe.[39] The Nice IGC stated that the Force would be empowered, "Where NATO as a whole is not engaged, to launch and conduct EU-led military operations in response to international crises." It would be "wholly answerable to the EU under the supreme political direction of the EU" and would "deal with NATO on an equal footing." The Presidency report on the European Security and Defence Policy stated that the EU would have "an autonomous capacity to take decisions and action in the security and defence field." Geoff Hoon, Britain's Defence Minister, said that there would be no geographical limits to its operations. Alain Richard, France's Minister of Defence, said that the force would enable the EU to develop global security responsibilities and that it must be able to deal with a 'high intensity crisis' by carrying out 'deep strikes'. Yet Blair claimed, "It's limited to peacekeeping and humanitarian tasks. It is not a conflict force."

The EU announced that this force would comprise 100,000 troops (240,000 in rotation), backed up by 400 warplanes, including Royal Navy Sea Harriers, and 100 warships. To make up for not joining the euro, Blair pledged the largest contribution to the Euro-army. Britain was to contribute 12,500 troops at any one time, with at least 25,000 (half the army) needed to sustain the force abroad for any longer than six months. This meant one brigade at any time, either armoured, infantry or air assault. Britain's contribution also included 72 combat aircraft (half the RAF's contingent), 18 warships including an aircraft carrier, two nuclear-powered submarines, four destroyers or frigates and an amphibious task group (half the Royal Navy's force), and artillery, attack helicopters and logistic support.

Some opposed the Euro-army because they believed that it would weaken NATO; others welcomed it for the same reason. Either way, backing NATO or backing the Euro-army, was to be complicit in rivalry. But the impact on NATO was not the point. An EU army could be a threat to Britain: the EU's leaders could use it against any country that wanted to leave the EU or whom they decreed to be insufficiently 'European'. As Jospin warned, "By pooling its armies, Europe will be able to maintain internal security ..." John Wilkinson MP agreed, "The greatest risk in the European Union's obtaining a defence role in its own right is that it will acquire an instrument for the potential physical coercion of recalcitrant member states – an armed capability against possible secessionist nations."[40]

5: Aid and development

In July 1973, the former President of the EEC Commission, Sicco Mansholt, said, "we are a rich man's club; we are discriminating against developing countries." The EU's relations with non-EU countries were exploitative. The EU produced ritual rhetoric about helping to relieve the debts, incurred by their rulers, owed by the countries of Asia, Africa and Latin America, but it did little.[41] The EEC's Director-General of Overseas Territories and Countries described the Lome Convention between the EEC and 70 African, Caribbean and Pacific (ACP) countries as 'a new form of European presence'. The EU sought to impose its own neoliberal priorities on these countries. Lome IV, 1990-1999, spent European Development Funds on 'structural adjustment support', that is, on making recipient countries adopt free market principles.[42]

EU development policy increasingly intervenes to promote capitalist forces abroad.[43] For example, in May 1996, Cuba rejected the EU's offered 'cooperation agreement' because the EU attempted to infringe Cuba's sovereignty. It insisted, as a condition of any agreement, that Cuba must move decisively towards a free enterprise system. The EU, far from challenging the illegal US blockade of Cuba, helped the US government to enforce the illegal Helms-Burton Act that tightened the blockade. (The US Congress passed this Act after Cuba shot down two Miami-based aircraft that had deliberately invaded Cuba's airspace.[44]) The Act punished non-American firms that invested in Cuban property confiscated, largely from organised crime syndicates, since the 1959 revolution.[45] In 1998, Blair agreed with Clinton that he would try to impose a tougher EU approach to Cuba.[46]

70% of the EU's foreign aid budget was tied to buying EU goods: workers' taxes subsidised EU firms. It brought more European private investment into extracting minerals, food and energy resources from the ACP countries. Its Development Fund invested not in industry but in cash crops and transport projects. EU food aid contracts are tied to purchases of goods produced by EU member countries at prices above the market rate.[47] It is also tied to neoliberal investment and trading agreements - access to strategic raw materials, free entry into domestic markets and ending pro-labour regulations. This is not aid or cooperation but subordination, the reproduction of imperialist relations.

This joint colonialism enabled the EU to impose its preferred economic policies on these countries, damaging their economies. It demanded that they remove agricultural subsidies while it paid huge subsidies to EU farmers. It dumped its agricultural surpluses on the ACP countries, undercutting their domestic food production, forcing down food prices and cutting their incomes. It used the World Trade Organisation and the World Bank to push these countries to open their markets to EU imports, but refused to open its own markets in return.

The less an underdeveloped country was tied to the EU, the better it has done. ACP exports fell from 6.7% of the EU market in 1976 to 3.4% in 1993. Other countries which received less of the EU's preferential treatment grew faster.[48]

Six months after the Asian tsunami, the EU had delivered barely a third of the aid that they promised. Oxfam reported that, across the region, most of the EU aid went to businesses and landowners. The poorest people benefited the least from the relief effort; they were also far more likely still to be living in refugee camps, where it was harder to find work or rebuild lives.

Section 6: Borders, immigration, race and asylum

The EU aimed to create a single border around itself, as every state has.[49] In June 1985, the leaders of France, Germany, Belgium, Netherlands and Luxembourg agreed at Schengen to abolish the frontiers between their countries, remove passport controls and define a single border around the area created by the signatory states. The Single European Market (SEM) and the Maastricht Treaty both led to more EU powers in this area, eroding national sovereignty. The SEM, which involves control of the labour market, could not be separated from control of immigration.[50] So the 1997 Amsterdam Treaty put Schengen into the EU acquis, giving the EU more powers to decide matters of immigration and asylum.[51] The Commission funded pro-migrant groups and bodies which supported EU, not national, decision-making on these matters.[52]

The EU wants labour, like capital, to move freely. Employers like to keep wages down, so they are prepared to import labour to do so. Trade unions exist to keep wages up, so they need to prevent competition from low-wage labour, whatever its source. Forced migrations add to the relative surplus-population of workers, undercutting wages and increasing unemployment.

Immigrants who are illegal and lacking in rights will be cheaper, much harder to organise and therefore more attractive to employers. This competition for work keeps wages low and conditions poor. So the trade unions have an interest in stopping immigration.[53] Employing immigrants as cheap labour also discourages the employer from investing in new equipment.[54] Immigration raises unemployment, particularly for badly-paid workers. It increases unemployment duration for almost all groups.[55] The steady influx of refugees into Germany in the 1950s kept wages low, even for skilled workers.[56] Restricting immigration, along with stronger trade unions and more generous social insurance, improves wages and conditions, reducing poverty and inequality, as in Canada.[57] Switzerland (not in the EU) has Europe's highest wages and lowest unemployment; it also has Europe's toughest immigration laws.

So the EU promotes free movement and wants more immigrants from outside the EU, claiming that the EU faced a 'demographic timebomb' due to a declining birth rate so that fewer workers would have to support more pensioners. It claimed that it needed 1.4 million new immigrants every year. This would save member states the trouble and expense of educating and bringing up these new members of the workforce. But EU members did not need new immigrants to rebuild their economies: 30 million people were unemployed in the eurozone countries, as many people without work as the entire populations of Ireland, Belgium and Denmark. In Britain, the government talked of having full employment, when even on their figures 1.5 million people were unemployed.

Further, emigration robbed poorer countries of vitally needed workers. The British government and its agencies procured skilled workers from countries where they were desperately needed, for instance health workers and teachers from South Africa and Zimbabwe. Emigration subsidises the receiving country, while the nation that trained them loses their valuable talents.[58]

Many used asylum seeking as cover for economic migration.[59] EU member governments agreed in the 1990 Dublin Convention on Asylum, "asylum applications can only be processed by the member state in which the asylum-seeker first arrives in the European Union."[60] This agreement was more honoured in the breach. In English law, as in international law, there is no right to asylum.[61] Every state is entitled to refuse or grant admission to nationals of other countries according to its own domestic laws, policies, and practices.[62] This was in line with international law, based on the practice of all other states.

By large majorities, British people opposed more immigration, opposed ceding control over immigration policy to the EU, thought that political refugees should not be allowed to stay indefinitely and wanted to keep passport controls between EU countries.[63] A Mori survey showed that two thirds of British adults thought that there were too many immigrants in the country, and an even greater number thought that asylum seekers came to Britain because it was seen as a 'soft touch'. The same survey showed that these beliefs had nothing to do with race or racism, and that only a tiny minority of British people were in any way racially prejudiced. 95% of white residents would not object if their employer was black or Asian. More than three quarters would be happy for a relative to marry a person of another race. 80% said that they would not be upset if their neighbour were of Asian or Afro-Caribbean origin; only 3% strongly agreed that they would be upset in these circumstances.[64]

Particularly in the more densely populated countries of the EU, like Britain and Holland, concerns about the growing numbers of immigrants and asylum seekers were widely raised. Many called for more effective immigration controls, while also opposing any racial biases in policy.

British people generally reject theories of racial difference and oppose racial discrimination. We know that there is no physical or biological basis for the concept of 'race'. We know that all human beings come from a single stock and belong to the same species.[65]

The human grief and misery caused by forced migration remains a concern to trade union movements who seek to support and integrate new immigrants while refusing to allow them to be used to drive down conditions long fought for. Compared to many countries in the EU, the work of the British trade union movement in this area is exemplary. Why then do some think that the EU can deal better with these matters than we can? But we have not yet tackled this problem at its political source.

By freeing the traffic of persons, goods and services while reducing border controls the EU has signally assisted the growth of transnational crime.[66] The EU's policy of ending border controls has also increased drug abuse in Eastern Europe: France's Observatory of Drugs and Drug Addiction reported in October 2002 that heroin, ecstasy and cannabis are now widely sold in the former communist countries. It noted that drug use there is approaching Western levels, and that EU enlargement would only hasten the process. It said, "The free market, the free movement of people, goods and capital, is a paradise for drug users and traffickers." The EU claimed that it was committed to tackling international crime: why then did it seek to loosen border controls? Reimposing border controls would restrict criminals' activities. Belgium and Luxemburg have both had to reimpose border controls to prevent influxes of illegal immigrants, proving that the Schengen agreement had failed. The Belgian interior minister admitted, "These controls are necessary to dissuade illegal arrivals in our country and to combat effectively the mafia-style networks that exploit these unfortunate people."

7: Religion

The EU's Soul for Europe programme, which started in 1991, declared, "the building of Europe has a spiritual and ethical dimension. The objective of Soul for Europe is to encourage contributions to the unification of Europe." It sought dialogue with 'faith groups' and promoted the understanding of EU policies. It was part of the European Commission's little-known 'Forward Studies Unit', whose aim was 'legitimising and constitutionalising the European Project'. The Commission granted £25 million a year to ecumenical pro-EU projects and to churches that promoted the EU. In 2004, it gave Soul for Europe 36,020 euros, Evangelische kirche der Union 13,919, Coordination Internationale des Jeunesse Ouvriere Chretienne 25,500, Ecumenical Forum of European Christian Women, Edinburgh 22,800, Federazione delle Chiese Evangeliche in Italia 25,000, Ecumenical Youth Council in Europe, Brussels 15,000, Jeunesse etudiante catholique 18,000, Pax Christi International Youth Forum 20,000, World Student Christian Federation, Oslo 25,000, Jeunesse ouvriere chretienne internationale 23,500. Funding applications were filtered through the Soul for Europe Screening Committee, whose membership was secret. As a result, the Church of England and all too many individual Anglican churches and ministers actively promoted Britain's absorption into the EU.

During the Convention on the Constitution, the Commission of the Bishops' Conferences of the European Community (COMECE) said that it wanted Europe's citizens to "trust in the values and objectives of European integration ... the centrality of the human being, solidarity, subsidiarity and transparent democracy."

Throughout the 20th century, the Roman Catholic Church backed every effort to create a single European state.[67] Indeed, the European flag with its halo of stars can be seen on many a Catholic portrait of the Virgin Mary. Pope Pius XII had helped Hitler's efforts to create a single European state: the Privy Chamberlain to the Pope, Franz von Papen, the Reich's Vice-Chancellor, smoothed Hitler's rise to power, explaining, "Nazism is a Christian reaction against the spirit of 1789." Pius blessed Mussolini's wars and colluded with the Nazi Ustashi in Yugoslavia in slaughtering 240,000 Orthodox Serbs and forcibly converting over 750,000.[68] In his 1944 Christmas message, Pius called for a single European state: "This organisation will be vested by common consent with supreme authority and with power to smother in its germinal stage any threat of isolated or collective aggression." In his 1952 Christmas broadcast, he announced his plan to unite Europe politically and the world religiously in a new Holy

Roman Empire, "a Christian order which alone is able to guarantee peace. To this goal the resources of the Church are now directed." Pope John XXIII also called for a European state, 'the Greatest Catholic superstate the world has ever known', and 'the greatest single human force ever seen by man'. The Papal Nuncio in Brussels described the EU as 'a Catholic confederation of States'.

The carefully chosen first Slavic Pope, John Paul II, repeatedly spoke of European unity on his sixty-plus propaganda journeys. His message was that European identity was 'incomprehensible without Christianity'. He sought strong Vatican influence on governments, as in the Middle Ages. In his address to the European Parliament in May 1985 he called for European unity. He designated Methodius and Cyril - the two saints who brought Christianity to the Slavic world in the ninth century - as Europe's patron saints. He told the European Parliament in 1988 of his wish that Europe might "one day expand to the dimensions bestowed on it by geography and above all by history". In October 1999, he started the process of canonising the EU's 'founding fathers', Alcide di Gasperi, Schuman and Adenauer, as their reward for founding it 'on Roman Catholic principles'.[69]

The ecumenical movement and its offshoots, disguised as a genuine conciliatory process, were part of the Vatican's secret strategy for the EU. In the early sixties, Cardinal Bea, President of the Vatican Secretariat for Promoting Church Unity, admitted, "The Church would be gravely misunderstood if it should be concluded that her present ecumenical adventuresomeness and opinions meant that she was prepared to re-examine her fixed dogmatic positions. No concessions in dogma can be made by the Church for the sake of Christian Unity."

Many leading pro-EU politicians in Britain are Catholics. For example, at the time of the first EU elections, the ardent pro-EU Catholic, Liberal Democrat Shirley Williams, linked the EU with her church's goal of assuming political and religious authority over everybody. The current Prime Minister's wife is a Catholic, and the Prime Minister is very close to Catholicism.

In the continent of Europe, 199 million people professed to be Roman Catholics; only 61 million people claimed a Protestant heritage. In the 1990s, the Vatican achieved its long-held ambitions to destroy

The EU Bad for Britain

Czechoslovakia by detaching Catholic Slovakia from the Protestant, Hussite Czech Republic, and to destroy Yugoslavia by splitting Catholic Croatia from the legally constituted state of Yugoslavia and the orthodox Serbs. Poland too has been thoroughly re-Catholicised through the Vatican's collusion with the Solidarnosc Movement, whose leader, Lech Walesa, an ardent Catholic, became President. The former Soviet Union fell apart into small states, some of which, including Ukraine and Lithuania, had large Catholic populations. The Vatican also used the EU to try to restore its influence in the Protestant Scandinavian countries and in Switzerland, the land of Zwingli and Calvin. The EU project represented a Counter Reformation to the nonconforming, tolerant and atheistic traditions established in Britain since the 16th century. In fact, Vatican hostility to Britain's independent-mindedness goes back to 1215; it denounced Magna Carta as 'abominable' and 'illicit' within ten weeks of its being signed! And it is maintained to the present day: in 1996 the Pope refused to condemn the IRA terrorists who were bombing London.

In April 2005 the EU gave a grant of several million euros to the Catholic Church in Poland.

8: Devolution and regionalisation

The EU's regionalisation policy sought to dissolve national identities by fostering regional autonomy.[70] The European Regional Development Fund, set up in 1975, was designed to create a 'Europe of the Regions', whereby power was leached away from national governments, not to the regions, but to those who controlled the central EU institutions. Neal Ascherson, who, like Charles Kennedy MP, leader of the Liberal Democrats, and Andrew Marr, the BBC's Political Editor, was a member of the Federal Trust Round Table, said, "increasing unity at the European surface and increasing diversity at regional level are in fact parts of a single development, the weakening of the nation-state ... that is why Maastricht not only designed fresh steps towards supranational unity, but also instituted the Committee of the Regions."[71]

Devolution too was the flip side of massive centralisation of power into EU bodies. The EU, not popular demand, drove the devolution programme.[72] The EU encouraged separatist movements to demand a Scottish parliament and a Welsh assembly, to divide Britain and undermine our democracy. In practice, devolution moved power not to the people but to politicians, and not even to anyone new. The Commission saw regionalism as integral to federalism. Regional bodies and supranational bodies complement each other since both undermine national governments.[73]

The EU also sought to centralise certain areas of production in different geographical regions spread throughout the continent. This promotion of 'clustering' undermined the ability of any one country to produce across a balanced range of industries.

The European Commission increasingly bypassed national government by dealing directly with 'subnational' authorities, i.e. regional and local government bodies. 'Subsidiarity' meant developing regional and local bodies at the expense of national bodies.[74] On the European Commission's map of the EU, available in local reference libraries, 'England' was missing.[75] The United Kingdom, Scotland, Wales and Northern Ireland were all identified, but England was not. In the Commission's view, Britain comprised 12 regions out of 111 in the EU: Scotland, Wales, Northern Ireland and London were each EU regions with their own elective assemblies, with varying degrees of autonomy and popular consent.

The Maastricht Treaty set up the Committee of the Regions to involve local government in the EU's legislative processes.[76] The Committee commented on draft laws on health, culture, the Structural Funds and whatever else the Council or Commission considered appropriate. It consisted of 222 representatives from local and regional authorities in the member states and an equal number of alternate members.

In April 1994, the Conservative government had created Government Offices for the regions, each under a Regional Director. In line with this policy, in March 1999 the Blair government passed the Regional Development Agencies Act. This created eight Regional Development Authorities (RDAs), business-led quangos, and non-elected regional assemblies comprising mainly businessmen and councillors. These bodies undermined the democracy of the country's internal structures; they undercut local councils and local organisations. Council taxpayers paid for them, yet any such taxpayer seeking some reference to them in reports and tax demands from his or her council, or exercising his or her curiosity in the local reference library, was likely to be disappointed. On 14 November 2001, Lord Falconer conceded that creating regional governments would mean abolishing one of the tiers of local government, the shire counties. In turn, this policy increased tensions between urban and rural areas.

Liberal Democrat policy supported the EU agenda of regionalisation, since it offered possibilities of political power forever unattainable at Westminster, as the Scottish Parliament showed. (Charles Kennedy had started his political life as a Scottish separatist, saying, "I am a Jacobite.") The Green parties also attacked national bodies, promoting the idea of a 'Europe of the Regions', seeking decentralisation within the EU. The Conservative party in theory opposed the regionalisation process, but in practice backed it. For example, the chair of the South East England Regional Assembly was the Conservative leader of Buckinghamshire CC, which maintained an office in Brussels.

The EU sponsored the Regional Development Agencies for lobbying for its Structural Funds. The funds were supposed to reduce social and economic inequalities, but as the Commission's First Cohesion Report, of 1996, revealed, "over the past decade regional differences in unemployment levels have increased, regional income disparities have widened and that the number of people living 'below the poverty line' has increased in several Member States, especially the UK, Italy and France."[77] More regionalisation will lead to even more inequality. We do not need lots of competing regional initiatives. We need different national policies, for full employment and industrial regeneration.[78]

As for the cash from the EU's Social and Regional and other funds, where did the money come from? If it came from our own pockets - as it almost certainly did - why did we have to get it back via the Brussels bureaucrats, who would surely have taken their commission? Why not cut out the middleman and spend the money ourselves? In the unlikely event that we were being subsidized from elsewhere in the EU, did we really want to be a charity case, eating from someone else's spoon - until a more deserving case came along and the subsidy suddenly dried up? The British have always been a stubbornly independent and self-reliant people.

Cross-border regions have been formed, for instance, parts of Southeast England region, Kent and West Sussex were part of a larger region called Pas du Calais Nord, centred on Lille. Other parts of the Southeast, and London, were part of an area called North Metropolitan, which extended to the North German plain.

Even apparently innocent affairs like town twinning promote the EU.[79] At town-twinning ceremonies, the mayors pledge to "join forces to help secure, to the utmost of our abilities, a successful outcome to this vital venture of peace and prosperity - European Union." Genuine civic aspirations for solidarity, reconciliation and internationalism have become perverted by the EU's more sinister centralizing agenda. The EU claims that it does not threaten existing national identities, but even the Nazis promised this: Professor Heinrich Hunke, the Economic Adviser of the Nazi Party, wrote, "The essence of the New Order: respect for national character".[80]

The EU has consistently pressed for regionalisation:[81]

1951 Council of European Municipalities and Regions (CEMR) founded

1965 First Commission Communication on Regional Policy

1969 Second Commission Communication on Regional Policy

1973 Conference of Peripheral Maritime Regions

1975 European Regional Development Fund

1979 First (Regional) structural reform funds

1984 First Conference of European Parliament/Regions

1984 Association of European Regions (AER) of Industrial Technology

1984 Second (Regional) structural reform funds

1985 Assembly of European Regions

1988 'Four Motors of Europe'

1988 Consultative Council of Regional/Local Authorities

1989 Third (Regional) structural reform funds

1991 CEMR becomes European representative of International Union of Local Authorities

1991 Second conference of European Parliament/Regions

1991 Charter of the Regions of the Community

1993 Fourth (Regional) structural reform funds

1994 Inaugural Session of Committee of the Regions (COR)

1996 AER declaration on regionalism

1996 Third Conference of EP/Regions (including COR)

1997 European Charter of Regional Self-Government

1997 Amsterdam Summit of the Regions and Cities of Europe

1998 Inaugural Session, COR 2nd Mandate

1999 Fifth (Regional) structural reform funds

As the Joseph Rowntree Foundation noted in 1996, "European programmes have put pressure on the UK to remedy its lack of regional structures." And the Campaign for English Regions says that regionalisation is all their own idea and nothing to do with the EU!

To get its way, the EU was still breaking up states' internal democratic structures to make them conform to the shape of the proposed new state. These policies would break Britain down into weak, mutually hostile regions that would be unable to stand up to the EU, imposing an unnecessary tier of regional government, devolution, a subordinate legal system and an emasculated local government. These changes were EU-driven, not democratically driven, though taking advantage of some people's misdirected aspirations for democracy.

If the EU and its Labour and Liberal-Democrat allies forced regional assemblies on us, they could force the Constitution and the euro on us too.

They know that they cannot convince us to vote for either, so they are trying to get them through by the back door by imposing an unnecessary and unwanted tier of regional government.

We have already forced Labour to back down on two of these three regional elections, in Yorkshire and Humberside, and the North West. The Chair of Yes4Yorkshire, Lord Haskins, told the Yorkshire Post in July that the referendum was 'unwinnable'. Yet Nick Raynsford, the Minister for Local and Regional Government, saw 'overwhelming support for a referendum'.

In the event, Labour got just 3,947 out of seven million people to back the proposed referendum for a regional assembly in the North West. John Prescott described this as 'significant and widespread interest'! The North East was the first English region to hold a referendum on establishing an assembly. People voted against, by 696,519 to 197,310. All 23 council areas in the region voted 'no'.

9: London, Britain's capital

Briefly, the status of London as Britain's capital city would change significantly in the euro-zone. Presently, it is a paradigm of a capital city with a balanced economy producing its unique character, and it is the most multiracial and integrated city in Europe. London is very different from the Continent's capitals. It is still at the heart of our economic life, as well as being Britain's political, financial, administrative, cultural and sporting capital. Despite all the hype about 'global cities' and 'European cities', London is still a national, rather than an international, economic centre, oriented towards our national economy and its own needs. Central London's main market areas are: the rest of Britain 40%, London 31%, the rest of the world 29%. The rest of Greater London's main market areas are: London 59%, the rest of Britain 32%, the rest of the world 9%.

It is still a centre of manufacturing excellence. In 1995, gross value added per manufacturing worker in London was £34,400, 13% higher than Britain's average. After the mid-1980s, London's manufacturing GDP increased significantly; its share of Britain's GDP was 15%, while it comprises only 12% of Britain's population.[82] This contradicted the Association of London Government's assertion that London is "a service-sector economy in which manufacturing is not now an issue of strategic importance." It has a trade surplus with the rest of Britain. It is also a net contributor to the EU, giving £3 billion to Brussels every year and getting back only £20 million.

In this chapter we have addressed many areas of concern in our common social life where we exercise our popular sovereignty. We have seen that a single EU state would end our sovereignty and our democracy.

Endnotes

[1]. Cited Daily Telegraph, 21 November 2001.

[2]. 1920 Horning vs DC.254 US 135.

[3]. 1969 U.S. v Moylan, 417 F2d 1002.

[4]. 1972 U.S. v Dougherty, 473 F2d 1113.

[5]. Cited page 1, Daily Telegraph, 30 November 1998.

[6]. The Magistrates Journal, September 2000.

[7]. Cited Sikh Times, Issue 152.

[8]. Frederick Engels, Special introduction to the 1892 English edition of Socialism utopian and scientific, Karl Marx and Frederick Engels, Selected Works, Volume 2, Foreign Languages Publishing House, Moscow, page 99.

[9]. Cited page 194, Peter Shore, Separate ways: the heart of Europe, Duckworth, 2000.

[10]. Cited page 28, Ambrose Evans-Pritchard, If this isn't a superstate in the making, then what is? Daily Telegraph, 15 November 2000.

[11]. Sunday Times, 3 September 2000.

[12]. See Desmond Dinan, Ever closer union: an introduction to European integration, Macmillan, 2nd edition, 1999, Chapter 17, pages 483-529.

[13]. Cited page 509, Desmond Dinan, Ever closer union: an introduction to European integration, Macmillan, 2nd edition, 1999.

[14]. Cited page 262, Charlotte Bretherton and John Vogler, The European Union as a global actor, Routledge, 1999.

[15]. Valerio Lintner, page 403, 'Overview: the European Union: the impact of membership on the UK economy and UK economic policy', Chapter 16, pages 399-430, in Tony Buxton, Paul Chapman and Paul Temple, editors, Britain's economic performance, Routledge, 2nd edition, 1998. Diana

Johnstone pointed out, "Anti-nationalism has been indispensable in the promotion of European unification. The more the European Union has been reduced to an instrument of transnational business and finance, the more it has been necessary, in public rhetoric, to stress its noble mission of putting an end to the national antagonisms that led to major European wars. The nation state has been stigmatised as the cause of war, oppression and violation of human rights. This interpretation overlooks both the persistence of war in the absence of strong states and the historic function of the nation state as the most effective existing framework for the social pact enabling citizens to build structures of social protection and cultural development, as well as to develop legal systems able to provide equality before the law and to defend citizens' rights. Demonising as 'nationalism' the only existing context for functioning institutionalised democracy obviously facilitates the dictates of 'the markets', which are innocent of nationalist prejudice." Diana Johnstone, page 15, 'NATO and the new world order: ideals and self-interest', Chapter 1, pages 7-18, in Philip Hammond and Edward Herman, editors, Degraded capability: the media and the Kosovo war, Pluto Press, 2000.

[16]. For details of the US state's record of forcible interventions in other countries' internal affairs, see David Schmitz, Thank God they're on our side: the United States and right-wing dictatorships, 1921-1965, University of North Carolina Press, 1999, Gabriel Kolko, Confronting the third world: United States foreign policy, 1945-1980, Pantheon, 1988, Thomas McCormick, America's half-century: United States foreign policy in the Cold War and after, Johns Hopkins University Press, 2nd edition, 1995, and William Blum, Killing hope: US military and CIA interventions since World War II, Black Rose, 1998. For two superb bibliographical overviews of American foreign policy, see Michael Hogan, editor, Paths to power: the historiography of American foreign relations to 1941, Cambridge University Press, 2000, and Michael Hogan, editor, America in the world: the historiography of American foreign relations since 1941, Cambridge University Press, 1995.

[17]. See Martin Feldstein, page 61, EMU and international conflict, Foreign Affairs, November/December 1997, Volume 76, Number 6, page 60-73.

[18]. Abby Innes, Czechoslovakia: the short goodbye, Yale University Press, 2001, page 219.

[19]. See Joanne van Selm-Thorburn and Bertjan Verbeek, 'The chance of a lifetime? The European Community's foreign and refugee policies towards the conflict in Yugoslavia, 1991-95', Chapter 10, pages 175-92, in Pat Gray and Paul 't Hart, editors, Public policy disasters in Western Europe, Routledge, 1998.

[20]. Cited page 243, John Peterson and Elizabeth Bomberg, Decision-making in the European Union, St Martin's Press, 1999.

[21]. See Colin Pilkington, Britain in the European Union today, Manchester University Press, 2nd edition, 2001, page 163.

[22]. See Peter Shore, Separate ways: the heart of Europe, Duckworth, 2000, pages 147-9.

[23]. Cited page 12, Daily Telegraph, 7 October 2000.

[24]. See, for instance, Brian Denny, German imperialism: Part 1, The Democrat, November-December 1999, No. 39, and Part 2. The Democrat, January 2000, No. 40, pages 6-7.

[25]. For details, see for example Irene Brennan's section, 'The implosion of the Russian economy', pages 97-100 of her 'Dialogue with Janus: the political economy of European Union-Russia relations', Chapter 5, pages 93-125, in Vassiliki Koutrakou, editor, The European Union and Britain: debating the challenges ahead, Macmillan, 2000. See also David Satter, Darkness at dawn: the rise of the Russian criminal state, Yale University Press, 2004, and Marshall I. Goldman, The piratisation of Russia: Russian reform goes awry, Routledge, 2003.

[26]. See Irene Brennan, 'Dialogue with Janus: the political economy of European Union-Russia relations', Chapter 5, pages 93-125, in Vassiliki Koutrakou, editor, The European Union and Britain: debating the challenges ahead, Macmillan, 2000.

[27]. Cited page 118, Irene Brennan, 'Dialogue with Janus: the political

economy of European Union-Russia relations', Chapter 5, pages 93-125, in Vassiliki Koutrakou, editor, The European Union and Britain: debating the challenges ahead, Macmillan, 2000.

[28]. See Neil Winn and Christopher Lord, EU foreign policy beyond the nation-state: joint actions and institutional analysis of the Common Foreign and Security Policy, Palgrave, 2001, pages 143 and 162.

[29]. For a full account, see Leo Dreapir and John Boyd, African resource wars of the 21st century: Sierra Leone-Zimbabwe-The Congo, Campaign Against Euro-Federalism, 2001.

[30]. See Richard Weight, Patriots: national identity in Britain 1940-2000, Macmillan, 2002, page 495.

[31]. See Gerard Prunier, The Rwanda crisis 1959-1994: history of a genocide, Hurst, 1995.

[32]. See Brian Denny, Belgium plans to recolonise Central Africa, The Democrat, July-August 2001, Number 54, pages 1-2.

[33]. Christopher Hill and William Wallace, page 10, 'Introduction: actors and actions', pages 1-16, in Christopher Hill, editor, The actors in Europe's foreign policy, Routledge, 1996.

[34]. See Desmond Dinan, Ever closer union: an introduction to European integration, Macmillan, 2nd edition, 1999, Chapter 17, pages 483-529. See also Peter Shore, Separate ways: the heart of Europe, Duckworth, 2000, pages 185-201.

[35]. Cited page 23, Peter Shore, Separate ways: the heart of Europe, Duckworth, 2000.

[36]. Cited page 149, Peter Shore, Separate ways: the heart of Europe, Duckworth, 2000.

[37]. Interview in the Independent, 4 February 2000. See Christopher Piening, Global Europe: the European Union in world affairs, Lynne Rienner, 1997, page 42. See also Martin Holland, 'The Common Foreign and Security Policy', Chapter 12, pages 230-46, in Laura Cram, Desmond Dinan and

Neill Nugent, editors, Developments in the European Union, Macmillan, 1999.

[38]. Cited pages 187-8, Peter Shore, Separate ways: the heart of Europe, Duckworth, 2000.

[39]. Peter Shore, Separate ways: the heart of Europe, Duckworth, 2000, page 191.

[40]. Hansard, 10 June 1999.

[41]. See Charlotte Bretherton and John Vogler, The European Union as a global actor, Routledge, 1999, page 126.

[42]. See A. Marin, 'The Lome Agreement', Chapter 22, pages 507-26, in Ali El-Agraa, The European Union: history, institutions, economics, politics, Prentice Hall Europe, 5th edition, 1998.

[43]. See Charlotte Bretherton and John Vogler, The European Union as a global actor, Routledge, 1999, page 136.

[44]. See John Peterson and Elizabeth Bomberg, Decision-making in the European Union, St Martin's Press, 1999, page 102. On the Helms-Burton Act, see their pages 102-3.

[45]. See John Peterson and Elizabeth Bomberg, Decision-making in the European Union, St Martin's Press, 1999, page 102.

[46]. See John Peterson and Elizabeth Bomberg, Decision-making in the European Union, St Martin's Press, 1999, page 103.

[47]. See Peter Gill, A year in the death of Africa, Paladin, 1986, page 69.

[48]. See M. Davenport, A. Hewitt and A. Koning, Europe's preferred partners? How the ACP countries should develop their trade, The ACP-EU Courier, 1995, Number 156, page 63. See also James Petras and Henry Veltmeyer, Globalization unmasked: imperialism in the 21st century, Zed Books, 2001, pages 121-2 and 128-38. See also Michael Maren, The road to hell: the ravaging effects of aid and international charity, Amazon Press, 1997.

[49]. See Desmond Dinan, Ever closer union: an introduction to European

integration, Macmillan, 2nd edition, 1999, pages 439-50.

[50]. See Andrew Geddes, Immigration and European integration: towards fortress Europe? Manchester University Press, 2000, page 84.

[51]. See Andrew Geddes, Immigration and European integration: towards fortress Europe? Manchester University Press, 2000, Chapter 5, pages 110-30.

[52]. See Andrew Geddes, Immigration and European integration: towards fortress Europe? Manchester University Press, 2000, pages 143-5.

[53]. See John Rex, page 67, in 'Transnational migrant communities and the modern nation-state', Chapter 4, pages 59-76, in Roland Axtmann, editor, Globalization and Europe: theoretical and empirical investigations, Pinter, 1998.

[54]. See Tom Bower, Gordon Brown, HarperCollins, 2004, pages 344-5.

[55]. See Rudolf Winter-Ebmer and Josef Zweimuller, page 263, 'Immigration, trade and Austrian unemployment', Chapter 10, pages 250-67, in Michael Landesmann and Karl Pichelmann, editors, Unemployment in Europe, Macmillan, 2000.

[56]. See Stephen George and Ian Bache, Politics in the European Union, Oxford University Press, 2001, page 152.

[57]. See Andrew Card and Richard Freeman, 'Small differences that matter: Canada vs. the United States', pages 189-222, in Richard Freeman, editor, Working under different rules, New York: Russell Sage Foundation, 1994.

[58]. See Gregory DeFreitas, page 351, 'Immigration, inequality, and policy alternatives', Chapter 14, pages 337-56, in Dean Baker, Gerald Epstein and Robert Pollin, editors, Globalization and progressive economic policy, Cambridge University Press, 1998.

[59]. See John Rex, 'Transnational migrant communities and the modern nation-state', Chapter 4, pages 59-76, in Roland Axtmann, editor, Globalization and Europe: theoretical and empirical investigations, Pinter, 1998.

[60]. Simon Hix, The political system of the European Union, Macmillan, 1999, page 314.

[61]. See Guy Goodwin-Gill, The Refugee in International Law, Clarendon Press, 1998, pages 202 and 204.

[62]. See J. G. Starke, Introduction to International Law, Butterworth, 10th edition, 1989, page 360.

[63]. See Social and Community Planning, British and European social attitudes: how Britain differs: the 15th report, Ashgate, 1998.

[64]. 'Too many immigrants' for majority of Britons, Daily Telegraph, 23 October 2000, page 4.

[65]. See Luigi Cavalli-Sforza, Paolo Menozzi and Alberto Piazza, The history and geography of human genes, Princeton University Press, 1994, pages 19-20. See also Ashley Montagu, Man's most dangerous myth: the fallacy of race, Altamira Press, 1997, pages 14, 31 and 121.

[66]. See Paul Kapteyn, The stateless market: the European dilemma of integration and civilisation, Routledge, 1996, page 71. See also Tony Thompson, Gangland Britain, Coronet, 1996, page 287.

[67]. With acknowledgements and thanks to Professor Arthur Noble, for material derived from his lecture, 'The Conspiracy Behind The European Union: What Every Christian Should Know', delivered at the Annual Autumn Conference of the United Protestant Council in London on 7 November 1998. See also Romano Prodi, Europe as I see it, Polity Press, 2000, pages 45-7.

[68]. For details, see John Cornwell, Hitler's Pope: the secret history of Pius XII, Viking, 1999.

[69]. See Adrian Hilton, The principality and power of Europe: Britain and the emerging Holy European Empire, Dorchester House, 2nd edition, 2000, pages 38-9.

[70]. On the regions, see Justin Greenwood, Representing interests in the European Union, New York: St Martin's Press, 1997, 'Territorial interests',

Chapter 9, pages 218-41.

[71]. Local government and the myth of sovereignty, Charter 88 Sovereignty Lecture, 25 February 1994.

[72]. See Desmond Dinan, Ever closer union: an introduction to European integration, Macmillan, 2nd edition, 1999, page 321.

[73]. See Desmond, Dinan, Ever closer union: an introduction to European integration, Macmillan, 2nd edition, 1999, pages 320 and 322.

[74]. See page 134, in Neill Nugent, 'Decision-making', Chapter 7, pages 130-50, in Laura Cram, Desmond Dinan and Neill Nugent, editors, Developments in the European Union, Macmillan, 1999. See also Justin Greenwood, Representing interests in the European Union, New York: St Martin's Press, 1997, page 223.

[75]. Michael Knight produced an excellent paper, The Balkanisation of Britain, to which I am indebted for the next three paragraphs.

[76]. For details on this Committee, see Neill Nugent, The government and politics of the European Union, Macmillan, 4th edition, 1999, pages 285-8, and Desmond Dinan, Ever closer union: an introduction to European integration, Macmillan, 2nd edition, 1999, pages 320-3.

[77]. Tamara Hervey, European social law and policy, Longman, 1998, page 192.

[78]. See John Mohan, A united kingdom? Economic, social and political geographies, Arnold, 1999, page 198.

[79]. See the EU's publication, 'A Europe of Towns and Cities: A Practical Guide to Town-Twinning'.

[80]. Introduction to Nazi lectures in 1942, in, Nazi plans for European Union: in their own words. Part 1: Economic face of the new Europe, Democrat Publications, 2002, page 3.

[81]. From the web site of the Brussels Committee of the Regions.

[82]. See Southern and Eastern Council of the TUC (SERTUC), The future of

manufacturing: a strategy to support the development of manufacturing in London, the South East and the East of England, SERTUC, 2001.

Chapter 4: The EU and its institutions

1: EU institutions - what kind of state?

A. The European Commission

B. A supranational civil service

C. The Council of Ministers

D. The European Council

E. The European Parliament

F. The European Court of Justice

G. Other EU bodies

2: Corruption

3: Forming a state ...

4: But not a democratic state

5: Enlargement

1: EU institutions - what kind of state?

Sometimes it appears that the EU seeks to win by sheer boredom, by a creeping crawling fumbling barrage of acronyms, endless red tape and labyrinthine bureaucracy. But its Directives, rules and Regulations are more than just a catalogue of ineptitude and bumbledom; they have a sinister consistency. In this section we seek to show how its institutions work - or not, as the case may be!

What kind of creature is this EU state-in-the-making? The EU functions like a giant corporation, "like an integrated economic system with a single centre of overall decision making" as the European Roundtable of Industrialists' former Secretary-General Keith Richardson accurately described it.[1] The Commission is its Board of Directors, the European Parliament its shareholders' meeting, the European Court of Justice its firm of solicitors. Each EU body is less democratic than its equivalent in each EU member state. As Sicco Mansholt, a former EU Commission President, summed up, "the ordinary democratic decision making process as we know it in the individual state does not exist in the Community." Its unelected quangos make the laws: its elected parliament doesn't. Its powerful bodies are unaccountable: its accountable ones are powerless. The EU takes away not only our national sovereignty and independence, but also our democracy.

A. The European Commission

The European Commission, an appointed not an elected body, is the EU's executive.[2] It intended to be, as Jacques Delors said, the 'beginning of a European government'.[3] The Commission described itself as 'the driving force behind European integration'.[4] It seizes every opportunity to expand the EU's powers.[5] Other EU leaders saw the Council as the core of the future government. None saw national governments or parliaments, still less the peoples, as the rightful sources of sovereign power or democratic authority.

The Commission is the EU's main legislator. It sets the agenda for the EU, initiates policy and produces much of the specific content of EU laws. The Council of Ministers, supposedly responsible for passing laws, only decides 15% of them. In 2001, 85% of EU laws were delegated, through 18 directives, 600 regulations and 651 decrees, produced by the Commission's 'comitology' system of 450 committees, its 1,000 expert committees and another 300 working groups.

It has 20 commissioners, two each from the larger member states and one each from the other nine. Member states' governments nominate the Commissioners and the European Parliament approves them for a period of five years.

The Commissioners elect a President from among their number.[6] The President is a member of the European Council, and also of the General Council of Foreign Ministers and of EcoFin, the Council of Finance Ministers, two of the EU's most powerful bodies.[7] The Maastricht

Treaty strengthened the President's position by giving him a five-year term and ruling that member governments could not dismiss the holder during that period. Previously the period of office was two years. The other 19 commissioners have responsibilities for various portfolios such as agriculture, transport, the budget, etc.[8] The commissioners normally meet once a week as the College of Commissioners and take decisions by majority vote. Each Commissioner has a cabinet of assistants; the rule is that no Commissioner should have more than six A-grade staff in his cabinet.[9] By tradition, all members of the cabinets - bar one - are the same nationality as the Commissioner. In 2001, the British Commissioners were Neil Kinnock, Vice President for Institutional Reform, and Chris Patten, Commissioner for External Relations. Now Peter Mandelson is the Commissioner for Trade. The Commission has 20,000 staff.

Commission Regulations are often the stuff of comedy. Number 2931/94 'Fixing the aid for the supply of breeding rabbits on the Canary Islands' must be one of the best. This subsidised some Canary Islanders who had the tricky job of getting rabbits to breed![10]

The EC Driving Licence Directive 91/439 is also a classic: "In general an additional driving test will be required for each category or subcategory of entitlement. But there remain certain exceptions to this where drivers have already passed one test which involves trailer entitlements for a larger or equivalent size vehicle. This will mean that passing a test for subcategory C1+E or D1+E will upgrade category B entitlement to B+E. But a test pass for C1+E will upgrade subcategory D1, if held, to D1+E. But a test pass for D1+E will not upgrade C1 to C1+E because the trailer size for D1+E tests is smaller than that required for a C1+E test. Passing a test for category C+E will upgrade category B entitlement to B+E and will also confer entitlement to C1 and C1+E and, if category D1 or D is held, will upgrade this to D1+E or D+E. A test passed for category D+E will upgrade category B and subcategory D1 to B+E and D1+E respectively. But it will not upgrade C1 or C entitlements because the trailer size required for a category D test is smaller than that required for a C+E or C1+E test."[11] Well, that clears up the problem!

The commissioners are not under the authority of their national governments, but must act in the interests of the EU as a whole. They swore an oath of office to renounce all defence of national interests. For British Commissioners, this meant breaking their prior oaths as Privy Councillors. A commissioner's salary in 2004 was £143,893, plus a residence allowance of £24,000, plus a relocation payment of £23,915, plus an entertainment allowance of £7,000, adding up to £198,808 a year.

The Commission's main role was 'guardian of the Treaties', and of the acquis communautaire, all the Treaties, policies, laws, directives, regulations, rules and judgments ever produced by the EU. By 2005 it ran to about 130,000 pages! By Article C of the Maastricht Treaty, members had to accept the acquis in full or leave. The acquis meant the constant, cumulative and one way accrual of authority by the Commission. The EU has never returned any powers to national parliaments. The Westminster Parliament has never overturned a single EU law. All the parliamentary scrutiny of EU legislation was just a charade.

The Commission could issue directives and regulations that were directly and immediately binding on all members, and it did so in abundance. (In theory, regulations were directly binding, imposing both means and ends on member states, while directives bound them on just the purposes. However, the ECJ ruled in Van Duyn v Home Office (1974) that directives too should have direct effect.) In 1998, for instance, it issued 773 new regulations, 44 directives and 537 decisions. It could also issue 'derogations' to member states wishing to bypass the rules of the Treaties.

The Commission's second main task is administering the EU's funds, about £55 billion a year. Its third and probably most far-reaching job is to initiate EU policy. It has the sole power to initiate, draft and propose laws for the Council of Ministers' deliberation. It is the only EU institution present at every stage of the legislative process. If the Council wishes to depart from the Commission's proposals, it must be unanimous, otherwise the Commission prevails.

The Commission is also responsible for implementing the Council's decisions. It investigates alleged infringements of the acquis and instructs member states to comply. It can also refer matters to the European Court. It can act upon complaints by member states or individuals or act on its own initiative. Its other roles are mediating between member states, representing the EU to third parties, and 'playing the role of supranational conscience'.[12] The Commission has autonomous powers under which it could act without reference to the Council in areas such as the Common Agricultural Policy and customs union. Anand Menon, Director of the European Research Institute, wrote to the *Financial Times*, on 1 March 2005, "I should point out that the European Commission is appointed and not elected. If it were elected, British business would have what it now lacks - a good reason to be sceptical of the merits of European integration. As it is, the main regulatory and bureaucratic authority in the European Union remains - mercifully - free from electoral pressures. It is also worth noting that continued British resistance to the notion of an elected Commission has been one of the reasons that such elections have never occurred."

The Commission worked closely with the most powerful corporate grouping in the EU, the European Roundtable of Industrialists.[13] This comprised 45 Chief Executive Officers of the biggest firms in Europe, including Royal Dutch/Shell, British American Tobacco, Siemens, Bayer, Krupp, Fiat and Hoffmann-La Roche. It was founded in 1983 to push for EU unification and to shape the EU to big business demands.[14] It led on proposing the Single European Market, deregulation, privatisation and flexible labour markets.[15] It founded the Association for Monetary Union in 1987, business's pressure group for EMU. It was the driving force behind forming the Transatlantic Business Dialogue in 1995, in which the European Commission and the US Department of Commerce combined to remove environmental, safety, health and worker regulations in Europe.[16] For example, during the passing of the tobacco directive, the Liberal, Christian Democrat and Socialist groups each tabled identical amendments supporting the tobacco companies – a lobbyist's dream!

Also influential in the EU were the Union of Industrial and Employers' Confederation of Europe (the European employers' organisation) and the EU Committee of the American Chambers of Commerce. The EU's giant firms were hand in glove with the EU's institutions.[17] Firms have far more access to EU bodies than any other organisations.[18] The employers created many PR agencies and corporate think tanks to influence the EU.[19] Of the EU's 700 'Eurogroups', lobbying groups, 490 represented firms.[20]

The EU displays activism on environmental issues largely because this enables it to expand its range of powers over ever more areas.[21] So the Commission makes every effort to keep a 'common environmental policy' on the EU's agenda.[22] But after two decades of EU environmental activism, the EU's own 5th 'Environmental Action Programme', published in 1993, noted a 'slow but relentless deterioration of the environment'.[23] Water quality is worse: as the Commission said, "Over the last 20 years, the state of the Community's water resources has not improved. ... Far more examples exist of deterioration in quality than of improvements."[24] Yet the EU's capital city of Brussels still has no functioning sewage system and no sewage treatment plant!

B. A supranational civil service

The EU's permanent staff functioned as a new top grade of civil service over the national civil services, whose work they directed. This achieved Monnet's aim: he had wanted the EU's staff "to remain a nucleus and confine itself to organizing and stimulating the work of others. For the rest, it could rely on the national civil services ... The French Modernization Plan had proved that authority could best be exercised by small teams ... A few hundred European civil servants would be enough to set thousands of national experts to work, and to make the powerful machinery of firms and Governments serve the aims of the [Schuman] Treaty. It was on this model, at least, that I was going to try to frame the first Community institutions."[25] It was more than a few hundred, more like a few tens of hundreds, but otherwise the result was much as Monnet wanted. After Prodi's 1999 reforms, the EU's administration comprised the Commission services: 23 Directorates General, and 15 Special Services, including the Secretariat General and the Legal Service.[26] Eurostat, the EU's statistical office, grew in importance.[27] The EU had in 1998 28,000 permanent staff, 14,000 of whom were at the administrative level.[28] More than 25,000 national civil servants were directly involved in the EU policy process. Increasingly, they worked under EU direction implementing EU, not national, decisions. The Commission contracted out many administrative tasks and key areas of policy to about a thousand unelected and unaccountable quangos, the vilely named 'comitology'.[29]

C. The Council of Ministers

The Council of Ministers is the EU's formal decision-making body.[30] The Commission proposes and initiates, but the Council disposes and decides. It considers the initiatives presented to it by the Commission. It takes decisions by majority vote, except where there is provision for qualified majority voting (QMV), whereby countries cast different numbers of votes – a system designed to ensure that if two large countries sided together they could not block a decision. The Single European Act extended the range of issues for which QMV was valid, and reduced the right of veto by member states. The Nice Treaty added another hundred kinds of occasions when QMV was deemed appropriate. The Council is made up of representatives from each member country, but they do not have to consult their national parliaments before taking decisions.

EU-supporter Michael Heseltine wrote, "A major defect in the machinery of Europe is the inability of national parliaments to influence events. Ministers may be held accountable to the House of Commons but only *after* the votes have been cast in the Council of Ministers. ... the national parliaments ... are altogether outside the decision-making process. ... The United Kingdom Parliament finds it hard enough to exercise effective control over its own government. It would be idle to pretend that it has any influence over the institutions of the European Community. It is equally unrealistic to believe that it could *ever* have effective control, or that other national parliaments, singly or acting together, could create an effective control mechanism."[31] Yet just seven pages later he proposed, "What we need is the democratic authority of national parliaments brought to bear upon the institutions of the European Community."[32]

The EU Treaties transferred policy-making powers away from national parliaments to the Council. As Philip Allot MP told the House of Commons, "The Council has virtually no political legitimacy. It is accountable to no one. Its relationship to the Commission is irretrievably obscure. It is more of a cabal than a cabinet, more of a permanent diplomatic conference than a senate. And yet it legislates profusely."[33]

D. The European Council

The European Council (or 'Summit') is the term for the meetings of the heads of state and government of the member states and the Commission's President, which occurs at least twice a year.[34] Like the Commission, the European Central Bank and the Court of Justice, the Council takes its decisions in secret. The Council's Secretariat-General is central to the continual process of Treaty reform (playing a key part in drafting the new EU Constitution) and in making the EU's foreign, security and military decisions. It has developed into a quasi-executive agency making policy in its own right. The EU has created military structures in the Council secretariat, including its own military staff. Article D of the Maastricht Treaty required the Council to 'provide the Union with the necessary impetus for its development, and to define general political guidelines'.[35]

E. The European Parliament

The European Parliament is not a legislature: it could not introduce or enact laws.[36] It meets for one week in every month. It holds its sessions in Strasbourg; its committees meet in Brussels and its administration is based in Luxembourg. Moving the tons of papers and hundreds of Members of the European Parliament (MEPs) and staff from city to city costs huge sums. Its total running costs are £850 million a year. It consists of 626 members elected on a national basis: the first direct elections were held in 1979. Britain has 87 members elected by constituencies and we contribute £56 million a year to the costs of running the Parliament. MEPs have high salaries and expenses, and very high rates of absenteeism.

Neither the Parliament (nor the Council of Ministers) can initiate or draft legislative proposals: only the Commission can do this. It can ask the Commission to draft legislation in any areas that it feels needed EU action. Its powers are limited to the right to ask questions of the Commission, to be consulted by the Commission, to investigate complaints of misadministration in the other institutions and to reject elements of the budget. It can give its opinion on proposed laws and propose amendments. But "The Council is not legally obliged to take account of the opinions or amendments emanating from the Parliament."[37] Neither the Parliament, nor national parliaments, can overturn decisions made by the Commission or the Council of Ministers. The Parliament acquired some new powers under the Single European Act and the Maastricht Treaty, including the right to veto the accession of new states to the EU and the right to veto laws in 14 policy areas, such as education and culture, by absolute majority. This is the 'co-decision procedure'. But it failed to make the Commission more accountable.[38]

MEPs do not represent their constituents, or their constituencies. Articles 189 and 190 of the Treaty Establishing the European Community lay down that they must represent the 'peoples of the States brought together in the Community'. EU elections are run on the party list method and MEPs are elected by proportional representation. The EU aimed to make Britain 'converge' with the other EU members and proportional representation, like all Blair's constitutional 'reforms', makes Britain more like the other EU members. Far from reducing the democratic deficit, PR gives the party leaders powers to choose all the candidates and decide the order in which they are listed. This increases their powers of patronage, and takes elections even further away from the electors.[39]

Parliament's grouping of MEPs into socialist, Christian Democrat, etc., regardless of the nation they came from, was the first attempt to undermine the concepts of the nation and of national interest. Article 191 of the Maastricht Treaty stated, "political parties at European level are important as a factor for integration within the Union. They contribute towards forming a European awareness and to expressing the political will of citizens of the Union." Nowadays, the EU does not talk of 'political parties at the European level', but of 'European political parties', a very different idea, whereby national political parties become mere sections of EU-wide organisations. It is also proposing that the EU state funds pro-EU political parties. So British taxpayers could find themselves paying for the activities of parties opposed to their interests and wishes – not very democratic! The 'Party of the European Left' and 'Respect: the unity coalition' deserved no more support than the right-wing 'European People's Party': they all wanted to get on the EU gravy train.

Under Article 191 of the Nice Treaty, the Council of Ministers has the power to ban political parties from speaking in the European Parliament. Parties that refuse to develop 'European awareness' will have their public funding rights removed.

The European People's Party, of which the Conservative Party's MEPs are 'allied members', and the Socialist Group, which includes all the Labour Party's MEPs, support the strengthening of the European Parliament, at the expense of the national parliaments. They also support the Constitution for Europe. Some other MEPs, who claim to oppose the EU and its Constitution, find that their membership of the European Parliament compromises their independence of mind.

The Parliament's procedures are hardly models of democracy: absentees are counted as having voted for the resolution, which encourages MEPs to do even less for their money. It veers from endless speechifying without resolution to absurdly hasty voting: once, 287 votes were taken in an hour!

The Parliament's role is to provide some democratic cover to the EU, yet it is clearly undemocratic. The answer is not to demand a sovereign European Parliament with greater powers; this would only increase the EU's ability to ride over our democratic powers. Where undemocratic bodies transgress national sovereignty, the answer is to reassert that sovereignty.

Naturally enough, people across the EU did not like being railroaded into a new state and responded by abstaining in the Euro-elections. In the June 1999 Euro-elections, only 49% of European voters voted (in 1979 the turnout 63%; in 1984, 61%, in 1989, 58.5% and in 1994 56.4%). The downward trend was clear. The turnout in Britain was 23% in 1999, down from 36% in 1989 and 1994, and 33% in 1979 and 1984. Opinion polls told a similar story. For instance the euro has never been popular in Germany: ever since 1977, only about a third of the German people favoured the move towards a single currency; by mid-1998, only 28% supported the euro, and 44% opposed it.[40] The EU's leaders pressed on regardless: Prodi said, "I am not embarrassed to suggest that, sometimes, the answer to the concerns of a disillusioned European public is not less Europe but more."[41]

F. The European Court of Justice

The European Court of Justice (not to be confused with the European Court of Human Rights) said that its job was 'overcoming the resistance of national governments to European integration'. Its decisions were final and binding, taken in secret and by a simple majority. Yet this Court has enormous power over all the EU member nations. Its decisions overruled national law in areas under the EU's competence. An ECJ judge rightly described it as 'a court with a mission' to extend the EU's powers as widely as possible. The Court had a vested interest in extending its own powers, as it has consistently done. It should not be judge and jury in its own interest.

It sits at Luxembourg and consists of fifteen judges, assisted by nine Advocates-General. Any doubts or disagreements about the meaning, function or interpretation of EU laws and Treaties are referred to the Court. Cases brought before it include breaches of the Treaties, disregard of EU directives or regulations, and assessments of the compatibility of member states' laws with EU law. It can issue compliance orders to member states, which must be obeyed within a strict time limit.

Its deliberations are never made public, so there is no way of knowing about the quality of its reasoning or about the strength of any dissenting voices. The other EU court, the Court of First Instance, rules on disputes concerning the EU institutions and their staff, competition rules and the European Coal and Steel Community.[42]

The ECJ's decisions overrule national law in areas under the EU's competence.[43] In the 1960s and 1970s, the Court's consistently federalist decisions played a major role in unifying the EU, continually taking away member states' sovereignty.[44] In 1963, the Court stated in the Van Gend en Loos case, "the Community constitutes a new legal order in international law for whose benefit the states have limited their sovereign rights, albeit within limited fields, and the subjects of which comprise not only Member States but also their nationals."[45] The Court's decisions promoted EU unification even more than the EU Treaties did.[46] Its decisions were not legal judgements, but political decisions which the EU's leaders backed because they gave the EU more powers and assisted its drive towards a single state. The judgements also enhanced the powers of the Court.[47]

In 1964, the Court ruled that states' accession to the Treaty of Rome permanently limited their sovereign rights: "The transfer by the States from their domestic legal system to the Community legal system of the rights and obligations arising under the Treaty carries with it a permanent limitation of their sovereign rights, against which a subsequent unilateral act incompatible with the concept of the Community cannot prevail."[48] In 1972, the Heath government, by signing the Treaty of Accession, signed us up to the EU's entire acquis - forty-three volumes of European legislation, more than 2,900 regulations and 410 directives. These all became binding upon Britain, despite never having been scrutinised or debated by parliament.[49]

In 1974, the Court ruled that EU Directives, as well as Regulations, should be directly effective in member states.[50] Consequently, as Lord Scarman stated, Britain was now 'part of a legal system which not only confers a right but imposes a duty in certain circumstances to invalidate legislation'.[51] In 1978, it ruled, "every national court must ... apply Community law in its entirety ... and must accordingly set aside any provisions of national law which may conflict with it."[52] In the 1991 Factortame case, the Court ruled, "Under the terms of the 1972 Act, it has always been clear that it was the duty of a United Kingdom court to override any rule of national law found to be in conflict with any directly enforceable rule of European law."[53] Also in 1991, the Court ruled that some parts of the Treaty were so important that member states could never modify them.[54] The same year, the Court acted ultra vires in ruling that EU workers without a job could move to other EU member states to look for work.[55] Parliament cannot refuse to accept Community law or repeal it, unless Britain cancels the Treaty of Accession and withdraws from the EU.[56]

Illusions about the European Court of Justice paralleled illusions about the Charter. We could use some Court decisions about health and safety, equal pay, and protection for part-time workers. But if we decided that the decisions were good, why did we need the Court's say-so to enforce them? And if they were bad, then the Court was even less useful. Relying on laws encouraged a slovenly, dependent, even slavish mentality. From our own experience we knew that nothing of worth was given away. There was no such thing as a free lunch, as employers were so fond of saying.

G. Other EU bodies

The EU generously funds bodies that promote the EU and its federalist agenda, e.g. the 'Our Europe' Association, Journalists in Europe (£150,000 in 2000), the European Movement (more than £6 million), the International Federation of Europe Houses, European Integration in Universities, the Prince programme, the European Trade Unions Congress (£180,000) and the European Women's Lobby (£220,000).

The EU also tries to use culture to legitimise its rule, to integrate Europe's nations into a single European state and to transform us all into Europeans. The Maastricht Treaty created 'European citizenship', and extended the EU's legal writ to education, youth and public health. Its 'Culture Article' 128 gave it the right to intervene in cultural matters. In 1990, the EC launched its 'Jean Monnet Project', setting up 1722 university teaching programmes in 'European integration studies', and establishing 409 'Jean Monnet Chairs'. As a fairly predictable result, most academic studies of the EU 'tend to be of an uncritical and even laudatory nature'.[57] An academic entitled the Jean Monnet Professor of European Integration - a political programme summed up in a job title - was hardly likely to retain academic objectivity in his teaching and writing.

The EU has set up other committees, including the Economic and Social Committee, an advisory body consisting of 222 representatives from the various economic and social sectors in the member states.[58] It is divided into three groups - employers, workers and various interests, such as the professions, consumer organisations, agriculture, small and medium-sized enterprises and transport. It draws up opinions on all draft legislation referred to it by the Commission. But its reports usually sit, unread, in Council meetings. The Council ignores the ESC.[59]

The Conciliation Committee is made up of members or representatives of the Council or Parliament in equal numbers. It is convened when the Council and the Parliament disagree on a proposal for legislation and it tries to draw up and approve a joint text that satisfies both bodies. The Committee of Permanent Representatives of the Member States (COREPER) is made up of national civil servants who initially discuss legislative proposals.[60] The Court of Auditors oversees the EU's finances, but has no power to correct abuses or punish wrongdoers.[61] The

European Investment Bank provides loans on a non profit-making basis for capital investment that is supposed to help the EU to achieve balanced development.[62]

2: Corruption

Where there was no democracy, corruption could breed, away from the light of public accountability. Consequently, fraud was rife in the EU. The European Commission could not account for £17 billion spent on 'structural projects', and fraud amounted to at least £6 billion a year, about 10% of the EU budget, according to the House of Lords Select Committee on the European Communities.[63] The Committee of Independent Experts reported in March 1999 that fraud, irregularities, cronyism, mismanagement, cover-ups, collusion and evasion of responsibilities ran throughout the Commission: "The studies carried out by the Committee have too often revealed a growing reluctance among the members of the hierarchy to acknowledge their responsibility. It is becoming difficult to find anyone who has even the slightest sense of responsibility."[64] The Report exposed how patronage, fraud and corruption had become institutionalised in the Commission.[65] Commissioner Neil Kinnock put forward a package of reforms to deal with these problems. A report on its effects concluded, "little or nothing has changed … the new Commission is just like the old."[66]

EU rules ban its civil servants from reporting to the European Parliament any alleged corruption, irregularities or fraud. In August 2002, the European Commission's former chief accountant, Marta Andreasen, claimed that the EU budget was 'massively open to fraud'. She said that there was a 'dangerous failing at the heart of the system' because of a 'complete lack of compliance with basic and minimum accounting standards'. She stated, "Unlike the issues surrounding Enron and WorldCom, where you can at least trace transactions and accounts, you cannot do so within the EU accounts as there is no system in place for tracing adjustments and changes to figures presented." Characteristically, the Commission responded by attacking Ms Andreasen's character and qualifications, not by responding to her criticisms. She was suspended for going public with her concerns.

Since 1999, the EU's Court of Auditors has been reporting that the accounting system is at risk because of its computer system's insecurity and other failures. But as it said, "The Commission has been warned about them but to date has not taken any remedial action."[67]

Paul van Buitenen, an assistant auditor in the Financial Control Directorate, alleged that the Leonardo programme, with its £400 million budget for 1995-2000 and its £2 billion budget for 2000-04, was riddled with favouritism, nepotism and corruption. The EU suspended him on half pay, banned him from auditing and severely reprimanded him. Pauline Green, the Labour MEP and leader of the Socialist Group, urged the European Parliament to sack him. The accused Commissioners however kept their full £130,000 a year salaries and their pensions. The EU was more concerned to stop the report than the fraud. The proposed Corpus Juris would make van Buitenen's brave action illegal: its Article 6 bans disclosing secrets pertaining to one's office.

In 2004, the European Court of Auditors 'qualified' the accounts on all but 10% of the EU's 100 billion euro budget, for the ninth year running. The auditors pointed to 'significant errors in terms of legality and regularity', in other words, fraud. This followed the scandal at Eurostat, the EU's statistical bureau, where an auditor investigating secret funds kept by Eurostat directors found that missing or destroyed records made it impossible to track what had happened to £3 million. Prodi then promised yet another action plan and a public prosecutor to fight fraud across the EU.

The Court of Auditors found that it could not audit the EU accounts because there were so many inconsistencies and omissions. Many accounts were retrospectively doctored; whistleblowers were harassed, suspended and demoted. The worst fraud was in the Common Agricultural Policy, whose payments to farmers were 'materially affected by error'. Farmers were claiming for more land than is cultivated, overdeclaring livestock numbers and illegally reimporting produce after pocketing export subsidies. In 2003 the Commission wrote off 1.1 billion euros as 'irrecoverable debt' even though it had 'no knowledge of the detail of the transactions in question'.

The all-party Public Accounts Committee in Parliament reported that the precise level of fraud and corruption in the EU budget was difficult to measure given the complexities of the accounts.[68] In 2003, member states reported 'irregularities, including alleged fraud' to the value of €922 million to sleaze watchdog OLAF, a figure which is even higher than when it was first set up in 1999. But as the member states are not obliged to report in a consistent manner, or differentiate between fraud and other irregularities, the figure may be much higher and there is no reliable way of measuring progress.

The report concludes that "accountability and audit arrangements of the European Union have been characterised by inertia among the institutions. The high levels of fraud and irregularity generally thought to exist in the European Union operations have seriously damaged the Community's reputation. The fact that the European Court of Auditors has qualified the Union's accounts for ten successive years gives credence to this view. We believe that obtaining a positive Statement of Assurance is hopeless without dramatic changes to the Common Agriculture Policy and the Structural Funds to make them simple to control, thereby avoiding the high levels of fraud and error."

The Committee reports that by 2003 the EU budget was €98.3 billion and Britain's gross contribution was €15.2 billion. It suggested that "the scale of [the Court of Auditors'] work is totally inadequate given the importance of ensuring the effective use of Community funds", noting, "No independent review of the Court's work has taken place since it was set up in 1977" and that unlike Britain's National Audit Office, "the Court does not report on its own performance to anyone".

In April 2005, MEPs rejected proposals to tighten the auditing of their expenses and to introduce basic auditing procedures. The reform package would have closed a number of loopholes that allow MEPs to embezzle funds.

Their current pension system allows MEPs to pay their own private contributions to their pensions out of their office and travel expenses. However, there is no mechanism to ensure that they repay the money that they owe back into their expenses fund. They also rejected a proposal to impose sanctions against MEPs who commit serious fraud. They even voted down the idea of publishing on the internet what expenses MEPs are allowed to claim.

They will still not have to produce their tickets to claim travel expenses, allowing them to claim for expensive first-class journeys that they have not made. MEPs can each make about £800 a week on their travel allowance, which is based on the most expensive notional air fare rather than on the Ryanair flight they usually take. They can pocket a further £2,400 a month on their 'general expenses allowances', which remain unscrutinised. They get £10,000 a month of secretarial allowance, much of which goes to their family members. They get £180 a day just for signing the attendance register, even without attending their Parliament. (No wonder the press are now forbidden to photograph MEPs claiming their daily allowance!)

All these perks are tax-free and they are all on top of the generous salaries that MEPs pay themselves. British MEPs get £57,485, which is of course untaxed.

MEPs' uncontrolled personal expenses disable them from acting against corruption in the other EU bodies. If they started to root out CAP fraud, the spotlight would soon be turned on their own dodgy dealings. It is impossible to reform the EU because it is institutionally corrupt.

3: Forming a state ...

The European Communities' own publication, The ABC of Community Law, states, "The EC has areas of responsibilities which together constitute essential attributes of statehood." It says, "the EU is itself not yet a finished product", but that it is "in the process of acquiring a status similar to that of an individual state."[69] The EEC's founders built the drive towards a single state into its foundations. Its founding charter, the Treaty of Rome, undermined member nations' sovereignty: by Article 189(2), "A regulation shall have general application. It shall be binding in its entirety and directly applicable in all Member States." The EEC superimposed its laws on every member state's national laws. This contradicted the confident promise in the 1971 Heath White Paper, "The common law will remain the basis of our legal system, and our courts will continue to operate as they do at present." The very act of joining the EEC compromised our national sovereignty.

Writers of the standard textbooks on the EU acknowledge that its goal is a single state.

John McCormick - the evolution of the EU's bodies "is having the effect of slowly building a confederal Europe ... steadily taking on the characteristics of a new level of government to which the member states and their citizens are subject." And, "If Europe is not yet federal, it is federalising."[70]

Colin Pilkington - "it must be accepted that the UK has surrendered both parliamentary and national sovereignty through the act of joining the European Union."[71] Surrendered, but not irretrievably.

David McKay - "All the events which have occurred since 1999 have reinforced my original conviction that what the Europeans were doing at Maastricht was close to the equivalent of the deliberations of the Founding Fathers of the United States at Philadelphia between 1787 and 1788. In this sense, Maastricht represented a sea change in the history of European integration which has no equivalent either in the Treaty of Rome, the Single European Act or the more recent Treaty of Amsterdam. In effect, the negotiating parties were in the business of creating a new federal state." And, "The Treaty on European Union was just that – an effort to create a new, federal state, involving the removal of the most fundamental of the nation state's domestic functions – macroeconomic policy – and its transfer to the supranational or federal level. There is, simply, no precedent for this in the history of international institutions." He concluded, "We should be in no doubt, therefore, that unusual though it is, what we are dealing with in Europe is an emerging federal state."[72]

William Wallace - "The EU is a collective political system, not an intergovernmental regime. Almost all European scholars start from this assumption. ... Policy-making within the EU may thus be described as post-sovereign. It spills across state boundaries, penetrating deep into previously domestic aspects of national politics and administration. It embodies the principle of mutual interference in each other's internal affairs, now extending even to mutual inspection of each other's judicial procedures."[73] He summed up that the EU "incontestably represents a new level of government."[74]

Kenneth Armstrong and Simon Bulmer - "European integration has now produced a system of government with state-like features. ... the

EC's acquis communautaire, i.e. the accumulation of supranational legal and political integration, and supranational nation-building. ... European integration is a process of state development."[75]

Martin Holland - Monnet's "comprehensive conceptualization of Europe encapsulated both internal and external integration in which foreign policy was an essential element. While the EU has yet to realize all of Monnet's ambitions, the underlying motivations are still central to the current integration process."[76] He also wrote, "supranationalism has been resilient and made significant advances which cumulatively have progressively undermined national sovereignty. ... Membership of the Community does necessitate limitations being imposed on a state's former absolute sovereignty. ... the EU is about political integration par excellence."[77]

Neill Nugent, Jean Monnet Professor of European Integration at Manchester Metropolitan University - "The most obvious price states pay for membership of the EU is a substantial loss of national decision-making powers. In some policy spheres – such as agriculture and external trade – most decisions are now taken at the EU level, whilst in many other spheres – such as environmental policy and competition policy – decision-making responsibilities are shared between the EU and the member states."[78]

Cris Shore - "a federalist vision of Europe has been implicit in the ethos and organisational structures of the European Community ever since its creation. ... To most critical observers it seems quite evident that the European Community has acquired most of the characteristics of a state, however much some might wish to deny this. ... The process of cumulative integration through functional 'spillover' that was so clearly described by the early theorists of European integration is, de facto, laying the foundations of a centralised European state. That is what EU leaders have long aspired to create, and that is what the neofunctionalist strategy – or 'Monnet method' – was designed to achieve."[79]

Helen Drake - "the founders built the contours of a federal system of which the logic, although such may not have been the intention, was that the Commission might one day become the government of a federal Europe."[80] As we saw earlier, the founders explicitly intended such an outcome. Generally, political agents do intend the results of their actions, and we should certainly hold them to have so intended.

Laura Cram, Desmond Dinan and Neill Nugent - "For many practitioners and observers, EMU provides irrefutable evidence that a state of some kind is emerging at the European level. EMU may also be said to provide evidence of the seemingly remorseless incrementalism of the integration process."[81]

Ali El-Agraa - "The approach in this book continues to be one of perceiving the EU as an evolving and dynamic institution whose integrative process will not cease until the realisation of the founding fathers' dream: the establishment of a United States of Europe."[82]

Brigid Laffan, Rory O'Donnell and Michael Smith wrote a book whose intended theme was that "the Union is not evolving towards a federal superstate but is an arena of deep economic integration governed by a prismatic policy characterised by innovation, experimentation, pragmatism, decentralisation and delegation." Yet they concluded, "the Union begins to go beyond regulation and market creation into core attributes of statehood, money, borders and security."[83]

Volker Bornschier summed up the common finding, "In our understanding, the Single European Act marks the transition to statehood ... the European state." He concluded that the EU is 'a supranational state'.[84]

Section 4: ... but not a democratic state

What kind of a state was it? We have seen that its institutions are less democratic than those of its members. Sicco Mansholt, a former EU Commission President, summed up in 1973 how he saw the European Community: "The Commission proposes, the European Parliament gives opinions, the council decides – and without more ado, the individual citizen is committed ... the ordinary democratic decision making process as we know it in the individual state does not exist in the Community." EU-supporter Michael Heseltine admitted, "The other notable characteristic of present political arrangements is that they are about as ineffective and as unaccountable as they could be. ... the institutions themselves are totally incapable of adjusting to that change. We have federalism by stealth ..."[85] (Unaccountable, incorrigible, deceitful - he could be describing himself!)

The authors of the standard textbooks on the EU, who are almost all EU-enthusiasts, agreed that it was not democratic. We cite their judgments, which constitute what criminal lawyers call 'admissions against interest'.

George Ross - "the European Commission, whatever its good intentions [!], has pushed new Europeanization forward through the long-consecrated 'Monnet method' of promoting integration by stealth, convinced that it was doing good for European peoples behind their backs."[86]

Wyn Grant - "The weakness of the European Parliament in relation to the CAP reflects a lack of democratic accountability in the decision-making procedures of the EU as a whole."[87]

Ken Endo - "Admittedly, any direct comparison of the EU with a fully fledged democracy is seriously misleading, since the Union is not such a democracy."[88]

Andrew Geddes - "as it stands the EU is not a democracy and its citizenship provisions are not particularly extensive."[89]

Desmond Dinan - "The democratic deficit will not be solved simply by giving the European Parliament more powers."[90]

Stefano Fella - "The EU appears all the more undemocratic to many because it entrenches a framework of economic rules which could arguably be described as containing an ideological bias in favour of free-market deregulation and untrammelled competition, for example in restricting the power of national governments to aid ailing industries."[91]

Kathleen McNamara wrote bluntly of 'the democratic deficit inherent in European integration'.[92] Geoffrey Denton referred to 'the vast democratic deficit at European Union level'.[93] As Cris Shore summed up, "with its single currency, its Central Bank and treaty control over money supply and borrowing, the EU takes on the powers of a sovereign state, albeit a transnational state without a democratic government."[94]

Most importantly, the EU corrupted member states' institutions. In Britain, for instance, as Lord Owen observed, "Those who watch *Breakfast with Frost* saw on 16 January this year the Prime Minister revealing how he interprets his role. 'I will decide the issue of monetary union. I'm the Prime Minister who's got responsibility for it, according to the British national interest.' Professor Peter Hennessy, who writes with authority on the British constitution, wrote about Blair's TV appearance, 'I treated this as a significant expression of his view of the functions of being Prime Minister, and one that did not accord with traditional notions of the constitutional limits of the job.' He then went on to add, 'Yet his words occasioned no great surprise.' It is true that we have acquiesced in more power accruing to the Prime Minister and the Party Whips and less power to Cabinet and Parliament."

In Britain, the new cabinet system of local government was patterned on the EU model. When councils' executive bodies meet secretly and exclude the public, other councillors and the trade unions, it undermines democracy.

Not only is the EU undemocratic, but the government's efforts to force us deeper into it distorted democracy. Successive governments' determination that Britain should become part of a single EU state, whatever the views of the majority of the British people, showed their contempt for democracy.[95]

The leaders called this process of creating a new state 'integration' or 'unification', but it was not a freely willed union of peoples; no member government had ever fought an election on the policy of forming a single EU state, nor had any member government, until 2005, ever asked its people to ratify the idea in a referendum. It was not union but empire, a newly created state power seeking to subordinate and incorporate previously sovereign states.

Some EU supporters accepted that fewer people supported the EU now, and recognised that more support was necessary to legitimate a democratic state. Some claimed that this lack of support proved that they were not really building a state, but it proved instead that they were not building a democratic state. The ruling classes drove the whole project, not the people, whom the EU's leaders saw as backward, ignorant 'xenophobes'.

The EU Commission's 'strategy of integration by stealth' was undemocratic.[96] Roy Hattersley told Panorama in March 2002, "We stopped telling the truth in order to subscribe to the political concept." For instance, in November 1991, ex-European Commissioner Lord Cockfield, said, "the British people had no moral right and probably no legal right" to resist the EU's demands. Pascal Lamy, Delors' chef de cabinet, said, "The people weren't ready to agree to integration, so you had to get on without telling them too much about what was happening."[97] Pierre Cot, a French socialist MEP, opposed sending copies of the Maastricht Treaty to the Danish people, saying, "It is a mistake to let people read the treaty; they will only misunderstand it."[98] William Wallace described the EU's "opaque policy process and a technical and non-transparent series of policy outcomes, drafted in terms accessible to expert elites but beyond the interest or understanding of the broader public."[99] Yet the EU's effects were not beyond our understanding: we understood them all too well, which is why few support it.

Yet some claimed that the EU was already democratic. Martin Holland wrote, "Popular support, whether for foreign policy or economic policy, is the fundamental condition on which integration is based."[100] Brigid Laffan summed up, "The European Union is not suffering from a crisis of democracy or legitimacy. The claim that the EU is undemocratic is fallacious." But she went on, "It is likely, however, that it will produce a system with less substantial institutions and processes of democracy than is customarily found at national level."[101] This seems to accept the justice of the critics' claim.

Section 5: Enlargement

Instead of seeking justice and democracy by addressing these problems, the EU chose to seek more power by adding twelve new members - Bulgaria, Cyprus, the Czech Republic, Estonia, Hungary, Latvia, Lithuania, Malta, Poland, Rumania, Slovakia and Slovenia. The ten countries of Central and Eastern Europe had large and growing trade deficits with the EU. They had all suffered the effects of neo-liberal 'shock therapy' (all shock, no therapy). Education and R&D budgets were cut; the much-heralded foreign investment was largely just foreign firms buying plant to catch existing markets; under the huge privatisation programmes, firms were sold for next to nothing to asset-strippers, speculators and crooks.[102] The European Commission's 2000 Enlargement Strategy Paper noted the increase in 'trafficking in women and children' in a number of states, and summed up, "corruption, fraud and economic crime are widespread in most candidate countries, leading to a lack of confidence by the citizens and discrediting the reforms."[103]

By increasing competition, enlargement lowers wages, welfare benefits and living standards across the EU. It meant that people from the ten new 'accession states' would be able to work legally here. The Blair government favoured this uncontrolled immigration, this 'free movement of labour', which would increase the numbers of immigrants from East to West Europe, driving down our wages and conditions and worsening our social services.[104] Every other EU member, except Ireland, put some controls on this inflow.[105] When Spain, Portugal and Greece joined the EU in 1986, employers forced down wages, conditions and social service standards across the EU, and forced up the costs of the CAP and the CFP.

If the CAP had been extended to cover the new entrants, it would have forced a massive increase in the EU's budget, to pay for the hugely increased costs of the CAP and regional funds, estimated by the EU as an extra £25 billion. The Commission itself admitted, "The next enlargement ... will inevitably provoke a deterioration in the budgetary positions of all the current member states."[106] There were more farmers in Poland, four million, than in the rest of the EU combined, so if the CAP covered Poland, it would bankrupt the EU! So the Commission announced in January 2002 that Eastern Europe's countries would have to wait ten years before they could get the agricultural subsidies available to current member states; until then, they would get just a quarter of the going rate.[107] This would give the heavily subsidised agricultures of earlier EU members ten years to destroy the agricultures of Eastern Europe through unfair competition.[108] Naturally, this unequal treatment angered the peoples of the applicant countries, making them think again about the value of EU membership.

Entry did not improve their industrial and service sectors: their economies were not 'convergent' with the economies of the present EU members, so euro membership is causing extraordinary difficulties. Their entry has widened the gap between the EU's economies and increased political tensions in the EU. As Helmut Schmidt predicted of Poland, "Within six months of joining the EU, Poland will be wiped out, because in the fields of marketing, productivity and so on, it is far from being able to compete."[109] This was true of all the other new entrants too. They provide cheap labour and raw materials; they are living-in servants to the EU's masters. As ex-Minister for Europe Peter Hain put it, "enlargement is a means by which the economic interests of capital will continue their dominance over the social interests of labour."[110] Enlargement allows the EU to exploit the poorer Eastern European countries as sweatshops and mines.[111]

This was why the German government, in particular, wanted enlargement. Germany already dominated Eastern Europe: its drive to the East was a significant motor in EU development. As Immo Stabreit, a former German ambassador to France, said, "It is only natural that the eastern part of the continent will become our preoccupation for years to come because Germans see this as a matter of historical destiny. The most fundamental priority we have is trying to integrate all of Europe."[112] Enlargement will increase Germany's dominance.[113] The Labour government wanted to enlarge the EU, and include Turkey, in order to strengthen both the market and the USA's influence in the EU.

But Wilhelm Nolling, former council member of the Bundesbank, warned, "The truth is that the enlargement of the EU is looking increasingly complex and risky, not least because of the establishment of Economic and Monetary Union. The potentially destabilising effects of the single currency beg the question both whether Western Europe can cope with a batch of new members and, even more pertinently, whether Western Europe is going to be a hospitable environment for the transition economies of central and eastern Europe."[114]

Nor was enlargement remotely democratic. It reduced national democracy and sovereignty in the member states. None of the peoples of the member states had wanted enlargement. Enlargement could wreck the EU.[115] Its drive for enlargement conflicted with its drive for union: the wider, the weaker.[116]

Endnotes

[1]. Cited page 9, Caroline Lucas and Mike Woodin, The euro or a sustainable future for Britain? A green critique of the single currency, New Europe, 2000.

[2]. For details, see Neill Nugent, The government and politics of the European Union, Macmillan, 4th edition, 1999, Chapter 6, pages 101-42, and Desmond Dinan, Ever closer union: an introduction to European integration, Macmillan, 2nd edition, 1999, pages 223-35.

[3]. Cited page 144, Cris Shore, Building Europe: the cultural politics of European integration, Routledge, 2000.

[4]. Submission to the 2000 IGC, cited page 11, Neill Nugent, The European Commission, Palgrave, 2001.

[5]. See Elizabeth Bomberg, Green parties and politics in the European Union, Routledge, 1998, page 127. See also Justin Greenwood, Representing interests in the European Union, New York: St Martin's Press, 1997, page 263.

[6]. On the President's role, see Desmond Dinan, Ever closer union: an introduction to European integration, Macmillan, 2nd edition, 1999, pages 206-13, and Neill Nugent, The European Commission, Palgrave, 2001, Chapter 3, pages 62-81.

[7]. See Ken Endo, The Presidency of the European Commission under

Jacques Delors: the politics of shared leadership, Macmillan, 1999, page 37. On EcoFin, see Kenneth Dyson, The politics of the Euro-zone: stability or breakdown? Oxford University Press, 2000, page 73.

[8]. On the Commissioners, see Desmond Dinan, Ever closer union: an introduction to European integration, Macmillan, 2nd edition, 1999, pages 213-8. On the College of Commissioners, see Neill Nugent, The European Commission, Palgrave, 2001, Chapter 4, pages 82-118. On the role of the College's Secretary General, see his pages 146-55.

[9]. On the cabinets, see Neill Nugent, The European Commission, Palgrave, 2001, Chapter 5, pages 119-33.

[10]. See Christopher Booker and Richard North, The castle of lies: why Britain must get out of Europe, Duckworth, 1997, pages 40 and 157.

[11]. Cited page 8, Christopher Booker and Richard North, The castle of lies: why Britain must get out of Europe, Duckworth, 1997.

[12]. Kenneth Armstrong and Simon Bulmer, The governance of the Single European Market, Manchester University Press, 1998, page 74.

[13]. On the ERT, see Michael Nollert and Nicola Fielder, 'Lobbying for a Europe of big business; the European Roundtable of Industrialists', Chapter 7, pages 187-209, in Volker Bornschier, editor, State-building in Europe: the revitalization of Western European integration, Cambridge University Press, 2000.

[14]. See Maria Cowles, page 503, Setting the agenda for a new Europe: the ERT and EC 1992, *Journal of Common Market Studies*, 1995, Volume 33, pages 501-26.

[15]. See ibid, page 522.

[16]. See Guglielmo Carchedi, For another Europe: a class analysis of European economic integration, Verso, 2001, pages 31-4.

[17]. See David Coen, The evolution of the large firm as a political actor in the European Union, *Journal of European Public Policy*, 1997, Volume 4, Number 1, pages 91-108.

[18]. See Justin Greenwood, Representing interests in the European Union, New York: St Martin's Press, 1997, pages 1-2. See also his Chapter 5, Business interests, pages 101-32.

[19]. See Sonia Mazey and Jeremy Richardson, pages 123-4, in 'Interests', Chapter 6, pages 105-29, in Laura Cram, Desmond Dinan and Neill Nugent, editors, Developments in the European Union, Macmillan, 1999.

[20]. See Sonia Mazey and Jeremy Richardson, 'Interests', Chapter 6, pages 105-29, in Laura Cram, Desmond Dinan and Neill Nugent, editors, Developments in the European Union, Macmillan, 1999.

[21]. See Justin Greenwood, Representing interests in the European Union, New York: St Martin's Press, 1997, page 180. On environmental interests and interest groups, see his pages 180-92.

[22]. See Janne Matlary, Environment policy in the European Union, Macmillan, 1997, page 10 and 'Towards a Common Environmental Policy', Chapter 4, pages 58-78.

[23]. Cited page 409, Desmond Dinan, Ever closer union: an introduction to European integration, Macmillan, 2nd edition, 1999.

[24]. Cited page 45, Elizabeth Bomberg, Green parties and politics in the European Union, Routledge, 1998. See also Wyn Grant, Duncan Matthews and Peter Newell, The effectiveness of European Union environmental policy, Macmillan, 2000, page 201.

[25]. Jean Monnet, Memoirs, Collins, 1978, page 373.

[26]. See Neill Nugent, The European Commission, Palgrave, 2001, pages 135-46.

[27]. See Kenneth Dyson, The politics of the Euro-zone: stability or breakdown? Oxford University Press, 2000, pages 70-1.

[28]. For details, see Desmond Dinan, Ever closer union: an introduction to European integration, Macmillan, 2nd edition, 1999, pages 218-23.

[29]. See pages 98, 104 and 108 of John Lambert and Catherine Hoskyns,

'How democratic is the European Parliament?' Chapter 5, pages 93-116, in Catherine Hoskyns and Michael Newman, editors, Democratizing the European Union: issues for the twenty-first century, Manchester University Press, 2000. See also Simon Hix, The political system of the European Union, Macmillan, 1999, page 42.

[30]. For details, see Neill Nugent, The government and politics of the European Union, Macmillan, 4th edition, 1999, Chapter 7, pages 143-76, and Desmond Dinan, Ever closer union: an introduction to European integration, Macmillan, 2nd edition, 1999, pages 254-65.

[31]. Michael Heseltine, The challenge of Europe: can Britain win? Weidenfeld and Nicolson, 1989, pages 25-6.

[32]. Michael Heseltine, The challenge of Europe: can Britain win? Weidenfeld and Nicolson, 1989, page 33.

[33]. Cited page 82, Stefano Fella, 'A Europe of the peoples? New Labour and democratizing the European Union', Chapter 4, pages 65-92 in Catherine Hoskyns and Michael Newman, editors, Democratizing the European Union: issues for the twenty-first century, Manchester University Press, 2000.

[34]. For details about the Council, see Neill Nugent, The government and politics of the European Union, Macmillan, 4th edition, 1999, Chapter 8, pages 177-204, and Desmond Dinan, Ever closer union: an introduction to European integration, Macmillan, 2nd edition, 1999, pages 237-54.

[35]. See Fiona Hayes-Renshaw, page 24, in 'The European Council and the Council of Ministers,' Chapter 2, pages 23-43, in Laura Cram, Desmond Dinan and Neill Nugent, editors, Developments in the European Union, Macmillan, 1999.

[36]. See Valerio Lintner, page 401, 'Overview: the European Union: the impact of membership on the UK economy and UK economic policy', Chapter 16, pages 399-430, in Tony Buxton, Paul Chapman and Paul Temple, editors, Britain's economic performance, Routledge, 2nd edition, 1998. For details of the Parliament's roles, see Neill Nugent, The government and politics of the European Union, Macmillan, 4th edition, 1999, Chapter 9, pages 205-

41, and Desmond Dinan, Ever closer union: an introduction to European integration, Macmillan, 2nd edition, 1999, Chapter 10, pages 267-300.

[37]. Klaus-Dieter Borchardt, The ABC of Community Law, Office for Official Publications, the European Communities, cited page 31, Is Europe becoming a superstate? Keith Marsden, *European Journal*, January/February 2001, Volume 8, Number 3, pages 30-2.

[38]. See Richard Weight, Patriots: national identity in Britain 1940-2000, Macmillan, 2002, page 515.

[39]. See Colin Pilkington, Britain in the European Union today, Manchester University Press, 2nd edition, 2001, page 162.

[40]. See Simon Bulmer, Charlie Jeffery and William Paterson, Germany's European diplomacy: shaping the regional milieu, Manchester University Press, 2000, page 94.

[41]. *Die Welt*, 22 July 2000.

[42]. For details, see Neill Nugent, The government and politics of the European Union, Macmillan, 4th edition, 1999, pages 275-6, and Desmond Dinan, Ever closer union: an introduction to European integration, Macmillan, 2nd edition, 1999, pages 312-5.

[43]. See Trevor Hartley, Constitutional problems of the European Union, Oxford: Hart Publishing, 1999, page 11.

[44]. For details, see Neill Nugent, The government and politics of the European Union, Macmillan, 4th edition, 1999, Chapter 10, pages 242-78. See also Kenneth Armstrong and Simon Bulmer, The governance of the Single European Market, Manchester University Press, 1998, pages 46-8, 66-70 and 79-81, and Desmond Dinan, Ever closer union: an introduction to European integration, Macmillan, 2nd edition, 1999, pages 301-12.

[45]. Case 26/62 NV Algemene Transport-en expeditie onderneming Van Gend en Loos v. Nederlandse Administratie der Belastingen [1963] ECR. See also Desmond Dinan, Ever closer union: an introduction to European integration, Macmillan, 2nd edition, 1999, pages 303-4, and Trevor Hartley, Constitutional problems of the European Union, Oxford: Hart Publishing,

1999, pages 24-6.

[46]. See Trevor Hartley, Constitutional problems of the European Union, Oxford: Hart Publishing, 1999, pages 25 and 135. See also Helen Wallace, page 23, 'The institutional setting: five variations on a theme', Chapter 1, pages 3-37, in Helen Wallace and William Wallace, editors, Policy-making in the European Union, Oxford University Press, 4th edition, 2000.

[47]. See Trevor Hartley, Constitutional problems of the European Union, Oxford: Hart Publishing, 1999, page 41. See his Chapter 2, 'The European Court: an objective interpreter of Community law?' Pages 22-42.

[48]. Case 6/64 Costa v. ENEL [1964] ECR, 1141.

[49]. See Colin Pilkington, Britain in the European Union today, Manchester University Press, 2nd edition, 2001, page 78.

[50]. In Van Duyn v. Home Office, Case 41/74, [1974] ECR 1337. See Trevor Hartley, Constitutional problems of the European Union, Oxford: Hart Publishing, 1999, pages 27-9 and 48.

[51]. Cited page 102, Colin Pilkington, Britain in the European Union today, Manchester University Press, 2nd edition, 2001.

[52]. Simmenthal v. Commission, cited page 304, Desmond Dinan, Ever closer union: an introduction to European integration, Macmillan, 2nd edition, 1999.

[53]. Factortame v. Secretary of State for Transport (no. 2) [1991], cited page 86, Colin Pilkington, Britain in the European Union today, Manchester University Press, 2nd edition, 2001.

[54]. Opinion 1/91, re the European Economic Area Agreement [1991], ECR, I-6079, cited page 36, Renaud Dehousse, The European Court of Justice: the politics of judicial integration, Macmillan, 1998.

[55]. In, The Queen v. The Immigration Appeal Tribunal, ex parte Antonissen, Case C-292/89, [1991] ECR 1-745, see Trevor Hartley, Constitutional problems of the European Union, Oxford: Hart Publishing, 1999, pages 45-8.

[56]. See Colin Pilkington, Britain in the European Union today, Manchester University Press, 2nd edition, 2001, page 87.

[57]. Gerard Delanty, Inventing Europe: idea, identity, reality, Macmillan, 1995, page x.

[58]. For more on this Committee, see Neill Nugent, The government and politics of the European Union, Macmillan, 4th edition, 1999, pages 279-85, and Desmond Dinan, Ever closer union: an introduction to European integration, Macmillan, 2nd edition, 1999, pages 317-20.

[59]. See Desmond Dinan, Ever closer union: an introduction to European integration, Macmillan, 2nd edition, 1999, pages 317-8 and 319.

[60]. For more on this Committee, see Neill Nugent, The government and politics of the European Union, Macmillan, 4th edition, 1999, pages 149-50.

[61]. For more details, see Neill Nugent, The government and politics of the European Union, Macmillan, 4th edition, 1999, pages 298-302, and Desmond Dinan, Ever closer union: an introduction to European integration, Macmillan, 2nd edition, 1999, pages 315-7.

[62]. For more on the Bank, see Neill Nugent, The government and politics of the European Union, Macmillan, 4th edition, 1999, pages 289-93, and Desmond Dinan, Ever closer union: an introduction to European integration, Macmillan, 2nd edition, 1999, pages 323-6.

[63]. House of Lords Select Committee on the European Communities, 12th Report 1993-4, Financial control and fraud in the Community, HMSO, 1994.

[64]. Committee of Independent Experts, First Report on Allegations Regarding Fraud, Mismanagement and Nepotism in the European Commission, Brussels: European Parliament, 15 March 1999. Cited page 217, Neill Nugent, The government and politics of the European Union, Macmillan, 4th edition, 1999. On the Report, see Paul van Buitenen, Blowing the whistle, Politico's Publishing, 2000, pages 150-73.

[65]. See Cris Shore, Building Europe: the cultural politics of European

integration, Routledge, 2000, page 203.

66. *Die Welt*, 5 April 2000, cited page 156, Adrian Hilton, The principality and power of Europe: Britain and the emerging Holy European Empire, Dorchester House, 2nd edition, 2000.

67. Controls over EU's £62 billion budget 'worse than Enron', *Independent*, 2 August 2002, page 10.

68. Eighteenth Report of the House of Commons Committee of Public Accounts, Session 2004-05, HC 498.

69. Klaus-Dieter Borchardt, The ABC of Community Law, Office for Official Publications, the European Communities, cited page 30, Is Europe becoming a superstate? Keith Marsden, *European Journal*, January/February 2001, Volume 8, Number 3, pages 30-2.

70. John McCormick, Understanding Europe: a concise introduction, Macmillan, 1999, pages 87-8 and 118.

71. Colin Pilkington, Britain in the European Union today, Manchester University Press, 2nd edition, 2001, page 87.

72. David McKay, Federalism and European Union: a political economy perspective, Oxford University Press, 1999, pages vii, 73 and 22.

73. William Wallace, pages 530 and 532, 'Collective governance: the EU political process', Chapter 19, pages 523-42, in Helen Wallace and William Wallace, editors, Policy-making in the European Union, Oxford University Press, 4th edition, 2000.

74. William Wallace, page 406, 'Less than a federation, more than a regime: the Community as a political system', in William Wallace, Helen Wallace and C. Webb, editors, Policy-making in the European Community, Wiley, 1983.

75. Kenneth Armstrong and Simon Bulmer, The governance of the Single European Market, Manchester University Press, 1998, pages 7, 46 and 49.

76. Martin Holland, page 235, in 'The Common Foreign and Security Policy', Chapter 12, pages 230-46, in Laura Cram, Desmond Dinan and

Neill Nugent, editors, Developments in the European Union, Macmillan, 1999.

[77]. Martin Holland, European integration: from Community to Union, Pinter, 1994, pages 87, 185 and 206.

[78]. Neill Nugent, The government and politics of the European Union, Macmillan, 4th edition, 1999, pages 471.

[79]. Cris Shore, Building Europe: the cultural politics of European integration, Routledge, 2000, pages 15-6, 209 and 211.

[80]. Helen Drake, page 232, in 'The Commission and the politics of legitimacy in the European Union', Chapter 12, pages 230-49, in Neill Nugent, editor, At the heart of the Union: studies of the European Commission, Macmillan, 2nd edition, 2000.

[81]. Laura Cram, Desmond Dinan and Neill Nugent, page 355, in 'The evolving European Union', Chapter 18, pages 353-65, in Laura Cram, Desmond Dinan and Neill Nugent, editors, Developments in the European Union, Macmillan, 1999.

[82]. Ali El-Agraa, The European Union: history, institutions, economics, politics, Prentice Hall Europe, 5th edition, 1998, page xxii.

[83]. Brigid Laffan, Rory O'Donnell and Michael Smith, Europe's experimental union: rethinking integration, Routledge, 2000, pages viii and 201-2.

[84]. Volker Bornschier, editor, State-building in Europe: the revitalization of Western European integration, Cambridge University Press, 2000, pages xii and 278.

[85]. Michael Heseltine, The challenge of Europe: can Britain win? Weidenfeld and Nicolson, 1989, page 19.

[86]. George Ross, page 181, in 'European integration and globalization', Chapter 10, pages 164-83, in Roland Axtmann, editor, Globalization and Europe: theoretical and empirical investigations, Pinter, 1998.

[87]. Wyn Grant, The Common Agricultural Policy, Macmillan, 1997, page 176.

[88]. Ken Endo, The Presidency of the European Commission under Jacques Delors: the politics of shared leadership, Macmillan, 1999, pages 71-2.

[89]. Andrew Geddes, Immigration and European integration: towards fortress Europe? Manchester University Press, 2000, page 58.

[90]. Desmond Dinan, Ever closer union: an introduction to European integration, Macmillan, 2nd edition, 1999, pages 298.

[91]. Stefano Fella, pages 86-7, 'A Europe of the peoples? New Labour and democratizing the European Union', Chapter 4, pages 65-92, in Catherine Hoskyns and Michael Newman, editors, Democratizing the European Union: issues for the twenty-first century, Manchester University Press, 2000.

[92]. Kathleen McNamara, The currency of ideas: monetary policy in the European Union, Cornell University Press, 1998, page 175.

[93]. Geoffrey Denton, page 151, 'The Federalist Vision', pages 97-153, in Ian Taylor, Austin Mitchell, Stephen Haseler and Geoffrey Denton, Federal Britain in federal Europe? The Federal Trust, 2001.

[94]. Cris Shore, Building Europe: the cultural politics of European integration, Routledge, 2000, page 94.

[95]. See Richard Weight, Patriots: national identity in Britain 1940-2000, Macmillan, 2002, page 469.

[96]. See Neill Nugent, The European Commission, Palgrave, 2001, page 221.

[97]. Cited page 18, Cris Shore, Building Europe: the cultural politics of European integration, Routledge, 2000.

[98]. Cited page 101, Cris Shore, Building Europe: the cultural politics of European integration, Routledge, 2000.

[99]. William Wallace, page 533, 'Collective governance: The EU political process', Chapter 19, pages 523-42, in Helen Wallace and William Wallace, editors, Policy-making in the European Union, Oxford University Press, 4th edition, 2000.

[100]. Martin Holland, page 243, in 'The Common Foreign and Security Policy', Chapter 12, pages 230-46, in Laura Cram, Desmond Dinan and Neill Nugent, editors, Developments in the European Union, Macmillan, 1999.

[101]. Brigid Laffan, pages 347-8, in 'Democracy and the European Union', Chapter 17, pages 330-49, in Laura Cram, Desmond Dinan and Neill Nugent, editors, Developments in the European Union, Macmillan, 1999.

[102]. See Guglielmo Carchedi, For another Europe: a class analysis of European economic integration, Verso, 2001, pages 187-9.

[103]. Cited page 22, Ambrose Evans-Pritchard, 2003 deadline call for larger EU, *Daily Telegraph*, 9 November 2000.

[104]. See Peter Shore, Separate ways: the heart of Europe, Duckworth, 2000, pages 138-40. See also John Mohan, A united kingdom? Economic, social and political geographies, Arnold, 1999, page 187.

[105]. Kate Hudson, Social democracy and post-communism: the Hungarian example, *Labour Focus on Eastern Europe*, 1996, Number 54, page 64.

[106]. The European Commission, Agenda 2000 Volume 1, page 84, cited page 536, A. Marin, 'The Lome Agreement', Chapter 22, pages 507-26, in Ali El-Agraa, The European Union: history, institutions, economics, politics, Prentice Hall Europe, 5th edition, 1998.

[107]. EU farm policy upsets east Europeans, *Guardian*, 31 January 2002, page 12.

[108]. See Martin Fletcher, EU selling us short, say Polish farmers, *The Times*, 7 February 2002, page 13.

[109]. Cited page 148, Mary Kaldor, 'Eastern enlargement and democracy', Chapter 7, pages 139-55, in Catherine Hoskyns and Michael Newman, editors, Democratizing the European Union: issues for the twenty-first century, Manchester University Press, 2000.

[110]. Peter Hain, Ayes to the left: a future for socialism, Lawrence & Wishart, 1995, page 162.

[111]. See Doug Henwood, Wall Street: how it works and for whom, Verso, 1997, page 112.

[112]. International Herald Tribune, September 1999.

[113]. See Jeffrey Harrop, The political economy of integration in the European Union, Elgar, 3rd edition, 2000, page 310.

[114]. Everything you ever wanted to know about the Euro, New Europe, 1999.

[115]. See Franklin Dehousse, Amsterdam: the making of a treaty, Kogan Page, 1999, page 30.

[116]. See Jeffrey Harrop, The political economy of integration in the European Union, Edward Elgar, 3rd edition, 2000, page 18. See also Franklin Dehousse, Amsterdam: the making of a treaty, Kogan Page, 1999, pages 21, 24 and 28-30.

The EU and its institutions

Chapter 5: The costs of EMU - lower growth, lower wages, fewer jobs

1: The costs of EMU

2: The five tests

3: EMU's effect of increasing flexibility in the labour market

4: EMU's effect of worsening growth and unemployment

*   "To bolster the pillars of the European economy, the ECB is intent on using its authority to promote a reform of European labor markets, wage cartels and welfare state. ... Amid the grand rhetoric of the midnight changeover, *one of Mr Duisenberg's most revealing comments came when he said Europe needed to adopt American-style free market policies.*"[1]

*   In the eurozone, unemployment is high and rising, and national economies are either growing slowly or shrinking; in Britain, unemployment is relatively low, growth relatively high. The unemployment rate in the eurozone is twice Britain's.

1: The costs of EMU

The cost of Britain's joining the euro would be £36 billion, £650 for each of us. A 1999 Bank of England report estimated that every year that we stayed in the euro would cost us £9 billion. Losing sovereignty over interest rate decisions could mean losing more than one per cent of national income every year. The Bank stated, "Monetary union requires one official interest rate. That may entail some countries setting their rate at a level that they would not otherwise have wanted." It also concluded that entering the euro would make the economy less, not more, stable. Mike Lazenby, Director of Britain's largest building society, the Nationwide, said, "It is a myth that entry will bring cheaper mortgages ... there is nothing to say that joining EMU will push mortgages down to European levels - we could see them rise slightly in the short term."[2]

Further, EMU's policies were neoliberal.[3] EMU would promote deregulation and privatisation and would worsen unemployment and destroy industry.[4] The United Nations Conference on Trade and Development, UNCTAD, forecast zero economic growth under EMU.[5] A report from the EC's Economic and Social Committee warned, "In the light of the Commission's analysis, a scenario could be imagined in which the Euro exchange rate is initially fixed at a level quite different from that suggested by the fundamentals of the European economy in all its diversity. The European Central Bank could in fact be obliged to impose an excessively tight monetary policy and to raise interest rates in response to financial market scepticism as to the objective of price stability arising as the result of policies pursued by certain countries."

These warnings proved accurate. From 1992 to 1999, the core EU member governments stayed in the ERM and continued to impose harsh deflationary policies, causing 10% plus unemployment and low growth averaging only 1.8% a year. Under EMU, the Bank kept interest rates high, so euro members suffered zero growth or worse – the French and Italian economies actually shrank in 2003. Even euro-supporters like Hugo Young acknowledged the Bank's 'absurdly deflationary targeting'.[6] The Bank worsened Europe's 2001-02 slump by keeping interest rates high. In February 2002, the European Economic Advisory Group's first annual report warned that the ECB's 2% target ceiling for inflation 'may simply be too tight' and could push Germany 'to the verge of deflation'.[7] Just like the International Monetary Fund, the ECB pursued deflationary policies even at the cost of slumps. There were other similarities: neither was responsible to national governments; job creation was off both their agendas, and both were mandated to focus on inflation, not on wages, jobs or growth.[8]

Immediately after the May 1997 election, the Labour government gave control over interest rate policy to the Bank of England and to a new, supposedly independent, Monetary Policy Committee. But Chancellor Gordon Brown instructed the Committee to achieve low inflation, in line with the European Central Bank's single remit. The EU enthused over the government's decision. Alexandre Lamfalussy, President of the European Monetary Institute, called it 'music to my ears', saying that it was an important step towards meeting the Maastricht convergence criteria.[9]

The high euro helped to keep the semi-detached pound too high: the Bank of England, under Brown's tacit orders, shadowed the euro, just as Lawson had covertly, and damagingly, shadowed the Deutschmark. These excessive interest rates hurt our manufacturing industry.[10] Under Blair, 1,000,000 manufacturing jobs were destroyed between May 1997 and April 2005, a rate of 10,000 a month, twice as bad as under Thatcher. As the TUC noted, "The short term consequences have been a stronger pound, putting more pressure on the manufacturing sector and worsening the growing trade deficit."[11] Being inside the euro would only add to the slaughter.

After the 1997 election, the pound rose sharply against European currencies but fell against the dollar. This meant that industry suffered the worst of both worlds: most British imports of fuel and raw materials were priced in dollars, so the pound's fall against the dollar added to industry's costs, but its strength against the euro made it hard to export to EU member countries. In the first year after the euro's introduction, the pound rose by 12% against the euro, making our exported goods dearer and imports from the EU cheaper.

Entering the euro would also damage investment prospects by allowing institutions to invest more in foreign assets. Fund managers typically invested over half their portfolios in home markets. After 1 January 1999, the EU allowed them to invest this proportion in the ten other countries in the euro zone. It was estimated that if Britain joined the euro, this looser investment regime could lose us $500 billion in equity investment, which would flow into continental European equities. This huge capital flight would further damage British industry. Also, firms would have to invest an estimated £36.2 billion in updating business systems and retraining staff to prepare for the euro. It was estimated that the euro's introduction cost banks in the eurozone a whole year's profits.[12]

Some, particularly in industry, wanted us to enter the euro because they wanted cheaper money to aid export sales - so a lower pound would meet their needs. There was no guarantee that entering the euro would mean cheaper money. The EU has not yet determined at what rate we would enter (if we chose to enter, in ignorance of what the rate would be). We have seen what punishment the core EU governments inflicted on their own peoples - why should they treat Britain any better? Trade unionists who think that entering the euro would benefit them should consider this scenario: if the euro rose against the dollar (and it could, since some believe it is undervalued), money would become dearer and selling to the US market would be even harder. So the result of entering the euro could be an increased exchange rate. This would mean 'several years of near-zero increases in nominal wages in the trading sector', as Samuel Brittan of the Financial Times warned.[13]

A single currency would be followed by a single taxation system and a single economic policy for all member countries, both dictated by the EU. As Onno Ruding, the Chairman of Citicorp, observed in the EC Tax Review, "Monetary Union requires ... a willingness to reduce national sovereignty over taxation as well." Gordon Brown misled Parliament when he said that there was 'no question of giving up our ability to make decisions on tax and spending'. If Britain joined the euro, we would be at the mercy of market forces as far as economic performance is concerned, devoid of any instruments of economic policy, and with depressed regions dependent on the largesse of the EU's central administration.[14]

In 1997, the Council of Ministers secretly demanded that the new Labour government "strictly implements its budgetary policy" by "maintaining a vigorous control of public expenditure." (By Article 104c(7) of the Treaty, the Council's 'recommendations' to member governments 'shall not be made public'.) The EU would have to harmonise taxation because of its commitment to freedom of movement: if taxes were not harmonised, people could move to wherever taxes were lowest. If we abolished the pound and joined the euro, we would be forced to 'harmonise' our taxes upwards. A report by the European Parliament suggested that Britain would have to raise income tax by 2p or cut £12 billion from public spending if we joined the euro.[15] The £400 billion a year that we in Britain raised in tax paid for our public services, but in a single EU state, the EU's leaders would decide where to spend the taxes, and this would not have to be where they were raised.

In February 2001, the EU's finance ministers, including Gordon Brown, scolded the Irish government for daring to have its own economic policy. Brown, whom some supposed to be the most euro-sceptic Cabinet minister, supported the EU against a government asserting - rather late - its sovereignty. James Buchan commented in the Guardian, "Meanwhile, the European reprimand to Ireland last week revealed, for the first time, the vast political scope of the single currency. European finance ministers (including, I regret to say, the British) told the Irish government that it should not cut taxes and raise spending in its 2001 budget because that might lead to inflation and destabilise the euro. ... In 1999, the Irish government abandoned for all time its monetary sovereignty to the European central bank but still thought it could tax and spend as it pleased. Last week's events suggest that the proponents of European federation in Germany and the Benelux countries may get what they always wanted: the euro will slowly reduce national governments, at least in their economic activities, to ciphers."[16]

If Britain joined the euro 'for all time', we too would lose control over tax and spending. In January 2002, the Commission opposed the government's plans to borrow to pay for hospitals, schools and transport; it demanded that Britain cut public spending or raise taxes by £10 billion a year.[17] But while we were outside the euro, we could ignore EU demands and instructions. Inside, we would be bound and the cost of joining would be £10 billion of public spending cuts, for starters. The British people continued to hold up the EU's schemes by staying hostile to the euro.

2: The five tests

The Labour government set five key tests that it said must be met before we could enter the euro:

"1. Are business cycles and economic structures compatible so that we could live comfortably with Euro interest rates on a permanent basis?

2. If problems emerge is there sufficient flexibility to deal with them?

3. Would joining the monetary union create better conditions for firms making long-term decisions to invest in Britain?

4. What impact would entry have on Britain's financial services industry, especially the City?

5. Will joining the Euro promote higher growth, stability and a lasting increase in jobs? This is the fundamental test."[18]

The tests as a whole were, firstly, not quantitative; there was no objective, checkable pass mark. In October 2000, Charles Kennedy said that he thought that we had already passed the five tests; Blair said that he thought that we hadn't. Who could tell who was right? Secondly, the tests were speculative: how could you test something before trying it? Joining the euro would be a leap in the dark.

The tests did not include reform of the European Central Bank's undemocratic practices and secretive procedures, nor of the deflationary Stability and Growth Pact, nor of the disastrous Common Agricultural Policy. Nor did they include any of the many other objectives that the government claims to seek. If the tests are deemed 'passed', our entry would be unconditional; there would be no bargaining or negotiation – we would go into the whole unreformed, unreformable set-up.

Let us look at the tests one by one.

Test 1. "Are business cycles and economic structures compatible so that we could live comfortably with Euro interest rates on a permanent basis?"

This test acknowledged the permanence of the decision, but how could we know that our business cycles and economic structures would be 'permanently' compatible? Business for Sterling's Memorandum to the

Treasury Select Committee of 26 July 2000 showed how much Britain's economy differed from those of the other EU members:

"40. In many significant aspects, Britain's economy is structurally divergent with the Eurozone. Studies by the IMF and the Treasury have shown that since we left the ERM, Britain's economy has been much more convergent with North America than with the Eurozone. In a summary of available evidence in July 1999, the IOD concluded that the UK/USA GDP correlation coefficient was 0.8, but the UK/Eurozone coefficient was -0.3.

41. Barclays Capital analysed the tests in September 1999 and concluded that: "UK growth has been fairly poorly correlated with euro-area activity. That is largely because the UK is relatively less reliant on trade with the EU than the EMU-5." Barclays concluded that the Chancellor's Five Tests could not be met in the life of the next Parliament and therefore advised that membership in that period be ruled out.

42. There is no evidence of long term convergence. Since Britain left the ERM, the pound/dollar relationship has been the most stable of any major currency relationship in the world. The pound has historically been far more stable against the dollar than against the deutschmark/euro. It is therefore no surprise that this relationship has continued since the euro's launch.

43. The pound/dollar relationship reflects the fact that our business cycle is more in line with North America than the Continent, and it also reflects the greater importance of the dollar for Britain's trade and investment. The Eurozone accounts for 45 per cent of our current account earnings (Pink Book, 1999) but only 27 per cent of foreign direct investment (ONS, 1999). Joining the euro would therefore bring us stability for Eurozone trade and investment at the cost of increased instability for dollar based trade and investment. The increasing globalisation of trade and investment flows, spurred by e-commerce, will increase the importance of the dollar. This is a substantially different picture than that for the Eurozone where intra-Eurozone trade and investment are relatively more important.

44. There are many other significant differences between the British and Eurozone economies:

— Britain is the EU's only major oil exporter; therefore changes in the price of oil affect us differently. The ECB recently cited the impact of the euro's fall on the rise of the price of oil in the Eurozone, demonstrating how global effects affect us differently.

—Britain has higher homeowner occupation, finances by variable rate mortgages making our economy much more sensitive to short term interest rate changes."

In sum, our economy is not 'converging' with the other EU members' economies. Britain's economy is and would remain different: we have a greater range of industries, a more efficient agriculture, a larger financial sector, oil and gas resources and uniquely fertile fishing waters. This divergence would break the Eurozone apart. As John Smith, then the Labour Party's Shadow Chancellor, told Parliament in January 1991, without convergence, "monetary union ... would create unbearable strains within the Community, threatening fragmentation rather than integration."[19] Lasting convergence of different countries' business cycles is impossible, because different nations' economies develop unevenly.[20] Political and economic shocks would still affect different countries in different ways; for instance, the Russian economy's difficulties affect Germany far more than France. The Commission conceded that the EU was not an 'optimal currency area'.[21]

Test 2. "If problems emerge is there sufficient flexibility to deal with them?"

This is the only one of the tests that is practical, and the answer has to be NO. Under the euro there is a single interest rate across the whole eurozone: this alone prevents any flexibility. A 'one-size-fits-all' interest rate must suit all members worse than their own individually chosen rates would. For instance, in 1998 German interest rates were low because of the recession and high unemployment, and the other EU member countries had to converge with them at 3%. This did not suit them. The Chief Economist of the Irish Central Bank, for example, said that the 'one size fits all' interest rate was "totally inappropriate for Ireland . . . Much of the EMU project is actually built on foundations of sand." Under the euro there is an irrevocably fixed exchange rate for all members. How could this be more flexible than floating exchange rates for each? Without flexibility, we could not meet any of the other four tests: we would not be able to live comfortably with euro interest rates, encourage investment, aid the financial services industry or promote growth and jobs.

Test 3. "Would joining the monetary union create better conditions for firms making long-term decisions to invest in Britain?"

Britain increased its lead over other eurozone countries in the past decade in terms of attracting foreign investment. Inward investment continued to increase after we decided not to join the euro. Figures from the Department of Trade and Industry showed another record year for inward investment in 1999, up from £207 billion to £244 billion. Half of this came from the USA, only a quarter from the whole of the EU. By March 2000, the stock of inward investment had risen to £250 billion. Sir David Wright, chairman of the government export body British Trade International, said, "There is nothing in these figures which suggests that the attitude of foreign companies is being significantly affected by the policy on the single currency." Stephen Byers, when Secretary of State for Trade and Industry, stated that Britain outside the eurozone was still extremely attractive to inward investors: "I genuinely can't see any sign of inward investment dropping off because of Britain not being in the euro."[22] This contradicted all the scare stories from the pro-euro lobby that investment was flooding out of Britain. By contrast, a net £125 billion of capital left the eurozone between June 1999 and June 2000 – another significant economic divergence.

Test 4. "What impact would entry have on Britain's financial services industry, especially the City?"

The British Bankers Association estimated that entering the euro would cost the British finance industry at least £914 million, largely due to the costs of changing information technology systems. In the longer run, it would raise unemployment in retail banking and in the whole finance sector. Ben Daniels of UNIFI, the union representing the workers in insurance and banking, wrote, "The impact of EMU on the retail banking sector can therefore be summarised as introducing the possibility of greater cross border competition and hence merger activity in the medium to long term. ... were the UK to join it is clear that these pressures would grow, hence putting pressure on staff and employment levels in this area." Of the euro's effect on the whole finance industry, he wrote, "Euro-Fiet (now UN-Europa) estimates that as a result of the single currency and continued restructuring in the industry there will be a net long term loss of over 200,000 jobs in the industry Europe-wide." The Bank of England would also be affected: "Inevitably some functions will be lost or reduced and there is likely to be some fall in the employment levels of the European central banks."[23]

Business for Sterling's Memorandum pointed out, "Far from suffering outside the Eurozone, the City has prospered:

— London handles 32 per cent of global foreign exchange business - Frankfurt and Paris have a combined 9 per cent.

— London is the number one location for fund management ($2 trillion under management) - Frankfurt is twelfth.

— 118 of Europe's biggest 500 companies have HQs in London compared with 9 in Frankfurt.

— 537 foreign banks are registered in London. Frankfurt has 225.

— The euro was meant to precipitate a swing in the balance of power towards Frankfurt, but since the launch of the euro in January 1999, London has increased its lead in euro bond issuing and foreign equity trading. "I have every confidence in the ability of the City to thrive in this competitive environment . . . and in that context suggestions that we should be somehow artificially disadvantaged are irrational." Eddie George, 7 December 1999.

— "London will no doubt remain the leading centre in Europe thanks to its advantages of size, excellently qualified personnel, and the attractive tax, legal and cultural environment." Rolf Breuer, Chairman of Frankfurt Stock Exchange, January 1999.

— The rigidity of Frankfurt's planning and labour laws constrain the development of the large floorplate buildings required by major financial firms.

— English is the language of international commerce and it is this factor, combined with London's cosmopolitan appeal, that makes it easier to attract internationally mobile financial services staff to London rather than Frankfurt.

— London accounts for 20 per cent of all global cross-border lending ($1900 billion) while German banks (not all based in Frankfurt) account for 9 per cent.

— The value of share transactions on the London Stock Exchange is over twice as large as Frankfurt's.

— London has the highest number of foreign stocks listed of any stock exchange and accounts for 65 per cent of all turnover of such stocks, compared to the German stock exchange's 4 per cent.

— London has specialist markets which Frankfurt does not - International Petroleum Exchange, London Metals Exchange, ship broking and registration, and a liquid bullion market."

A report by the University of Reading concluded, "Almost all our findings point to the continued dominance of the City of London as the European financial centre. There are threats . . . None of them seem sufficient to overcome the critical mass of the markets, the diversity of markets, services, labour and business space, and the cosmopolitan appeal of London when compared to Frankfurt. It would take an unprecedented combination of mismanagement and misfortune for London to lose its position to Frankfurt, no matter how enormous the efforts made by the latter."[24]

The pro-euro lobby warned that the City of London would lose investments and jobs if Britain refused to scrap the pound and sign up to monetary union. Yet the City thrived outside the euro zone after it was launched on 1 January 2000 and increased its share of business. Lord Levene, the outgoing Lord Mayor of London, pointed out that Britain's membership of the euro was not the key to whether banks and other financial institutions decided to continue to do business in Britain. Experience had taught Lord Levene, who had earlier warned that London would lose out as a result of our not joining the euro.

Further, WTO rules permitted free flows of capital. Whether Britain had the pound or the euro as its currency did not count much to those who bought and sold currencies. Some claimed that the euro would curb the speculators by reducing the number of currencies for them to play with, but the number of currencies did not matter to speculators: a smaller number of currencies would no more curb speculation than a smaller field of horses would curb betting. There was no evidence, nor likelihood, of the euro's increasing international exchange rate stability.[25] The euro has gone up or down by as much as 10% in a month against the pound, the dollar and the yen. The dollar and the yen have both been far more volatile against the euro than against the pound. Consistently high euro/dollar volatility would mean that, if we joined the euro, our currency volatility against the dollar would increase, especially since we trade more with the USA than any other EU member does.

So the euro would not bring a stable interest rate to aid our industry, nor would it curb the speculators. A single currency, by ending national currencies in the eurozone, ended speculation on one European currency against another, but it increased capital flows between the eurozone and everywhere else, threatening the euro's stability and therefore interest rate stability.[26] The euro would behave as the ERM did.

Besides, why did the five tests single out the fate of the financial services industry? Finance capital is not as powerful as it seems. As Michael Mann wrote, "Electronically transmitted claims to economic ownership slosh relatively freely and transnationally across the world, their 'paper' value exceeding the value of all global trade by a factor of three hundred or more. Such astronomical sums are misleading, the result of the same stocks, bonds, futures, etc. being traded many times during a day. Whatever the real economic power such transnational capital possesses, it is far less than its nominal value might suggest. Moreover, there is some regulation of finance capital. This still operates principally through the stock exchanges, the accountancy practices and the commercial laws of individual nation-states."[27] Far more people were employed in manufacturing than in financial services, and, as we have seen, manufacturing industry was far more significant to Britain's future. Why did the tests not single out manufacturing industry? The tests did not even mention it, an omission that revealed the Government's interests and intentions all too clearly.

Test 5. "Will joining the Euro promote higher growth, stability and a lasting increase in jobs? This is the fundamental test."

To make EMU credible to the markets, the Bank kept interest rates high, flattening economic growth, adding to unemployment and cutting wages, living standards and investment. The euro was a key part of this deflationary policy package.

Outside the euro, we had higher growth and lower unemployment than eurozone members. In the euro zone, average unemployment was 11% in May 2005. The average for the EU as a whole is lower because Britain, Sweden and Denmark, the three EU members who have not joined the euro, have lower rates. Even so, by 2004 in Britain 7.8 million people were classed as either unemployed or as having withdrawn from job search (economically inactive), 250,000 more than in 1997. Since 1990, we had a threefold increase in the numbers of those receiving incapacity benefit, up to 2.7 million, costing £16 billion a year.[28]

Business for Sterling's Memorandum observed, "Throughout the EU, there is also a tendency to disguise the already poor unemployment figures by encouraging people to disappear from the labour market altogether, particularly via early retirement. This, however, only adds to the long term burden on bankrupt pension systems." It concluded, "Joining the euro in the foreseeable future would therefore increase unemployment in Britain substantially." Job losses in the EU rose steadily during the EMU-dominated decade of the 1990s. The chapter on employment in the Amsterdam Treaty and the special jobs summit in Luxembourg in November 1997 were gestures, with no practical effect.[29] German unemployment went above five million early in 2005. For all of us, including trade unionists, the euro's impact on employment was surely the fundamental test, and the euro had already failed this test. The nations have to take responsibility for job creation, since the EU has failed to do so.

A European Commission report presented to the European Parliament on 21 January 2004 admitted the problems. The EU had promised to become 'the most competitive knowledge-based economy in the world by 2010', and the euro was supposed to be the key to this advance. But the report said, "there are significant problems which hold back the entire strategy and which hinder the return of strong growth." The areas where the EU lagged were jobs, productivity and investment. It admitted that the intermediate target for jobs would not be met by 2005 and that both the growth rate and public investment were falling. It concluded,

"The European Union's efforts to catch up with the United States are at a standstill."

Business for Sterling's Memorandum summed up their conclusions about the five tests, "BfS does not believe that the Chancellor's Five Tests can be met in "clear and unambiguous" fashion in the next Parliament: there is no prospect of sustainable structural convergence with the Eurozone in the foreseeable future; the Eurozone is insufficiently flexible already and Britain joining would exacerbate this problem; and inward investment and the City would be harmed more by joining the euro than by staying outside. Overall, we believe joining would increase unemployment."

The Financial Times' economic commentator, Martin Wolf, analysed the Chancellor's five tests and concluded, "Assessment of the economic tests gives nothing close to a decisive yes. It never could. The status quo is far safer. Whether that will influence Mr Blair's or Mr Brown's largely political decision is another question."[30] On the tests, Wolf concluded:

"Convergence: "The Bank of England is virtually certain to do a better job of stabilising Britain than the European Central Bank, since the UK would only be a sixth of the ECB's monetary area. Convergence remains incomplete even within monetary union. The Bank of England still feels it necessary to impose higher short-term rates than those of the Eurozone, although a strong pound exerts persistent disinflationary pressure."

- Flexibility: "a floating exchange rate always tends to give greater flexibility to relative prices, in response to shocks, than an irrevocably fixed exchange rate."

- Investment: "There is little evidence that failure to join the single currency has up to now adversely affected investment in the UK. In 1999, business investment in the UK was a higher share of GDP than Germany and France. The UK also remains the highest recipient of foreign direct investment in the EU."

- The City: "So far it seems that the City remains the thriving home to the biggest and most sophisticated financial markets in the European time zone. It is far from evident that failure to enter EMU has proved a decisive disadvantage to the City, at least so far."

- Jobs: "The fifth test was whether joining EMU would promote higher growth, stability and a lasting increase in jobs. On the basis of the examination of the first four tests, the answer is not a decisive yes."

Larry Elliott, the Guardian's economics editor, summed up a study by Barclays Capital, published on 11 June 2001, which stated that Britain failed four of the five tests, "Britain's deep structural differences with the economies of the eurozone mean that it will pass only one of Gordon Brown's five tests for entry into the single currency during the next five years. ... the only risk to the UK of not joining monetary union would be a loss of inward investment, but that the lack of compatibility would result in premature entry hitting growth and jobs. ... Britain's economy remained strikingly different from the rest of the eurozone. It argued that economic growth was poorly correlated with that of the euro area core (Germany), and that Britain reacted to economic shocks in a different way." The report concluded, "This is not the basis for a successful monetary union as it implies a need for independent monetary policy."[31]

In sum, Britain did not meet the five tests. The EU's economies were diverging, as Duisenberg admitted.[32] We had more economic flexibility than the eurozone; investment into Britain was rising, the City of London was flourishing and unemployment was lower than in the eurozone.

We have to defend Britain's sovereignty and independence and continue to reject the euro. It would certainly be bad for the economy and jobs, and, as even the government-commissioned GGC/NOP report admitted, the euro is a 'threat to national identity and decision-making'.

3: EMU's effect of increasing flexibility in the labour market

EMU meant perpetuating Thatcherism, imposed through permanent deflation and a flexible labour market, both enforced by the Labour government. The Amsterdam Treaty sought above all to coordinate national employment policies by 'freeing' the labour market.[33] Blair kept Thatcher's anti-trade union laws, designed to prevent workers in different workplaces, firms and industries from acting together to defend each other against threats to their wages, working conditions and job security. These laws made it illegal for unions to act as unions. Labour's 1997 election manifesto promised that it would be foremost in 'promoting flexible labour markets' across the EU. This meant tearing up the protective rules that trade unions had won. It meant minimal restraints on employers and minimal rights for workers. Brown said that he was fighting unemployment by imposing flexible labour markets, but flexible labour markets made it easier for the employer to sack people.

John Edmonds, General Secretary of the GMB union, wrote, "If the politicians of Europe have nothing to offer working people but an unregulated labour market with rising insecurity and ever more powerful employers, trade union support for the single currency must be forfeit because there will be no benefit to justify the risk."[34] But we in Britain are already in an unregulated labour market, and entering the euro would not miraculously make it regulated! Edmonds supports early euro entry without conditions: if we followed his lead, we would find ourselves in the euro and in no position to stop Blair from fastening an unregulated labour market on the whole EU.

If Britain joined the euro, this would harm Europe's workers, for the EU would use the flexibility and deregulations of the British labour market against them. As Ben Daniels of UNIFI pointed out, "EMU is likely to lead to the further decline of national sectoral agreements in Europe and the rise of company level bargaining."[35] Growing EU control over national level industrial relations could lead to what has been called 'virtual collective bargaining'. Inside the euro the employer could compare wages more easily, find the lowest and drive wages down to this level.

The World Bank frankly stated, "Increasing labor market flexibility - despite the bad name it has acquired as a euphemism for pushing wages down and workers out - is essential in all the regions of the world ... The most important reforms involve lifting constraints on labor mobility and wage flexibility, as well as breaking the ties between social services and labor contracts."[36] Jacques Santer, then President of the European Commission, told the CBI in May 1995, "we must keep all our relative international costs as low as possible to maximise our competitivity." Santer's successor Prodi called for 'greater flexibility and lower labour costs' to develop the Mezzogiorno, Italy's south, but also to solve the EU's unemployment problem.[37]

The authors of the standard textbooks on the EU agreed that the euro would make labour markets more flexible, worsening wages, conditions and employment levels. For example, Valerio Lintner wrote, "If there are no different currencies, their values cannot of course change, and, in the absence of devaluation, differences in competitiveness must either be balanced by falls in living standards (if there are flexible labour markets which permit wages to fall in response to a decline in the demand for labour) or by unemployment (supplemented, to the extent that labour is mobile, by migration as workers follow the geographical distribution of jobs) and a decline in the level of economic activity and hence in material prosperity."[38] This was unusually frank in defining flexible labour markets as those that let employers cut wages and in showing that the euro would mean lower living standards, either through lower wages or more unemployment or more probably both, plus more forced emigration and economic decline.

Simon Hix concluded that EMU meant, "Publics must support structural reforms, be prepared to negotiate flexible wage rates, and be willing to cross borders to take up jobs."[39] Colin Crouch stated that in a single currency, "all adaptations must be made by reductions in unit labour costs - whether directly through reductions in labour costs, or indirectly by labour improving its productivity. This imposes an enormous burden on labour. ... European labour markets are becoming deregulated, and the competitive pressure of the single currency is strengthening these tendencies considerably."[40] Dinan pointed out, "most national governments are beginning to introduce more wage and labor flexibility, however haltingly. The advent of monetary union increases the pressure on them to do so."[41] Professor Norbert Berthold of Wurzburg University wrote that the euro could only succeed if governments slashed trade union powers and privatised the remaining social services: the resulting flexible labour markets would cut jobs and wages. What Ben Daniels wrote of the finance sector applied to the others too: "the introduction of a single currency will lead to a desire for a more co-ordinated working week across the finance sector in Europe in some specific activities. This will create a desire from employers for employees to be prepared to work more flexible hours."[42]

Freeing up labour markets also meant cutting labour's benefits. To justify their attacks on unions, jobs and welfare, employers and politicians claimed that over-regulated job markets caused unemployment: for example, the OECD Jobs Study 1994 blamed the EU's poor employment record on union power and welfare costs. Yet the OECD's own figures showed that the association between employment and social spending is practically zero: the size of the welfare state does not worsen international competitiveness.[43]

The EC produced its first social action programme as early as 1974 - measures to achieve full employment, equal treatment of men and women in the workplace, better living and working conditions, and worker participation in industrial decision-making.[44] But these worthy aims were just rhetoric: Keith Richardson, the Secretary-General of the European Round Table of Industrialists, admitted, "If politicians feel it is important to get the chapter referring to the desirability of full employment and they think it will help public opinion we don't really object. It won't help jobs, but it won't do much damage providing of course that it remains related to aspirations."[45]

The Commission's White Paper 'Growth, Competitiveness, Employment' of June 1993 outlined its aim to 'create at least 15 million new jobs by the year 2000'.[46] However, the European Council dropped this goal in December.[47] Yet the Madrid Council meeting of December 1995 solemnly proclaimed, "job creation is the principal social, economic and political objective of the European Union and its Member States."[48] Santer said that employment was the 'grand projet mobilisateur' of his Presidency, and on 31 January 1996 he called for a 'European Confidence Pact for Employment'. But the 1996 Council in Florence rejected plans to invest in transport and communications. The EU's idea of creating jobs was to cut wages and worsen conditions: European Council meetings discussed employment only to commit the EU repeatedly 'to restrain wage growth and dismantle labour market rigidities'.[49] Prodi relied on private enterprise, not EU policy, to solve the EU's huge unemployment problem.[50]

The employers wanted changes that would roll back the social and economic gains achieved by trader unions over many decades. Some academics backed these proposals. Vinals and Jimeno, for example, wrote, "several labor market institutions seem to have been responsible for the less than satisfactory performance of European labor markets, both by contributing to sustained wage pressures and by slowing down the speed with which wage growth decelerates in the presence of worsening economic conditions. Among the labor market institutions discussed, three stand out: collective bargaining, job security legislation, and unemployment benefits systems." This admitted that trade unions and the laws that they have won had prevented wage cuts - quite a compliment, even if backhanded! They then proposed worse conditions and benefits: "the further deregulation and liberalization of nontraded goods and services sectors, when necessary, and the redesign of labor market institutions - such as job security provisions and unemployment benefits schemes - should be among the top priorities."[51]

Dinan wrote, "The cure for high EU unemployment should therefore be obvious: lower and shorter-lasting unemployment benefits, stricter tests for receipt of benefits, lower payroll taxes and other statutory charges, greater wage flexibility, less job protection, and the provision of earned-income tax credits. Taken together, these recommendations read like a recipe for what many Europeans decry as the callous Anglo-Saxon economic model, which, precisely because of its supposed social consequences - growing income inequalities, the emergence of a 'working poor' underclass, and the lack of a social safety net - a majority of EU member states are loath to embrace."[52] 'Supposed'?

Simonazzi and Villa also observed that these neo-liberal policies have increased unemployment, "overall, in Europe, the policies implemented have not produced the desired effects: unemployment has continued to increase ... In the USA, on the other hand, the end result of the 'job-creation miracle' has been rising inequality and falling real earnings. ... The European experience, and in particular the contrast between the UK and the other EC countries, seems to confirm that it is not sufficient to increase the degree of flexibility, weaken union power, decentralise the wage-setting process, and finally reduce the generosity of income support to job-seekers, in order to bring about the 'flourishing' of low-paid, poor-quality jobs. ... despite its much stronger commitment to deregulation, the UK economy has not engendered better job-creation capacity than the other EC countries: in the years 1980-93, the UK registered a contraction in total employment (-0.8 per cent)."[53] Tuire Santamaki-Vuori confirmed,

"International evidence suggests that removing the ability of people without jobs to claim welfare benefits risks compounding rather than solving the problem [of unemployment], pushing the unemployed off the official jobless count into economic inactivity rather than employment."[54]

Jeremy Richardson wrote, "Increasingly, we hear the argument that the winners at the Euro-level, more often than not, are business interests. As we near the end of the century, the EU is seen by many as a business-driven project. Whether or not one accepts this rather simple-minded argument, it is fairly clear, nevertheless, that trade unions and their members (and the many other workers not in unions) have tended to lose out. As the Single Market project has been driven forward, and as greater emphasis is placed on the need to increase Europe's competitiveness against the rest of the world, traditional trade union and citizen claims get pushed aside. In practice, the almost hegemonic view that Europe's competitiveness must be increased has been a euphemism for reduced social protection, weaker unions, and greater acceptance of the vagaries of market forces. ... the traditional model of economic citizenship in Europe is now under severe strain, with high and persistent levels of unemployment, a decline in the economic functionality of the social institutions that have sustained economic citizenship in the member-states, and the fragmentation of social coherence."[55] This summary showed how capital has used the EU to gain at workers' expense, even if it was 'rather simple-minded' to say so.

As Reder and Ulman noted, "continued European unification ... will reinforce prevailing trends towards the Community's economic integration and the attendant reduction of a member state's ability to protect its citizens from competition by producers in other member states. Further, if maintained the recently established regime of nearly fixed exchange rates should sharply reduce national governments' ability to protect output and employment by devaluing their currencies and offsetting idiosyncratic movements of national wage levels. The combined effect of these concurrent developments will be to weaken national unions' ability to influence terms of employment. The state's power to limit nonunion operations within its borders as well as to establish nontariff barriers to imports, to restrict immigration, and to impose wage and price controls has acted as a dike behind which unions have been able to set wages and other terms of employment that are greater than what they would otherwise have been."[56]

Dean Baker concluded that lack of demand, not inflexible labour markets, increased unemployment, "the conventional view - that the OECD countries have experienced slow growth and high unemployment in recent years because of the structures of their labour markets - is difficult to support. Instead, the main obstacle to more rapid growth would appear to be the lack of sufficient demand. Public policy should then focus primarily on the means to generate more internal demand rather than try to restructure the labor market. The evidence that insufficient demand is the immediate constraint on growth for most of the European nations is overwhelming. ... It is worth noting that, for most European countries, the unemployment rates have been even higher in the 1990s than in the 1980s. However much labor market rigidities might have contributed to increases in unemployment, it simply is not plausible that they have increased this rapidly, particularly at a time when the welfare state has been contracting in most of Europe."[57] Simonazzi and Villa summed up, "the higher the degree of flexibility, the higher is earning inequality, with all the related problems of poverty, deprivation and homelessness."[58]

Rebuilding countries would solve the problem of unemployment, by increasing demand. The employers' way - attacking trade unions, wages, and welfare - worsened the problem.

4: EMU's effect of worsening growth and unemployment

The closer that the EEC members got to economic and monetary union, the slower their economies grew. The West German 'economic miracle', like other countries' post-war economic recoveries, largely predated the EEC. The original six members grew faster before they founded the EEC than after: at the same time, Britain, which had not yet joined, increased its growth rate. (Contrary to the prediction of a 1961 Cabinet committee chaired by Macmillan: "But perhaps the strongest argument for joining the Six was based on the potential dangers of staying outside; as the Six consolidated, we would inevitably enter into a period of relative decline."⁵⁹)

When the original six had no form of EMU, from 1950 to 1969, they grew by 5.5% a year. When they linked their currencies in the 'snake', from 1969 to 1975, they grew by just 3.7% a year, falling from 6.9% in 1969 to minus 1.2% in 1975. From 1976, when the snake collapsed, to 1979, they grew by 3.6% a year, but when they again linked their currencies through the ERM, from 1979 to 1993, they grew by just 2.1% a year, falling from 4.7% in 1979 to minus 1% in 1993. The ERM gradually squeezed the life out of the EC's economies by keeping members' currencies too high and preventing them from boosting their economies by expanding the money supply.

The EU has never been achieved anything near to full employment. In 1981 unemployment in the EC-10 was 7.4%. In 1986 in the EC-12 it was 10.8%. In 1995 in the EU-15 it was 10.1% and in 2001 it was 7.4%. In 2005 in the EU-25 it was 8.9%.

For instance, unemployment in Greece rose to 10%, its debts and trade deficits soared and production fell. EU membership has led to a decline in Greek productivity, especially in agriculture and manufacture, an explosive public and external debt and a trade deficit.⁶⁰

Ireland experienced a boom for the owners of capital, a slump for those producing the wealth. Its uniquely low taxation of firms' profits, at 10%, not its euro membership, explained its growth. (Britain had the next lowest rate of taxation, at 30%.) This caused a huge influx of US capital, the highest level per head in Europe, bringing high US-style profits, rents, dividends and bonuses. But it also caused the lowest wages in the EU. Between 1987 and 1997, the share of profits, interest, dividends and rent rose from 31% to 41% of national income, while the share of wages, pensions and social security fell from 69% to 59%. This was not wealth trickling down, but being pumped up. So hospitals closed, school class sizes rose, public spending was cut, local authority house building virtually ceased and house prices rose out of sight. In response, white-collar trade unions grew rapidly and won widespread support: most of the population backed the 1999 nurses' strike for higher pay.

As the former President of the Commission, Sicco Mansholt, admitted in July 1973, the result was, "For the great mass of the population there has been no broad improvement in conditions generally and dissatisfaction is widespread." EEC members coped badly with the 1973-74 oil price shock: the US and Asian economies maintained their growth, unlike EEC members.

Under the European Monetary System, members were tightly bound. The famous Mitterand U-turn in 1983 was not forced by capital flight but by the EMS, which did not allow France to boost its economy by expanding the money supply. By contrast, the economies of Sweden and Norway, which were not in the EMS, grew throughout the 1970s and early 1980s, because they could keep their currencies floating.[61]

What did currency unification do to Germany when it reunited in 1990?[62] The West German government saw currency union as a political not an economic issue, just as the EU's leaders see the euro. They were determined to push for full union, whatever the costs - which were known in advance. They ignored all the warnings of economic disaster, just as the EU's leaders do now. In fact, the German government cynically promised the East Germans an economic miracle. The result was disaster. In 1990, East Germany's industrial output was just 46% of its 1989 level; unemployment soared to 32% in 1991-92. Monetary union brought higher taxes and higher interest rates.[63] Since the euro's introduction, Germany's unemployment total has risen by 200,000 to 5.1 million. For four years running, Germany has breached the EU's 'Stability and Growth Pact' (Stagnation Pact). In 2004, its government imposed an increase in the working week from 35 to 42 hours – equivalent to a 20% pay cut. So much for any belief that the EU somehow gives workers a legal entitlement to a shorter working week.

In 2005, 30 million people in the EU were unemployed, according to official figures. Forty per cent of them were less than 25 years old and had never had a job. The way that unemployment was counted in EU member states consistently underestimated the real totals. In Belgium, for instance, unemployment was officially 13% in 1986, but the real total was more like 25%.[64] And unemployment in the eurozone was on the rise. In Germany it rose from 6.6% in 1992 to 9.1% in 1999 to 12.6% in 2005, in France from 10.4% to 11%, and in Italy from 8.8% to 11.3%. In Spain in 2005 it was 10.4%, in Slovakia 16.9% and in Poland 18.3%. (One might even suspect that the US government backs the euro because it wants to cut down the industries of Germany, France and Italy.)

The OECD outrageously claimed that for the industrialised economies, the 'natural rate' of unemployment below which inflation would accelerate was 11%. So for the European Central Bank, which accepts this analysis, "the focus of monetary policy becomes to ensure, in practice, that unemployment is sufficiently high to reduce price and wage increases."[65] So to the EU, high unemployment is a success.

Any unemployment, never mind 11%, was a crime - countries needed goods and services, yet the people who could provide them could not find work. The EU was an accessory to that crime. It was not a full employment economy, nor was it on its way to full employment. Its treaties, particularly the Maastricht and Amsterdam Treaties, were designed to rule out even the attempt to achieve full employment.[66] The tight monetary and fiscal policies adopted to prepare for the euro worsened unemployment and cut growth.[67]

The Maastricht Treaty's criteria for joining EMU were deflationary: those countries that did not meet them had to deflate; those that met them were not obliged to reflate. As Peter Hain wrote back in 1995, the Maastricht Treaty's "imposition of monetarism is both deflationary and reactionary." He also pointed out the inevitable result: "The monetarism of the EU had generated mass unemployment ... " And, "a single currency would impose major restrictions upon the use of macroeconomic policy instruments which, without offsetting policies, would give rise to growing unemployment in less competitive regions."[68] In 1996 Ken Livingstone signed a statement titled 'Europe isn't working', denouncing the EU's failures on jobs and called on Blair to rule out joining the single currency. Like Hain, he has now switched to supporting the EU.

EMU's supporters promised that the euro would increase growth, but they had previously promised that the Single Market and the ERM would increase growth and we have seen how false those promises were. The Thatcher government claimed that the Single Market was 'Thatcherism on a European scale': EMU would be even more so. The employers wanted the Single Market, the ERM and EMU because they all freed capital at the expense of labour.[69]

The academic authorities agreed that this was so. Paul de Grauwe noted, "monetary integration will intensify competition and the liberalization dynamics in Europe."[70] Dyson and Featherstone wrote, "Public disquiet with the [Maastricht] Treaty had much to do with a growing sense that its consequences would be not so much 'controlled' as 'sauvage'; that EMU might not be so much a shield and protector against the forces of the global market as a means of institutionalising its imperatives."[71] In particular, finance companies wanted EMU, so that the money markets could use it to control wages and public spending. Dyson wrote, "The crucial enforcer of the sound money paradigm is the global financial markets. They act as vigilant external disciplines on the Euro-Zone's public sectors."[72]

In the euro, there would be no chance of revaluing the currency up or down to suit our needs. The only means of adjustment, when devaluations were forbidden, were wage cuts and mass emigration. The Bank of England's 1989 Report urged wage cuts: "With the reduction of exchange rate variability, it is important for the wage system to become more responsive to considerations of competitiveness." The Bank also observed, "For EMU to be sustainable, the economies of countries forming the union must be similarly competitive or else some countries would be faced with the equivalent of a constant balance of payments deficit which, in EMU, would be reflected in terms of stagnation and unemployment."

The Governor of the Bank of England, Sir Eddie George, pointed out that the euro would mean fewer jobs and lower growth. Business Week estimated that the euro would put one in twenty of Europe's industrial workers out of a job.[73] Adair Turner, then the CBI's Director-General, said in 1998, "The European public has not been fully prepared for the likely impact of monetary union. I think they've been given false assurances that EMU itself will directly create jobs and cure unemployment - an assertion without intellectual justification." Sir Nigel Wicks, the Treasury man who was Chair of the EU monetary committee, said, "I would not regard monetary policy as an instrument for solving unemployment." An internal European Commission paper said that EMU would cause massive unemployment.[74]

Professor Wilhelm Nolling, a Bundesbank Council member from 1989 to 1992, said, "Europe's most pressing challenge is combating mass unemployment. Yet monetary union would impose a costly straitjacket that would make a bad situation worse. Fixing exchange rates will remove a state's ability to make corrections needed to economic policies by changing the exchange rate. Instead of such flexibility the rigidities of monetary union would lead to more unemployment."[75]

Lucas and Woodin wrote, "Monetary union is also likely to result in ever-fiercer cross-border competition. The Euro makes the instant comparison of prices and productivity within the whole of Euroland possible, increasing the trend of relocations to the most competitive areas, and exacerbating the competition between countries and regions to attract investments. As a Morgan Stanley economist has remarked, 'If you remove currency as a safety valve, governments will be forced to focus on real changes to become more competitive: lower taxes, labour market flexibility, and a more favourable regulatory backdrop for business.'"[76]

Even Giles Radice, the Labour MP and Chairman of the European Movement, conceded, "EMU (sic) may not be what economists call an 'optimal currency area'."[77] So the prescribed 'one-size-fits-all' economic policy would cause great damage, particularly to jobs. As Tony Thirlwall wrote, "I know no one who believes that the current eleven countries of Euroland constitute an optimum currency area. This being so, monetary union is unlikely to lead to the real convergence of member countries. If anything, increased divergence is more likely. Therefore, greater regional divergence is also more likely given that regional disparities are more closely related to differences in performance between countries than to regional disparities within countries."[78] The European Central Bank would set an inflexible interest rate across the whole of the EU to minimise inflation, not to secure growth or full employment.

For example, on 31 August 2000 the Bank raised interest rates to 4.5%, when Ireland's inflation was 6% and rising and Spain's was 5%, so the Spanish and Irish governments welcomed the rise, but others were less keen. As Miguel Angel Garcia, a Spanish trade unionist, pointed out, "Spanish inflation and that of Ireland are punishing other countries." Heinz Putzhammer of the German Federation of Trade Unions said of the rise, "It's bad for business, dangerous for growth and recovery, and will not fight inflation." The rise was too small to curb Irish and Spanish inflation, while it added to the difficulties of economies mired in recession, like Germany and France.

We needed very different interest rates, even within a single country or region. For instance, directors seeking a loan in order to fund speculation or overseas loans should face penally high rates; those seeking funds to invest in production and jobs should be able to borrow money very cheaply.[79] A single fixed interest rate meant that governments' only economic tools were wage cuts and unemployment.

Trade unions were very concerned about the pound's high value and high interest rates, and some trade union members mistakenly saw the lower short-term interest rate regime in the EU as a consequence of the euro. It was not so, and the figures were misleading. The ECB set the eurozone's short-term interest rate relatively low, but this did not cure mass unemployment or secure major industrial investment. The important interest rate is the long-term interest rate, the rate over a 20-year period, which manufacturers use because it supports and guarantees longer-term industrial investment. This rate has been higher in the eurozone than in Britain for a long time.

The economist Christian Chabot wrote, "a few types of businesses do bear a disproportionate share of the burden. European firms that need to make significant euro-related transition investments but that don't accrue any of the compensating benefits from international trade, for instance, see little benefit from monetary union." He went on, "never forget that the majority of the world's firms still derive the bulk of their revenue from home markets. ... The euro's core economic effects appear to offer few significant benefits to such organizations." In Britain, the 80% of firms that depended on home sales would have to bear the euro's costs, but would get none of its (putative) benefits. He went on, "Other at-risk industries include the banking, insurance, telecommunications, transport, utilities, and pharmaceutical industries."[80] So the 'few types of businesses' that would lose out were the majority of European firms, plus these six important industries. Over the years, the EU had closed down or drastically cut back basic industries such as steel, textiles and fishing.[81] Now it appeared that the euro would finish off what was left!

Entering the euro would prevent us trading freely in all the world's markets and would prevent the kind of full employment economy that the trade union movement wanted. Europhiles liked to claim that nearly 60% of our trade was with the EU; in fact nearly 60% of our exports of goods, a very different matter, went to the EU. This equated to only 10% of our jobs and GDP being traded with the EU. 10% of our GDP went to the rest of the world. The other 80% of our jobs and GDP depended on the British economy. Why should the 10% going to the EU determine the fate of the other 90%?

We were told that 3.5 million British jobs depended on our exports to EU member countries. But 4.5 million EU jobs depended on exports to us since we were running a huge trade deficit with them. So we, in effect, supported a million EU jobs: they depended on us more than we depended on them. Anyway, we did not need to be in the EU to trade with it: more than 60% of Switzerland's exports went to the EU, but that did not make Switzerland join the EU. Norway, also not a member, had tariff-free access to EU markets. It sold 74% of its exports to EU countries and enjoyed record levels of exports to the EU even after it voted not to join. WTO rules forbid the EU to discriminate against the products of any country, and the EU's external tariff was only 6% on average, so if we withdrew from the EU, trade would continue and so would the jobs.

The National Institute for Economic and Social Research found that withdrawing from the EU would not cost jobs. The Independent reported this as '8 million jobs could be lost if Britain quits EU' (18 February 2000). The NIESR's director, Dr Martin Weale, responded that the Independent's claim was "absurd ... pure Goebbels. In many years of academic research I cannot recall such a wilful distortion of the facts." In the subsequent discussion, Gordon Brown claimed, "750,000 British companies export from Britain to Europe": the government's own figure was 18,000.

In 2001, the Ernst & Young Item Club, using the Treasury model of the economy, estimated that joining the euro at a rate of £1 to 1.53 euros would cut manufacturing output by an average of 0.5% a year in the first three years. It would cut our overall growth by 0.2% in the first year and by 0.3% in both the next two years. This would cost us about £8 billion in lost output, destroying more than 150,000 jobs. By the end of the three years, our unemployment rate would be 3.6% as against the 3.1% forecast outside the euro. Projections showed that joining at the rate of £1 to 1.63

euros would cause even more damage.[82]

In late 2004, the European Commission forecast that economic growth across the eurozone would be 2.1% for 2005. In April 2005 it had to revise that forecast down to a beggarly 1.6%.

Academic writers on the EU agreed that EMU would mean lower wages, fewer jobs and worse working conditions. The EU-enthusiasts Cram, Dinan and Nugent wrote, "Nor does the ECB's tight monetary policy and commitment to price stability necessarily sit easily with a social democratic economic approach. As it is, the ECB will have difficulty adopting a 'one-size-fits-all' policy for such a heterogeneous economic area as euroland. A central bank makes policy for a country or - in the case of the ECB - for a collection of countries, as a whole. It cannot make policy for a particular region, no matter how disadvantaged - for example, because it suffers higher than average unemployment - that region happens to be. In euroland, disadvantaged regions are likely to be entire member states whose populations are bound to resent the impression that unemployment in their country is the price being paid for low inflation throughout euroland."[83] This would not be an impression; it would be the reality.

Chabot wrote, "In the short and medium term, the euro does little or nothing to ease Europe's acute unemployment situation, despite a glut of political claims to the contrary."[84] Feldstein believed that the euro would worsen unemployment and inflation: "Indeed, the adverse economic effects of a single currency on unemployment and inflation would outweigh any gains from facilitating trade and capital flows among the EMU members."[85] The Guardian wrote that the euro would cut people's living standards: "The euro in their pocket will not go as far as the lira or the peseta used to, and they will have to tighten their belts."[86] The economist Susan Strange warned, "it could very well be that German monetary hegemony in the EU will doom European economies to prolonged slow growth, high unemployment and low competitiveness."[87] Bretherton and Vogler remarked, "the deleterious effects of the neoliberal economic policies necessitated by the convergence criteria" and 'the uncertain benefits of EMU itself'. They concluded, "EMU, and indeed enlargement, are policy areas whose long-term success depends, in part, upon the willingness of EU publics to tolerate economic sacrifices."[88] (This calls to mind the British government's World War Two slogan, 'Your sacrifices will bring us victory'.) As Colin Crouch summed up, "For national unions it is very bad news indeed if the single currency regime continues as it inevitably started: severely deflationary, monetarist, and neo-liberal."[89]

The euro would not even keep prices down. The European Economic Advisory Group's first annual report concluded, "contrary to a popular view, prices of individual goods will not converge to their lowest level in the euro area."[90] They pointed out that firms would take advantage of differing distribution and transport costs to charge what local markets could bear. And this proved to be true: car prices in Germany were 20% higher than the cheapest in the EU. As the Independent wrote, "The launch of the euro three years ago was supposed to usher in the great nirvana of lower prices by making the cost of goods transparent across the eurozone. Prices are meant to harmonise down to the lowest common denominator, since if retailers charge more in one country than another, consumers will simply hop across the border and spend their hard-earned euros where they buy the most. Well, it may be working for some things, but it is not working for automobiles. The latest car price comparisons from the European Commission show that little or no convergence has taken place. Indeed, in some instances, the differential between the cheapest and most expensive pre-tax prices in euroland has actually widened as the single currency has matured."[91]

In addition, the euro's introduction led to price rises of up to 10%, contrary to EU assurances that this would not happen. A Financial Times editorial argued, "policymakers, particularly the politicians, are not innocent victims of consumers' euro price misperceptions. They promised, contrary to almost all available academic evidence, that European prices would converge quickly downwards after the introduction of euro notes and coins as prices became much more transparent."[92] David Byrne, the Commissioner for Consumer Affairs, admitted in June 2002, "in some sectors, prices have increased at above average rates." In September 2002, the Treasury added a study on price differentials to its five tests.

Some in the labour movement argued that staying outside the euro would increase unemployment. The engineers' union, the AEEU, claimed that staying out would jeopardise jobs because we would lose inward investment and access to Europe's markets.[93] It also argued that joining the euro would help by ending transaction costs, but every businessman knew that these costs were avoidable and so in practice negligible.[94] Relying on inward investment would make Britain a branch-line economy, dependent for our industrial future on decisions made by outside investors investing here because of our low wages and high skills. Depending on outside business interests, far from assuring our industrial future, exposed us to dependence on economies themselves subject to slumps. We needed to rebuild our economy, using our own resources. As the South West TUC remarked, "Resources should not be wasted attracting poor inward investment which may be better used developing indigenous business."[95]

Manufacturing production has always been central to the trade union movement, and trade unions, particularly those in manufacturing, have always backed Britain's manufacturing industry, recognizing it as vital to Britain's future. How could they argue for a policy that would mean merging Britain into an EU state? It was no good for trade unionists to argue (quite rightly) on the one hand for British-made products, and on the other to bless the euro that threatened this domestic production.

The AEEU stated that joining the euro would reduce interest rates, but we could cut interest rates and lower the pound's value against the euro whenever we wanted. The union recognised that the European Central Bank was unaccountable and secretive, and called for making it more accountable and open. But this unaccountability and secrecy were written into the Maastricht Treaty.

Some proposed that we should accept the Treaty and then campaign to change it. But, as John Grahl noted, it was impossible to renegotiate the Treaty.[96] Yet while recognising that "no substantial deviation from the formulas was politically conceivable", he proposed that we should "accept the Maastricht agenda while proposing gradualist and, initially, piecemeal strategies for its amendment."[97] This was typical social democracy: accept the unacceptable, then pretend to soften its impact by proposing impossible reforms. He also wrote, "the Maastricht agenda ... is quite unworkable."[98] So why not say so, rather than telling people to accept it?

Endnotes

[1]. John Schmid, New era for ECB, International Herald Tribune, 2 January 2002. Our italics.

[2]. Sun, 28 May 1998.

[3]. See Kenneth Dyson, The politics of the Euro-zone: stability or breakdown? Oxford University Press, 2000, page 42.

[4]. See Kenneth Dyson and Kevin Featherstone, The road to Maastricht: negotiating Economic and Monetary Union, Oxford University Press, 1999, page 791.

[5]. Annual Trade and Development Report, UNCTAD, September 1996.

[6]. Hugo Young, Winning the referendum is the beginning not the end, Guardian, 3 May 2001, page 20.

[7]. See David Turner, ECB inflation target may act as straitjacket on economy, Financial Times, 18 February 2002, page 10.

[8]. See Joseph Stiglitz, Globalization and its discontents, Allen Lane, 2002.

[9]. Cited page 327, David Gowland and Arthur Turner, Reluctant Europeans: Britain and European integration, 1945-1998, Longman, 2000.

[10]. See Donald Macintyre, Mandelson: the biography, HarperCollins, 1999, page 416.

[11]. Give growth a chance, TUC, September 1999.

[12]. See Francesco Guerrera, Euro changeover costs banks a 'year's profit', Financial Times, 18 February 2002, page 10.

[13]. Samuel Brittan, Keep floating, stop worrying, Financial Times, 28 March 2002, page 25.

[14]. See Tony Thirlwall and Helen Gibson, Balance-of-payments theory and the United Kingdom experience, Macmillan, 4th edition, 1992, page 388.

[15]. See Faisal Islam and Oliver Morgan, UK back in the red by 2003, Observer Business, 25 November 2001, page 1.

[16]. James Buchan, Fools' gold? Guardian, 19 February 2001, G2, pages 2 and 4.

[17]. Larry Elliott and Charlotte Denny, Scorn for EU pleas on spending, Guardian, 31 January 2002, page 2.

[18]. See Labour Euro News, October 1998.

[19]. Cited page 224, Andy McSmith, John Smith: a life 1938-1994, Mandarin, 1994.

[20]. See Roland Axtmann, 'Globalization, Europe and the state: introductory reflections', Chapter 1, pages 1-22, in Roland Axtmann, editor, Globalization and Europe: theoretical and empirical investigations, Pinter, 1998.

[21]. See Desmond Dinan, Ever closer union: an introduction to European integration, Macmillan, 2nd edition, 1999, page 459.

[22]. Sunday Business, 18 February 2001.

[23]. Ben Daniels, The euro, UNIFI, 2001, pages 30 and 33.

[24]. The University of Reading, The Space Race, 4 May 2000.

[25]. See Kenneth Dyson and Kevin Featherstone, The road to Maastricht: negotiating Economic and Monetary Union, Oxford University Press, 1999, especially their discussion on 'EMU, Stability, and the International Monetary System', pages 797-9.

[26]. See Graham Ingham, Managing change: a guide to British economic policy, Manchester University Press, 2000, page 206. Our italics.

[27]. Michael Mann, page 194, 'Is there a society called Euro?' Chapter 11, pages 184-207, in Roland Axtmann, editor, Globalization and Europe: theoretical and empirical investigations, Pinter, 1998.

[28]. Tom Bower, Gordon Brown, HarperCollins, 2004, page 444.

[29]. Laura Cram, Desmond Dinan and Neill Nugent, page 356, in 'The evolving European Union', Chapter 18, pages 353-65, in Laura Cram, Desmond Dinan and Neill Nugent, editors, Developments in the European

Union, Macmillan, 1999. See also Desmond Dinan, Ever closer union: an introduction to European integration, Macmillan, 2nd edition, 1999, pages 183 and 404. On the EU's employment policy, see his pages 401-4.

[30]. Financial Times, 21 February 2001.

[31]. See Larry Elliott, UK 'fails four of five euro tests', Guardian, 12 June 2001, page 23.

[32]. The Times, 6 March 1999.

[33]. See Franklin Dehousse, Amsterdam: the making of a treaty, Kogan Page, 1999, page 39.

[34]. Roger Beetham, editor, The euro debate: persuading the people, Federal Trust, 2001, page 121.

[35]. Ben Daniels, The euro, UNIFI, 2001, page 35.

[36]. World Bank, World Development Report, 1995.

[37]. Romano Prodi, Europe as I see it, Polity Press, 2000, page 126; see also his page 77.

[38]. Valerio Lintner, page 118, 'Controlling Monetary Union', Chapter 6, pages 117-38, in Catherine Hoskyns and Michael Newman, editors, Democratizing the European Union: issues for the twenty-first century, Manchester University Press, 2000.

[39]. Simon Hix, The political system of the European Union, Macmillan, 1999, page 306.

[40]. Colin Crouch, 'Introduction: the political and institutional deficits of European Monetary Union', pages 1-23, in Colin Crouch, editor, After the euro: shaping institutions for governance in the wake of European Monetary Union, Oxford University Press, 2000, pages 19-20.

[41]. Desmond Dinan, Ever closer union: an introduction to European integration, Macmillan, 2nd edition, 1999, page 404.

[42]. Ben Daniels, The euro, UNIFI, 2001, page 31.

[43]. See Fritz Scharpf, Governing in Europe: effective and democratic? Oxford University Press, 1999, pages 127 and 130.

[44]. On social interests, see Justin Greenwood, Representing interests in the European Union, New York: St Martin's Press, 1997, pages 204-16; on consumer interests, see his pages 193-204.

[45]. Cited pages 16-17, Brian Denny, Politics of the euro: economics of the madhouse, Campaign Against Euro-Federalism, 2001.

[46]. Cited page 130, Helen Drake, Jacques Delors: perspectives on a European leader, Routledge, 2000.

[47]. See Helen Drake, Jacques Delors: perspectives on a European leader, Routledge, 2000, page 134.

[48]. Cited page 142, Helen Drake, Jacques Delors: perspectives on a European leader, Routledge, 2000.

[49]. Cited page 136, Helen Drake, Jacques Delors: perspectives on a European leader, Routledge, 2000. On the bad and worsening working conditions in the EU, see, for instance, Guglielmo Carchedi, For another Europe: a class analysis of European economic integration, Verso, 2001, pages 238-9.

[50]. See Romano Prodi, Europe as I see it, Polity Press, 2000, pages 53 and 96.

[51]. Jose Vinals and Juan Jimeno, 'Monetary Union and European unemployment', Chapter 2, pages 13-52, in Jeffrey Frieden, Daniel Gros and Erik Jones, editors, The new political economy of EMU, Rowman & Littlefield, 1998, pages 42 and 43.

[52]. Desmond Dinan, Ever closer union: an introduction to European integration, Macmillan, 2nd edition, 1999, pages 402-3.

[53]. Annamaria Simonazzi and Paola Villa, pages 52 and 70, 'Employment, growth and income inequality: some open questions', Chapter 3, pages 50-95, in Michael Landesmann and Karl Pichelmann, editors, Unemployment in Europe, Macmillan, 2000. On the vast and growing income inequalities in the EU, see, for instance, Guglielmo Carchedi, For another Europe: a

class analysis of European economic integration, Verso, 2001, pages 237-8.

[54]. Tuire Santamaki-Vuori, 'Labour market experiences of the long-term unemployed in Finland in the early 1990s', Chapter 14, pages 344-73, in Michael Landesmann and Karl Pichelmann, editors, Unemployment in Europe, Macmillan, 2000.

[55]. Jeremy Richardson, pages ix-x, 'Series editor's preface', pages ix-xi, in Paul Teague, Economic citizenship in the European Union: employment relations in the new Europe, Routledge, 1999.

[56]. Melvin Reder and Lloyd Ulman, page 38, 'Unionism and unification', Chapter 2, pages 13-44, in Lloyd Ulman, Barry Eichengreen and William Dickens, editors, Labor and an integrated Europe, The Brookings Institution, 1993.

[57]. Dean Baker, page 386, 'The NAIRU: is it a real constraint?' Chapter 16, pages 369-87, in Dean Baker, Gerald Epstein and Robert Pollin, editors, Globalization and progressive economic policy, Cambridge University Press, 1998.

[58]. Annamaria Simonazzi and Paola Villa, page 86, 'Employment, growth and income inequality: some open questions', Chapter 3, pages 50-95, in Michael Landesmann and Karl Pichelmann, editors, Unemployment in Europe, Macmillan, 2000.

[59]. Cited page 5, David Gowland and Arthur Turner, Reluctant Europeans: Britain and European integration, 1945-1998, Longman, 2000.

[60]. See Panos Tsakoloyanis, page 199, 'Greece: the limits to convergence', Chapter 8, pages 186-207, in Christopher Hill, editor, The actors in Europe's foreign policy, Routledge, 1996.

[61]. See Eric Helleiner, pages 145-7, 'Sovereignty, territoriality and the globalization of finance', Chapter 7, pages 138-57, in David Smith, Dorothy Solinger and Steven Topik, editors, States and sovereignty in the global economy, Routledge, 1999.

[62]. See Wolfgang Seibel, 'An unavoidable disaster? The German currency

union of 1990', Chapter 6, pages 96-111, in Pat Gray and Paul 't Hart, editors, Public policy disasters in Western Europe, Routledge, 1998.

[63]. See Stephen George and Ian Bache, Politics in the European Union, Oxford University Press, 2001, page 159.

[64]. See Lode Van Outrive, page 27, 'The disastrous justice system in Belgium: a crisis of democracy?' Chapter 2, pages 23-38, in Pat Gray and Paul 't Hart, editors, Public policy disasters in Western Europe, Routledge, 1998.

[65]. Mark Baimbridge, Brian Burkitt and Philip Whyman, 'The Bank that rules Europe: the European Central Bank and central bank independence', Chapter 6, pages 121-141, in Martin Holmes, editor, The Eurosceptical reader 2, Palgrave, 2002.

[66]. See Fritz Scharpf, Governing in Europe: effective and democratic? Oxford University Press, 1999, page 115.

[67]. See Malcolm Levitt and Christopher Lord, The political economy of monetary union, Macmillan, 2000, page 17.

[68]. Peter Hain, Ayes to the left: a future for socialism, Lawrence & Wishart, 1995, pages 167, 3 and 164.

[69]. See Stephen George and Ian Bache, Politics in the European Union, Oxford University Press, 2001, page 356.

[70]. Paul de Grauwe, Economics of monetary integration, Oxford University Press, 4th edition, 2000, page 223.

[71]. Kenneth Dyson and Kevin Featherstone, The road to Maastricht: negotiating Economic and Monetary Union, Oxford University Press, 1999, page 252.

[72]. Kenneth Dyson, The politics of the Euro-zone: stability or breakdown? Oxford University Press, 2000, page 31.

[73]. Business Week, 27 April 1998.

[74]. Financial Times, 16 August 1993.

[75]. Cited page 186, Martin Holmes, 'The single currency: evaluating Europe's monetary experiment', Chapter 10, pages 180-9, in Vassiliki Koutrakou, editor, The European Union and Britain: debating the challenges ahead, Macmillan, 2000.

[76]. Caroline Lucas and Mike Woodin, The euro or a sustainable future for Britain? A green critique of the single currency, New Europe, 2000, page 8.

[77]. Giles Radice MP, The case for the euro, Guardian, May 2000, page 12.

[78]. Tony Thirlwall, The euro and 'regional' divergence in Europe, New Europe Research Trust, 2000, page 25.

[79]. See Gar Alperovitz and Jeff Faux, Rebuilding America: a blueprint for the new economy, New York: Pantheon Books, 1984, pages 268-9.

[80]. Christian Chabot, Understanding the euro: the clear and concise guide to the new trans-European economy, McGraw-Hill, 1999, pages 130 and 156.

[81]. See Justin Greenwood, Representing interests in the European Union, New York: St Martin's Press, 1997, page 222.

[82]. Gary Duncan, Euro entry 'to cost £8bn', The Times, 21 January 2001.

[83]. Laura Cram, Desmond Dinan and Neill Nugent, page 357, 'The evolving European Union', Chapter 18, pages 353-65, in Laura Cram, Desmond Dinan and Neill Nugent, editors, Developments in the European Union, Macmillan, 1999.

[84]. Christian Chabot, Understanding the euro: the clear and concise guide to the new trans-European economy, McGraw-Hill, 1999, pages 110-1.

[85]. Martin Feldstein, EMU and international conflict, Foreign Affairs, November/December 1997, Volume 76, Number 6, page 60.

[86]. Wim must become Alice in Euroland, Finance notebook, Guardian, 27 June 2001, page 25.

[87]. Susan Strange, Mad money, Manchester University Press, 1998, p 74.

[88]. Charlotte Bretherton and John Vogler, The European Union as a global actor, Routledge, 1999, page 233.

[89]. Colin Crouch, 'National wage determination and European Monetary Union', Chapter 8, pages 203-26, in Colin Crouch, editor, After the euro: shaping institutions for governance in the wake of the European Monetary Union, Oxford University Press, 2000, page 208.

[90]. Cited, David Turner, ECB inflation target may act as straitjacket on economy, Financial Times, 18 February 2002, page 10.

[91]. Euro nirvana fails to work magic on car prices, Independent, 26 February 2002, page 17.

[92]. Price is right, editorial, Financial Times, 9 September 2002.

[93]. The case for the single currency, AEEU, February 1999.

[94]. See Lynden Moore, Britain's trade and economic structure: the impact of the European Union, Routledge, 1999, page 374.

[95]. The South West TUC, The South West can make it, 2000.

[96]. John Grahl, After Maastricht: a guide to European Monetary Union, Lawrence & Wishart, 1997, page 245.

[97]. John Grahl, After Maastricht: a guide to European Monetary Union, Lawrence & Wishart, 1997, pages 227 and 245.

[98]. John Grahl, After Maastricht: a guide to European Monetary Union, Lawrence & Wishart, 1997, page 245.

Chapter 6: Industrial inspiration

1: The economy

2: A future of manufacturing industry

3: Energy

4: Steel

5: The defence industry

6: Communications

7: Transport industries

8: Textiles

*   Under the second Blair government, 15,000 manufacturing jobs were destroyed every month. Compare this with under Thatcher, 5,000 such jobs every month, and under the first Blair government, 10,000 every month.

In this chapter, we try to show the EU's impact on Britain's industries and services. The coverage is inevitably uneven and illustrative.

1: The economy

Economically, the EEC has been a disaster for Britain. Entering the EEC meant investment abroad soared while industrial investment at home, and therefore output, fell.[1] From 1976 to 1980, £4.2 billion in capital left Britain. From 1972 to 1975, British investors put £1 billion into EEC countries, which invested only £296 million in Britain. Most of this went not into building new factories but into acquisitions and mergers. All research proves that most acquisitions reduce firms' value.

Growth in output per head in manufacturing fell from an average of 4% between 1961 and 1973 to just 0.7% between 1973 and 1979. Academic authorities agree that joining the EEC was bad for Britain. E. L. Grinols estimated that joining cost Britain 2-3% of GDP in the first six years.[2] Other authorities agree. Valerio Lintner concluded, "the best estimates tend to suggest that membership of the Community reduced UK output of manufactures and significantly worsened the trade balance in this area."[3] Alan Winters wrote that the "unavoidable conclusion is that British accession to the EC worsened her trade balance in, and reduced her gross output of, manufactures quite substantially. Even on the most conservative estimate it reduced output by at least £3 billion, about 1.5% of GNP, and the effect could easily have been twice that."[4] Lynden Moore wrote, "De-industrialization - that is, a decline in the proportion of employment in the manufacturing sector - had started in the late 1960s, but it was accelerated by Britain's entry to the EC. After entry, her output of manufactures fell because imports from the other EC Member States ousted her home-produced goods from her own market."[5]

Britain's policy of free trade in food imports, conducted since the 1840s right up to our entry into the EEC, resulted in cheap food, particularly from Commonwealth countries. EEC entry meant Common Agricultural Policy entry, raising food prices by 105% in the next three years, while other prices rose by 77%. Since the average family spent 30% of its income on food, these high food prices reduced workers' living standards. Naturally trade union members put in wage claims to keep their living standards up.

Opponents of the EEC, like Douglas Jay, argued that the EEC's higher food costs and free trade in manufactured goods would cause a growing trade deficit.[6] Prime Minister Heath, on the other hand, told us that joining would have 'positive and substantial' effects on Britain's balance of payments. Who was right? In 1970, we had a £385 million surplus in trade in manufactured goods with EEC countries; but ever since we entered the EEC, we have had a balance of payments deficit. The deficit in manufactured goods trade with the EEC rose from £500 million in 1973, to £2.6 billion in 1979 and £10.4 billion in 1989.

In 1982-83, Britain had its first-ever overall trade deficit in manufactured goods and we have been in deficit ever since. It rose from £3.345 billion in 1985 to £20.808 billion in 1988. In Thatcher's second slump, between 1988 and 1990, trade deficits averaged £18 billion a year. Britain's share of its own domestic market fell under Thatcher by 30%. Imports as a proportion of GDP rose from 29% in 1981 to 37% in 1988. In 1980, we exported one and a half times the capital goods that we imported; by 1989, we imported more capital goods than we exported.

The EU has always been bad for Britain's manufacturing industry. In the 16 years before we joined the EEC, our manufacturing output rose by a total of 67 per cent. After we joined, manufacturing output fell sharply: 1973's output level was not achieved again until 1988. Britain's share of world manufacturing output fell from 14% in 1960 to 9.1% in 1979 to just 6% in 1990. As a House of Commons Select Committee reported in 1984, "It is quite obvious that EEC membership has not provided the benefits to our manufacturing industry which were promised." Low manufacturing growth caused low overall economic growth. Britain's output grew by 3% a year between 1950 and 1973 but by only 2% a year from 1973 to 1989.

Under Thatcher, unemployment averaged 2.3 million from 1979 to 1991. Another 1.2 million people wanted work but despaired of finding it, so they did not sign on and were not counted in official statistics. Dividends rose by 73.2%. 40% of households had lower real incomes in 1989 than in 1979. Investment fell from 7% of GNP a year to less than 6% and manufacturing gross capital stock, vital for future industrial growth, did not grow at all, the worst record of any industrial country.

In 1990, the European Commission proposed, and in 1991 the EC

Council adopted, Thatcherite guidelines for EU industrial policy: policy must aim above all to provide a 'competitive environment' and ban the protection of any industry, however strategic.[7] The same policies produced the same results: in the 1990s, unemployment and profits rose across the EU while wages and investment fell. Merger mania caused huge job losses: between 1993 and 1995, the top one hundred firms' turnover rose by 25%, while they sacked 225,000 workers.

The EU imposed free trade. As a result, industry by industry, import penetration destroyed jobs (see table below)

Industry	Import penetration		Number of workers	
	1970	1988	1970	1988
Motor vehicles	5%	53%	532,000	235,000
Mechanical engineering	20%	46%	1,200,000	705,000
Textiles	15%	52%	634,000	216,000
Clothing and footwear	13%	43%	440,000	249,000
Chemical Industry	18%	42%	444,000	336,000

The following table shows that in three important manufacturing sectors - chemicals, aircraft and telecommunications equipment - our trade balance with the EU worsened during our first two decades of EU membership while our trade balance with the rest of the world improved. In machine tools, our trade balance with the EU worsened far more than our trade balance with the rest of the world.

	Trade balance with EC (£million) 1970	1989	Trade balance with rest of world 1970	1989
Chemicals	-58	-949	+299	+2891
Aircraft	+30	-82	+11	+428
Telecoms equipment	+3	-851	+61	+719
Machine tools	-10	-164	+55	-36

Britain paid much more into the EU than we received in every year except 1975, not coincidentally the year of the referendum. These were in effect taxes we paid to the EU, without our consent. In 1999, for instance, we paid £11 billion to the EU's budget, a fifth of its total, and got back just £5.5 billion. The most recent figures available - for the years 1999-2003 - show that Britain's total gross contributions to the EU, at 2003 prices, were £37.8 billion. Receipts were £20 billion. So our average loss was £3.6 billion a year. Since we joined the EEC, our cumulated net contribution is more than £100 billion.

The EU's leaders wanted to end our £3 billion a year budget rebate. We don't want a rebate – we want all our money back. But we cannot rely on Blair to defend Britain's interests: on 16 June 2005, Blair said that Britain's rebate was not up for negotiation; by 22 June he was saying that it could be traded away in return for reform of the CAP.

No British government has ever done a cost/benefit analysis of our membership. An IEA report of June 2005 estimated that Britain loses £200 billion a year, 20% of national income, from being a member of the EU, including paying much higher costs for manufactured goods. Of course, outside the EU, we could choose to manufacture the goods that we need.

It also includes the costs of the Common Fisheries Policy and of our chronic goods trade deficit with the EU (£20 billion in 2002). It costs us £20 billion a year to enforce the EU's regulations and directives (101,811 of them since 1973). The Common Agricultural Policy costs us £15 billion a year. The Bank of England says that joining the euro would cost us £10 billion a year in lost output, because we would lose all control over our monetary policy. The Treasury agrees that the costs of joining would outweigh the benefits. Changing from sterling to euro would cost £30-40 billion.

The EU is, like its offspring the proposed - and rejected - Regional Assemblies, a politically imposed expense, an extra unnecessary layer of bureaucracy, a waste of our money.

2: A future of manufacturing industry

Britain depends on manufacturing industry: it is vital to economic growth and higher living standards. Manufacture is by far the main way to convert knowledge into value. Productivity in manufacturing is 60% higher than in services. Most goods that industries buy are other manufactured goods, and this stimulates productivity growth throughout the economy.[8] In Britain, production and construction make up, on official figures, 40% of GNP, but this is an underestimate because the figures count transport and telecommunications as services not as industries.

The millions of skilled workers who work in mechanical engineering and instrument engineering, and all those who produce metal goods, office machinery, data processing equipment, and electrical and electronic equipment, are the key to our future industrial renaissance. Engineering provided 40% of Britain's entire manufacturing output, 10% of our whole GDP.

The economists Michael Kitson and Jonathan Michie concluded, "Manufacturing does matter. Firstly, much of the service sector itself will depend on the size and rate of growth of the manufacturing sector. Secondly, and as argued persuasively by Kaldor, processes of cumulative causation can lead to a spiral of decline which can spread out from manufacturing to other sectors, so that for example if deindustrialization creates a depressing environment for both investment and training, this will obstruct the processes necessary for any successful shift into new sectors. Thirdly, a deteriorating position in manufacturing trade creates a number of dangers, not least the deflationary macroeconomic policies that tend to follow any resulting balance of payments deficit or pressure on the currency. To reverse Britain's deindustrialization will require a sustained increase in manufacturing investment. Piecemeal policies – manipulating tax rates and allowances – will not be sufficient. What is needed is the implementation of a macroeconomic and industrial strategy directed towards achieving sustainable economic growth, the root and branch reform of a financial system that has been failing British industry since Victorian times and an active industrial policy which will help foster the collaborative structures necessary to create a competitive and successful economy."[9]

Britain still depends on its manufacturing sector.[10] Manufacturing inspires the country by generating development across the economy. It acts as a conduit for technological change elsewhere in the economy. The important factor in generating growth in manufacturing is the ability to increase the knowledge intensity of investments across manufacturing, not just shifting resources into 'hi-tech' sectors.[11]

Further, we need manufacturing industry in order to maintain high-quality services. For the shift of employment to services to be developmental and not a shift to poverty, we must maintain mastery and control of manufacturing production.[12] Manufacturing creates high-wage and hi-tech jobs in both industry and services. In Britain, 2.4 million service sector jobs are directly linked to manufacturing. These supply services add value too, in 1994, for instance, adding £70 billion value, while manufacturing added £124 billion.

Similarly, in the USA, industries producing manufactured goods contributed half the country's wealth. Manufacturing creates 24% of its GNP, and a further "25% of US GNP originates in services used as inputs by goods-producing industries" as the 1983 Report of the President on the Trade Agreements Program pointed out.[13] And the wider services too need industry: three quarters of the service jobs in the USA, 60 million workers, depend on manufacturing production.

Manufacturing is not a minority pursuit, an ever-declining, increasingly unimportant, backwoods pastime, although some with vested interests argue that industry was unnecessary. For example, a New York Stock Exchange report of 1984 said, "a strong manufacturing sector is not a requisite for a prosperous economy."[14] Its evidence was the US 'surplus in services', $33 billion in 1982. But 77% of that figure was investment income - interest - from US loans to foreign firms, not profits made from exporting services. In 1979 the US state put financial services first. Paul Volcker, the Chairman of the USA's central bank, the Federal Reserve Board, said, "The standard of living of the average American has to decline."[15] And so it did. The consequent deindustrialisation has been cutting the incomes of three quarters of US families ever since.[16] Most people saw rising living standards as the whole point of an economy, and saw an economy that did not produce them as a failure.

Post-industrial services' start-up costs are low - but so are their real gains. IBM and then Microsoft made exceptional gains only because they temporarily monopolised the setting of standards for computer operating systems. Some argue that post-industrial services based on information provision are the only way forward, but it was estimated that basing the US economy on the information industries would cost 25 million jobs. Finance was a cuckoo in the economy's nest. Even the speculator George Soros called on governments to control the financial markets to 'stop the market destroying the economy'.

Countries committed to manufacturing, like Sweden, Austria and Switzerland, grew faster, had more jobs at higher wages and produced more exports than countries with governments committed to 'post-industrialism', like Britain.[17] What would distribution and transport workers have to move and storage workers to store, if we produced no real physical goods? Why would we need communications if we produced nothing that we could sell? What business would insurance workers insure, what incomes would bank workers bank, if we produced no goods?

Britain needs a manufacturing renaissance. We needed to produce modern means of production: machine tools, production machines that make hi-tech components and electronic materials, and equipment for the engineering, telecommunications, transport, textile, chemical and power-generating industries.[18] It was sad, but typical, that Japanese or Korean parent companies controlled eleven of the British Radio and Electronics Equipment Manufacturers' Association's fifteen members.[19]

As L. T. C. Rolt, our pre-eminent historian of industry, pointed out, "By the standards of our modern industrialised society the world's machine-tool industry is a small one, but it is of vital importance. For good or ill it has made possible the world in which we live today and in this sense it is the arbiter of tomorrow."[20] We need to produce textiles, especially polyesters and carbon fibres, pollution control equipment, shipping, high quality steel, robotics, microelectronics, plastics, new materials and biotechnology. Britain also needs to have a state-backed support service to aid research, spread knowledge and publicise the most useful current research, now all too often localised and secret. We need to organise the use of the best technology available. We need more and better education in technical subjects. We need to give new industries and new products time to grow, so we need to be able to protect our home market from imports when necessary.

Britain needs to reinvest in our manufacturing industry the surplus value produced here, savings for example. In 1979, life assurance and pension funds held only 1.9% of their assets overseas; under Thatcher, this rose to 19.8%. We should find ways to repatriate the £120 billion invested abroad, and to invest in manufacturing the other £480 billion held in pension funds. Britain needed to shift investment to industry: an extra £2.5 billion a year spent on R&D in industrial products and processes, embodied in additional plant costing £10 billion, would increase our GDP by 20%.

Every year, Britain's deficit in trade of manufactured goods reached a new record. But this deficit was not the manufactured goods sector's fault: this sector always runs a healthy surplus.[21] In 1994, for instance, it ran a £57 billion surplus: its exports were worth £135 billion (75% of our total exports), while it imported just £78 billion of raw materials, components and machinery. The services sector's vaunted trade surpluses became negative when its imports of manufactured goods - IT equipment, telecommunications equipment and office building fittings (all customarily debited to the manufacturing sector!) - were included. In 1994, for instance, it proclaimed a £4.8 billion surplus, but spent £8 billion on imports, so its real trading position was a £3.2 billion deficit. If Britain's central government, local government, major quangos and service industries bought their manufactured goods from British suppliers, this would help our manufacturing sector and put our trade in surplus. But the EU's Common Commercial Policy was designed to remove any national limits on non-EU imports.

Inadequate investment and education threatened our ability to produce these vital goods. Britain's industrially financed R&D is just 45% of our total R&D, the lowest among Europe's main economies. It is 68% in Switzerland. Also, British manufacturing's overheads - legal, financial and accounting services - were far dearer than elsewhere. As the TUC pointed out, "in every year since 1960 the UK has invested less as a share of GDP than the OECD average. As a result, UK workers have less capital stock behind them than in any other industrialised country."[22] In 1995, in the private sector, capital stock per worker was nearly 40% behind Germany and France and more than 20% behind the USA. In the public sector, capital stock per hour worked in Germany was three times more than in Britain, in France it was twice as much and in the USA it was 90% more. Throughout the 1990s, Britain's stock of fixed capital in relation to its main competitors continued to fall.[23]

The low spending approach adopted by Conservative and Labour governments did not lead to higher private investment and left us far behind our competitors. Despite the fact that the rate of return on capital was higher than at any time since 1960, the investment share in the economy in 2000 was lower than in 1990. Consequently, manufacturing output, exports and jobs all fell too. In 2001 alone, our manufacturing output fell by 2.3% and output from agriculture, forestry and fishing fell by 11.4%. Britain's capital stock had grown by just 2% a year since 1995. Dividends and bonuses grew far faster. In 2001, the pay of the Chief Executive Officers of the FTSE 100 companies rose by 15% on 2000 and their bonuses rose from 40% to 47% of their salaries.

But all Britain's needs for developing a balanced industrial base through planned, sustained investment clashed with the EU's aims. The EU wants to assist capital to organise production on an EU-wide basis, concentrating types of production in specific regions of the eurozone. No national economy would be allowed an integrated manufacturing base. The EU wanted to end all 'Made in Britain' labels. All goods produced by EU member nations must be labelled 'Made in the EU'.

Further, the EU denied governments the right to assist the economy. Article 93 of the EEC Treaty, then Article 88 of the Amsterdam Treaty, now Article III-167 of the Constitution, gave the Commission powers to end industrial support that 'distorts competition'. (Article III-167 says, "Any aid granted by a Member State or through State resources in any form whatsoever which distorts or threatens to distort competition by favouring certain undertakings or the production of certain goods shall, insofar as it affects trade between Member States, be incompatible with the internal market.") Under EU pressure, Britain's state aid to manufacturing fell by half between 1988 and 1992.

Even the German Chancellor, Gerhard Schroeder, attacked the Commission for pursuing 'neo-liberal' policies that undermined industry. In a clear reference to ex-University Professor Romano Prodi, Schroeder said in July 2002, "I have noticed a strange approach among those I'd like to call the professor in the Commission, or those who think they are, that exceeds even the neo-liberalism of the United States. There are strong forces in Brussels who think it is acceptable to neglect industry. But industrial production remains the basis of Europe's economic welfare, at a high level." (True, but what has he done about this?)

The Commission ruled that governments must end their 'golden shares' in former nationalised industries, like the British Airports Authority, British Airways, utilities like the National Grid, and defence and engineering firms. The - all too small - amount of national control given by 'golden shares' broke the EU's rules on free movement of capital. Getting rid of the 'golden shares' reduced nations' ability to defend these national industries against hostile foreign takeover. The Blair government welcomed the ruling. Blair also welcomed the EU's new code for company mergers, which imposed a single European market for financial services, making mergers and closures easier. It too reduces firms' ability to fend off hostile takeovers.

Some suggest cutting economic growth. Green activist Jonathon Porritt, for instance, claimed, "an increase in Gross National Product (GNP) inevitably means an increase in Gross National Pollution."[24] If it did, London would have dirtier water than during the Great Stinks and cholera epidemics of the 19th century, and worse air than in the great smogs of the 20th. Improving transport and housing adds to GNP and also creates jobs.[25] Germany has created 750,000 jobs in the last ten years by providing walking and cycling facilities and improving public transport and housing.[26]

As the TUC said, "Investment in a modern and efficient transport infrastructure is needed to help improve industrial efficiency and labour mobility as well as meeting wider environmental objectives. Investment in affordable social housing not only improves the welfare of the less well-off, it also can help improve labour mobility, take pressure off greenfield sites and encourage urban regeneration, and by increasing overall supply reduce inflationary pressures in the housing market."

We want our economy to grow, to provide more and better goods and services for our people. So we have to oppose the EU and its Constitution because they are preventing us doing this. The British people running a sovereign Britain could produce for ourselves a prosperous future and keep the best of our traditions. EU membership is not needed to cut unemployment or raise wages: Switzerland, not in the EU, has Europe's lowest unemployment and highest wages. Independence from the EU would be particularly good for British industry. The US International Trade Commission noted that leaving the EU would stimulate Britain's output and bring new jobs in mining, iron and steel, other manufacturing and services.

We want a full employment economy. This would increase GNP; for example, it is estimated that if the USA's 12 million unemployed had been in work in 1983, they would have added an extra $400 billion to the USA's GNP and an extra $125 billion in tax revenues, without raising taxes. Full employment would be based on balanced industrial production across a range of sectors, investment in good public services, free health and education services, publicly owned and accountable utilities and essential services, fairness at work and investment in industrial infrastructure, science and technology. We have a huge range of the raw materials that we need and can get the rest by trade.

Britain still lags in investment in human capital.[27] We seek a high-skill, high-wage, high-productivity, high-investment industrial base using the best education and training system, with advanced technologies and materials. We need an expanded programme of apprenticeships, an increased provision of basic skills and a comprehensive adult guidance service. As the TUC observed, the deregulated labour market, a result of Thatcher's anti-trade union laws retained by the Labour government, has "undermined the national training effort by directly reducing the incentive to train and by creating workplaces where the full potential benefits of training will prove difficult to realise."[28]

We need expanded provision of higher and further education. The TUC argued, "without a more substantial increase in public spending on post-16 education and training and a secure financial base for the sector, it is unlikely that the Government's objectives for widening participation can be met."

But improving skills, although vital, is not enough; these newly skilled people need productive jobs to go into. Profits made in Britain should be reinvested here, generating jobs here. There is far more British capital invested abroad, £2000 billions, than foreign capital invested here. That investment abroad exports jobs abroad.[29] The Treasury was right to argue, "Britain needs a period of higher investment than other leading economies if it is to begin to address the under-investment of the past."[30] We need to retrieve those overseas funds and put them to work here modernising plant and machinery, setting up new industries, rebuilding our transport, coal, oil and gas systems. We could take up the lead given by clothing and textile workers and say make it and buy it in Britain.

We could reclaim our waters for fishing and end the misuse of our farm land. Greater self-sufficiency in food could support a national programme of food consumption to improve health, starting with introducing good quality school meals.

We aim to strengthen the domestic economy and control the levers of decision making in politics and economics. We should keep control of our domestic rate of interest and the currency, so that we can pursue full employment and decent social policies. We could do what the Bundesbank used to do - charge those borrowing for vital industrial investment at lower interest rates than for ordinary borrowers. We need to socialise investment, control the money markets, control imports through state trading agreements and adopt a steady cheap money policy for investment.[31]

Having this economic sovereignty would keep us out of future crises created by capitalism's instability. Exchange controls would prevent the vast exoduses of footloose capital that caused 1997-98's economic crisis in East Asia.[32] Putting the real productive economy first would build up a trade surplus, in place of the present ever-increasing trade deficit. Keeping out of the euro would sustain our economy by keeping our reserves, rather than giving them away to the European Central Bank. We could then avoid short-term borrowing, which keeps us in debt and dependency.

Sovereignty also means that every nation has the right to decide with whom it traded. We should be able to trade freely with all 200 countries in the world, not just with the EU. We did not need to be part of an exclusive economic bloc. We need to control movement of capital and labour to ensure high rates of investment and a stable, increasingly skilled working class.

The Southern and Eastern Regional Council of the TUC concluded, "Far from being doomed to terminal decline, manufacturing can be the powerhouse of sustainable economic growth, economic regeneration and social regeneration in London, the South East and the East of England."[33] This was true of the rest of Britain too.

3: Energy

It was vital to our planned industrial renaissance that we control our energy sources - coal, oil, gas and electricity supply. Britain had by far the largest energy reserves of any country in the EU, but our EU 'partners' regard our oil and gas fields with the same covetous eyes as they regarded our fishing grounds. The Maastricht Treaty's Preamble 8, Title 2, describes our oil as a 'shared resource', trumping the Scottish National Party's claim to 'Scotland's oil'; their EU friends would take it. Balanced use of these resources must be central to planning Britain's future.

This would be more efficient than the present profit-driven anarchy.[34] Britain's energy industries gain when under national, not private, control.[35] Similarly, in the USA public electricity firms are consistently more efficient than private ones.[36] As a result of privatisation and deregulation, British utilities are caught in a feeding frenzy as gas, electricity and water firms devour one another. Foreign firms take advantage of the 'liberalisation': by 2004 US firms owned eight of the original twelve regional electricity firms. As American regulatory expert Gregory Palast said, "They just see the UK companies as cash cows and bring little investment into the UK. I can't see what the UK gains by giving up its strategic resources."

In 1989, the EU undertook to be using no more energy in 2010 than in 1988: by 2000, energy use had already risen by 11%. The Council of Ministers opposes tax incentives for firms to save energy and reduce pollution. The European Commission wants to end the EU's only programme of energy conservation ('Save'): in May 1996, EU energy ministers cut its funding by over two-thirds.[37] The Commission also wants to dump the only EU programme designed to find renewable sources of fuel ('Altener'): this is underfunded and has only non-binding targets.[38]

4: Steel

Thatcher called steel one of 'yesterday's industries'.[39] Yet iron and steel were vital to every advanced economy. Our remaining iron and steel industry was highly productive. But EEC restructuring made cash available only to cut down the industry; Corby, Consett, and Shelton Bar were all closed. Both the ferrous and non-ferrous founding industry followed the same path. Some of the trade union leadership rushed to Brussels for security, as a coward's castle, blaming the EEC while blessing it, much as today! While industry was closed, regional trade unions and the Labour Party pursued inward investment and regional government.

The Iron and Steel Confederation acted as an agent for EU integration, against the interests of its members. The employers' organisation, the European Federation of Iron and Steel Industries, was hand in glove with the EU. The Federation, like the European Federation of Pharmaceutical Industry Associations, is so deeply involved in governance mechanisms that its involvement bears the hallmarks of neo-corporatism.[40]

In 2002, the Blair government gave £60 million to an Indian company to support its efforts to buy Rumania's steel industry in order to run it down, in line with EU policy promoting privatisation. This firm then lobbied the US government to impose tariffs on steel imports, including those from Britain. Needless to say, the government had not even considered giving £60 million to support Britain's steel industry.[41]

5: The defence industry

The defence industry is our greatest reserve of the engineering skills we need to rebuild and retool our economy. We need to keep the ability to design and make our own arms. Yet successive governments' defence procurement policies have undermined the industry. For example, in July 1995 the Major government decided to spend £2.5 billion on buying US Apache helicopters, instead of investing this huge sum in our own helicopter industry.[42] The failure to unify the defence industry risks its serial destruction. Britain needs a merger between GEC and BAe to create a national defence champion able to compete globally.[43] But the EU aims to close our defence industry. Its Common Foreign and Security Policy was designed to lead to a single defence industry, located in Germany. In July 2000, the British, French, German, Italian, Spanish and Swedish governments signed a legally binding agreement that placed our arms industry under EU control. An inventory of all our military ordnance was made available to all EU member states, furthering the aim of developing a single EU defence industry.

6: Communications

In 1992, the European Court of Justice imposed 'liberalisation' of the telecommunications services market and ruled that the Commission's powers over competition policy included breaking up 'monopolies'. Industry expert Michael Calingaert wrote, "The first step was a 1988 directive terminating member states' exclusive rights to import, market and install terminal equipment, such as telephone sets, private branch exchanges, data transmission terminals and mobile phones. Such quick action was possible only because the Commission, over the objections of some member states, used an anti-monopoly provision of Article 90 TEC (now Article 86) to issue this directive on its own authority, rather than following the normal legislative procedure that requires approval by the Parliament and Council."[44] The Commission used powers given it by Treaty to bypass the European Parliament - a worrying precedent. Without this Commission coup, BT and Deutsche Telekom could not have cut huge numbers of jobs in the 1990s.[45]

In April 2005, BT announced that it had decided to award the whole £10 billion contract for renewing our network to overseas firms, snubbing Marconi. Yet BT had conducted a successful six-month trial with Marconi's advanced 'soft-switch' equipment and has conducted no similar trials with the contract-winning firms' equipment. The decision is likely to cost 2,500 jobs. The government's response? No action, no comment.

The Commission wants to deregulate and privatise all postal services. In 1997, it proposed a single market in postal services. In September 2000, the Blair government refused to defend the Post Office from this directive, reneging on its earlier promise to resist it.[46] In 2003 the Commission decreed that all mail weighing over 100 grams should be open to full competition. In 2006 the maximum will come down to just 50 grams. The Commission has set 1 December 2009 for completing a single market in postal services, the end of public post services. The Post Office's chief executive, John Roberts, warned that this would "make it impossible to continue with the bedrock principle of an affordable and uniform postal service available to every customer, no matter how remote their address, and irrespective of what distance domestic mail travels." Sweden's postal services were privatised in 1993; by 2000, a first class letter cost 71p.

7: Transport industries

An island with a major fishing fleet and dependent on a merchant navy to carry its trade needs to be able to build and repair ships. In 1993, 94% by weight of Britain's overseas trade was carried by sea, yet British-registered ships carried only 18%. Shipbuilding, like other modern manufacturing industries, needs large amounts of capital and production know-how. 'Post-industry' theorists have ignored this. John Naisbitt, for instance, predicted in 1980 that Brazil would soon overtake Japan as the world's leading shipbuilder - Brazil produces 0.6% of the world's output, Japan 37%!

As with iron and steel, EEC entry meant closure. The EU aided the rundown of shipbuilding: it offered various subsidies and an Intervention Fund to member countries if restructuring took place. It defined three kinds of shipyards: 'Merchant', which could get Intervention Funds, 'Composite Naval and Merchant', that got limited funding, and 'Naval', that got no funding. Once a yard declared its type, it could not change. Swan Hunter and Cammell Laird were composite yards. As the nationalised industry fell for this, the yards closed. Marine engineering, engine building and R & D all but disappeared. In 1985-86, the government privatised warship building, then sold off merchant shipbuilding. Privatisation destroyed what was left of the industry. By 1988, there were only 6,300 workers in the industry; in 1977, there had been 87,300.

In 1988, the Sunderland yards of British Shipbuilders employed 2,800 highly skilled workers, running some of the world's most technologically advanced yards. The Thatcher government closed these yards. It got £45 million redundancy aid from the Commission, on condition that the yard was permanently closed and that the government would not negotiate a return to shipbuilding, even by a private buyer. It rejected a potentially lifesaving order for ships from the Cuban line Mambira.[47] A senior civil servant told the Chairman of British Shipbuilders that Thatcher "wants rid of shipbuilding."[48] A government that wanted to end the industry was assisted by "a Commission intent on reducing shipbuilding capacity in the EC."[49] But the demand for shipping still existed: the world's fleet has more than doubled since 1970.

Britain's aerospace industry is the third largest in the world and is one of only three able to build entire planes on its own.[50] Overseas sales valued at £8 billion in 1991 accounted for 12% of world aerospace exports and yielded a trade surplus of £2.5 billion. Britain is also a leader in developing a high-velocity close air defence system. The EU, led by Germany, is trying to absorb our aerospace industry through 'collaborative' projects. It is vital that we keep our independent aerospace capability, both military and civil.[51]

The motor vehicle industry is a vital part of our manufacturing base; many other parts of industry feed into it and depend on it.[52] In 1970 import penetration of Britain's domestic market was only 5%. By 1990, after 17 years in the EU, it was 51%, by 1999, 70%. As a result, British output declined from 1.9 million cars a year in 1970 to 1.64 million in 2005. In 1973, British components made up 91% of each Ford, Vauxhall or Peugeot Talbot car, by 2005 just 20-25%. Jobs in our components sector fell by 16% since 1998 to 142,000 in 2005.

The Thatcher government's policy towards the motor industry was to encourage Japanese firms to produce cars here, at the cost of Britain's survival as a car-producing country.[53] The Association des Constructeurs Europeens d'Automobiles said in 1993, "The UK's preoccupation with attracting new transplant investments while ignoring the needs of the well established manufacturers may create new jobs in the short-term but will result in a net loss of jobs in the long-term. Independent automotive consultants and the EC Commission have calculated that in fact one new job created by a transplant operation in Europe destroys two existing European jobs."[54]

The EU continually interferes in our decisions about our motor vehicle industry's future. In 1988, the Commission attacked the Rover car group, using Article 88 of the Amsterdam Treaty. The Commission could now investigate if aid was compatible with Single European Market principles and demand changes, with the threat of court action if the national government did not comply. When British Aerospace bought the Rover car group, the Thatcher government agreed to the Commission's demand that Britain end its right to provide overdraft guarantees. This involved the 'abolition of the Parliamentary assurances which had been used to guarantee Rover Group's borrowings'. The government also agreed to other restrictions and reduced the funds to cover Rover group losses from £800 million to £469 million. In its eagerness to privatize Rover, the Thatcher government gave away sovereign national rights.[55]

Britain, like France, Italy, Portugal and Spain, had longstanding limits on the numbers of cars imported from Japan. But the Commission agreed with the Japanese government to end the quotas in 1999, hence the closures at Luton, Longbridge and Dagenham.

In the summer of 2000, when Rover was threatened with closure, the EU blocked any aid for BMW's Rover plants at Longbridge. The Labour government also refused to help, even though the costs of closure would have been 60,000 jobs and £2 billion a year in unemployment and social payments. The government would not provide the overdraft guarantees eventually obtained from an American bank. Blair even refused to put Rovers on the list of cars that government departments could buy.[56] The Department of Social Security and the Inland Revenue, two of the largest vehicle buyers in the government, signed three-year contracts to buy all their 12,000 cars from Ford, Vauxhall, Peugeot, Fiat, Nissan and Citroen, saying that their car purchasing complied with EU procurement guidelines! The Cabinet Office's approved list of ministerial cars did not include the flagship Rover 75, car of the year in 1999. Even the minister for the car industry, Alan Johnson, was not allowed to buy a Rover! The list also excluded the S-class Jaguar, another British-built car. The government was boycotting the products of our only national car manufacturers.

In 2005, the government let Rover fold, at the expense of 6,000 jobs and another 50,000 jobs in linked component suppliers. The government that gives the EU £30 million every day would not give Rover the £100 million it needed to survive.

Across the EU, the Commission only provides funds to the motor industry for privatisations and the consequent closures.[57] As it had long wanted, the Commission effectively polices this vital sector.[58] The industry's history proves that giving away control of our economy by joining the euro would add to the problems that our industries faced.[59]

Successive British governments have sabotaged the motor industry. By contrast, Japanese governments have advanced their motor industry by protecting their home market and offering low-interest loans, depreciation allowances and subsidies for buying machine tools.[60] As a result, by 1970 Japan's car production was second only to the USA's, and by 1980 it had become the largest vehicle producer in the world. We could adopt the same policies and not just for the motor industry.

British rolling stock desperately needs modernising, but the only suitable British factory, ABB's York Works, was closed down and the work given to a European firm. We could build the trains and rolling stock we needed at the factories in Derby and Birmingham. Buses too are supplied largely from outside Britain, and the EU was considering banning double-deckers on the grounds that their manufacture gave an unfair advantage to British firms, as these buses were only used in Britain.

These failures in the production of transport goods mean that we are not producing what we needed to move people and goods around Britain. Consequently, our transport systems are failing too.

Britain needs more public investment in developing a planned integrated transport system, not privatisation, liberalisation and fragmentation.[61] Market forces cannot achieve this, yet the EU enforces a free market policy in transport. The EU lets firms hijack transport proposals to meet business' demands.[62]

Regarding air travel, the European Parliament approved in July 2000 a plan to create a 'single European sky'. The Tory MEP Sir Robert Atkins introduced a report urging "the Council of Ministers to take the political decision that the Commission should develop a single sky over a single market ... run by a single European air traffic control." The idea was that all EU members should privatise their air traffic control agencies and that these should work under the direction of a new EU agency, Eurocontrol. The Blair government's part of this scheme included cost cuts of up to 36%, largely to be achieved by cutting staff. Directors of the National Air Traffic Services (Nats) told the government that this posed an unacceptable threat to safety. They pointed out that in the air traffic industry, "manning levels are absolutely critical to safety and service delivery."

The Civil Aviation Authority regulator expected cuts of between 16% and 29% in capital spending over the first five years of the privatised regime, undermining ministers' repeated claims that the sale's main advantage would be increased investment. The air traffic controllers' union, the Institution of Professionals, Managers and Specialists (IPMS) - now called Prospect - said, "At a stroke, these proposals blow away the Government's rationale for this privatisation. Even Nats managers acknowledge that cuts on this scale would impact on safety. These proposals would be devastating to Nats and dangerous to travellers. The Government should drop its plans immediately."[63]

Britain needs a publicly run, democratically accountable, integrated railway, instead of the 100-piece, privatised anarchy we endure. EU Regulation EC91/440 had ordered British Rail's fragmentation through privatisation.[64] It laid down in minute detail how railways must be managed: management and financing of the track must be totally separate from the train services and both had to be run on strictly commercial lines.[65] The Major government privatised the railways by means of a statutory instrument, the Railways Regulation 1992, whose preamble revealed that it had been introduced under Section 2(2) of the European Communities Act 1972.

Gerald Corbett, Railtrack's chief executive, admitted on BBC 2's Newsnight, "The railway was ripped apart at privatisation and the structure that was put in place was a structure designed, if we are honest, to maximise the proceeds to the Treasury. It was not a structure designed to optimise safety, optimise investment or, indeed, cope with the huge increase in the number of passengers the railway has seen."[66] (He omitted to mention that it also maximised the proceeds to Railtrack's directors and shareholders.)

The directors of the rail firms prioritise their shareholders' interests over safety and public service, cutting costs by sacking maintenance workers down from 31,000 in 1994 to 19,000 in 2000. The Blair government, like its predecessors, refuses to introduce the best safety system, the Automatic Train Protection system (first recommended in 1988) because it would cost too much, £2 billion.

Privatisation has not produced a better, more reliable and more punctual service. Rolling stock, track and signalling equipment are worse than under investment-starved British Rail. Even Railtrack had to admit that this fragmentation had reduced rail safety. Only the fares are top-rate. We had to pay the world's highest standard rail fares. Fares on the key London-Manchester route - a Virgin Trains monopoly - rose by 50% between 2000 and 2002.

Rail privatisation cost the country £6 billion. The taxpayer gave Railtrack £1000 million a year. Railtrack gave £350 million of this to its shareholders. Railtrack collapsed in October 2001 owing £1.8 billion to subcontractors and £700 million in bills and interest payments to bondholders and banks. In March 2002, the government gave the shareholders another £300 million. Winding up Railtrack cost another £4.8 billion.[67] Tested in practice, privatisation had failed.[68]

The government responded by trying to privatise London Underground, the prison service, education and the National Health Service, instead of respecting the 76% of us who want rail renationalised and the 89% who oppose handing public services over to private firms.

As usual, the government was responding to private finance rather than to the people, to democracy.[69] Under the renamed Private Finance Initiative known as Public Private Partnership (PPP), firms would be borrowing the money: why not let the public sector do that itself? But the government was committed in principle to PPPs, whatever their results. As Gordon Brown said, "the wealth-creating agenda and support for public-private partnerships, the encouragement of small business is central to everything we as a government will do." He also said, "The Labour Party is more pro-business, pro-wealth creation, pro-competition than ever before."[70] He proved this by cutting capital gains tax rates from 40p to 10p in the pound, a tax break worth more than £1 billion a year!

The other EU countries had earlier ignored the EU Directive on the railways.[71] But in November 2000, the Commission agreed to copy across the whole EU this 'British model' of privatising the railways. It proposed Regulation COM (2000) 7, 'Concerning public service requirements and the award of public service contracts in passenger transport', designed to open up 'closed markets' and promote a 'single European market in the provision of public transport'.[72] The Blair government urged Labour MEPs to oppose an amendment that would have excluded national rail systems from such compulsory competitive tendering. In January 2002, the Commission set up the European Railways Agency to integrate the organisation of all rail operations in the EU.

By EU directive, since 1993, road haulage has been fully 'liberalised'. Market forces dictate that lorries too big and heavy for our roads should dominate the freight business, carrying loads that should be carried by rail. The EU excludes transport workers from safety directives on working hours. Yet road accidents are the biggest single cause of sudden death at work: occupational road use is more dangerous than building work or mining.[73]

Of the 1,200 people killed on Britain's roads each year, 300 are working drivers. The TUC calls for road use to come under the health and safety laws. The TGWU in particular campaigns for better laws to protect drivers, supported by a campaign organised across Europe by the International Transport Workers Federation. Transport workers must negotiate better working time agreements, as airline pilots did early in 2000.

The EU policy of imposing extra taxes on fuels, ostensibly for environmental reasons, harms the transport industry, all those who depend on it for goods and all those who use any form of vehicle. High fuel taxes raise the cost of driving and do not cut fuel use.[74] Only direct controls on pollution, safety and fuel efficiency make manufacturers produce cleaner, safer and more efficient cars.[75]

The Labour government spends far less on London Underground than the previous Tory government: £816 million a year between 1997 and 2001, compared with £1.06 billion a year between 1992 and 1997. It keeps trying to privatise the Tube, despite massive popular resistance. The Financial Times called it an 'ill-conceived project'.[76] Yet the European Commission gave the scheme its blessing.[77]

8: Textiles

In 1994, the Uruguay Round of GATT negotiations ended the international Multi-Fibre Agreement, which had ensured some stability in textile production both here and abroad. This increased low-cost imports; consequently four million jobs have since gone from Europe's textile industries, 750 every day of 2004. A quarter of the world's textiles are now made in China. The system of import quotas ended on 1 January 2005, so Chinese and Indian textiles will flood into Europe. Trade Commissioner Peter Mandelson says that it is a good thing if imports rise as a result of fair competition.

In 2000, Britain's textile industry still had a turnover of £17.7 billion and exported £5.1 billion worth of products each year. In late 2000, the European Commission removed all limits on the remaining 62 types of textile imports - mostly 'dumped', sweatshop goods - in spite of the continuing tariffs that other countries placed on EU countries' exports. Also, major British retailers, such as Marks & Spencer and British Home Stores, which dominated the home market in a way unparalleled in the world, decided to use foreign, cheap-labour suppliers. This caused major job losses: in 1999, 41,000 textiles and footwear jobs ended.

In 1998, Bradford hosted a summit meeting of all parts of the British textile and clothing industry which set out a strategy for the industry. In summer 2000 the Textile and Clothing Strategy Group published 'A national strategy for the UK textile & clothing industry'.[78] This plan proposed closer ties between retailers and manufacturers achieving 'short lead times, short runs, quick response and flexible manufacturing', already features of best practice in Britain. It called on more British manufacturers to wake up to the potential provided by their workers' high-skill, high-value products. After all, if a third of their production in terms of value is exported, it must have an appeal to the rest of the world. The report also suggested taking advantage of high investment levels in fabrics and in technical textiles - those made mainly for industrial purposes - where Britain was at the forefront of expertise. These are prime candidates for expansion. The plan also called for supportive government investment, particularly in R&D, neglected at present.

The textile workers' initiative was a great step forward in industrial thought. It could become a model not only for textiles but also for regenerating manufacturing throughout Britain. To implement this, we needed to be able to sell throughout the world, while protecting our vulnerable industry from foreign competition.

Paul Gates, General Secretary of the knitwear and footwear union, KFAT, said, "We now need to build on this initiative; and we look forward to further measures being introduced in the near future. But manufacturers in the industry must seize this opportunity. They must improve their skills in areas such as design, marketing and e-commerce; and they need to look at developing niche products and value added goods. I accept it is a major challenge, but we must all work together."

KFAT consistently presses the government to buy only British-made textiles and footwear. But the Blair government unpatriotically supported foreign firms at the expense of the British textile industry. For example, the

The EU Bad for Britain

Ministry of Defence placed a £5.5 million order for army uniforms with a German firm. Unfortunately, the union undercuts its efforts to support the industry by backing the euro.

Endnotes

[1]. See Sidney Pollard, The development of the British economy 1914-1990, Arnold, 4th edition, 1992, page 336.

[2]. See E. L. Grinols, A thorn in the lion's paw: has Britain paid too much for Common Market membership? Journal of International Economics, 1984, Volume 16, pages 271-93.

[3]. Valerio Lintner, page 405, 'Overview: the European Union: the impact of membership on the UK economy and UK economic policy', Chapter 16, pages 399-430, in Tony Buxton, Paul Chapman and Paul Temple, editors, Britain's economic performance, Routledge, 2nd edition, 1998.

[4]. L. Alan Winters, page 328, Britain in Europe: a survey of quantitative trade studies, Journal of Common Market Studies, 1987, Volume 25, Number 4, pages 315-35.

[5]. Lynden Moore, Britain's trade and economic structure: the impact of the European Union, Routledge, 1999, page 372.

[6]. See Jay's superb essay, 'The free trade alternative to the EC: a witness account', pages 123-33, in Brian Brivati and Harriet Jones, editors, From reconstruction to integration: Britain and Europe since 1945, Leicester University Press, 1993.

[7]. See Desmond Dinan, Ever closer union: an introduction to European integration, Macmillan, 2nd edition, 1999, pages 394-5. On EU competition policy, see his pages 379-90; on EU industrial policy, see his pages 390-6.

[8]. See Gar Alperovitz and Jeff Faux, Rebuilding America: a blueprint for the new economy, Pantheon Books, 1984, pages 89 and 136.

[9]. Michael Kitson and Jonathan Michie, page 91, in Does manufacturing matter? International Journal of the Economics of Business, 1997, Volume 10. Number 1, pages 71-95.

[10]. See Mohammad Haq and Paul Temple, page 488, 'Overview: economic policy and the changing international division of labour', Chapter 18, pages 455-94, in Tony Buxton, Paul Chapman and Paul Temple, editors, Britain's economic performance, Routledge, 2nd edition, 1998.

[11]. See pages 91 and 92, Paul Temple, 'Overview: growth, competitiveness and trade performance', Chapter 4, pages 69-98, in Tony Buxton, Paul Chapman and Paul Temple, editors, Britain's economic performance, Routledge, 2nd edition, 1998.

[12]. See Stephen Cohen and John Zysman, Manufacturing matters: the myth of the post-industrial economy, New York: Basic Books, 1987, page 21.

[13]. Cited page 22, Stephen S. Cohen and John Zysman, Manufacturing matters: the myth of the post-industrial economy, New York: Basic Books, 1987.

[14]. Cited page 5, Stephen S. Cohen and John Zysman, Manufacturing matters: the myth of the post-industrial economy, New York: Basic Books, 1987.

[15]. Cited New York Times, 18 October 1979.

[16]. Gar Alperovitz and Jeff Faux, Rebuilding America: a blueprint for the new economy, Pantheon Books, 1984, page 90.

[17]. See Eamonn Fingleton, In praise of hard industries, Houghton Mifflin (US), Orion Business Books (UK), 1999.

[18]. Stephen S. Cohen and John Zysman, Manufacturing matters: the myth of the post-industrial economy, New York: Basic Books, 1987, pages 108-9

[19]. On the need to build our capacity in computing and electronics, see Nicholas Costello, Jonathan Michie and Seumas Milne, Beyond the casino economy: planning for the 1990s, Verso, 1989, pages 161-5 and 165-71.

[20]. L. T. C. Rolt, Tools for the job: a history of machine tools to 1950, HMSO, 1986, page 254.

[21]. For this paragraph, thanks to Stephen Bush, On the importance of

manufacture to the economy, Manchester Statistical Society, 1999.

22. Britain's public investment gap, TUC, September 1999.

23. See Tony Buxton, page 183, 'Overview: the foundations of competitiveness, investment and innovation', Chapter 8, pages 165-86, in Tony Buxton, Paul Chapman and Paul Temple, editors, Britain's economic performance, Routledge, 2nd edition, 1998.

24. Jonathon Porritt, Seeing green, Oxford, 1984, page 36.

25. For more on how improving services creates jobs, see, for example, Eban Goodstein, 'Malthus redux? Globalization and the environment', Chapter 12, pages 297-318, in Dean Baker, Gerald Epstein and Robert Pollin, editors, Globalization and progressive economic policy, Cambridge University Press, 1998.

26. See John Whitelegg, Critical mass: transport, environment and society in the twenty-first century, Pluto Press, page 219.

27. See Margaret Sharp, page 522, 'Technology policy: the last two decades', Chapter 19, pages 495-526, in Tony Buxton, Paul Chapman and Paul Temple, editors, Britain's economic performance, Routledge, 2nd edition, 1998.

28. Britain's skills gap, TUC, August 1999.

29. See Ali El-Agraa, The European Union: history, institutions, economics, politics, Prentice Hall Europe, 5th edition, 1998, page 471.

30. Cited in the TUC's 1999 Budget statement, TUC, 1999.

31. See B. W. E. Alford, Britain in the world economy since 1880, Longman, 1996, page 197.

32. Imposing exchange controls is both desirable and feasible, see Nicholas Costello, Jonathan Michie and Seumas Milne, Beyond the casino economy: planning for the 1990s, Verso, 1989, pages 53-5, 127-31, 135 and 269-70. See also Andrew Glyn, Capital flight and exchange controls, New Left Review, 1986, Number 155, pages 37-49.

[33]. The Southern and Eastern Regional Council of the TUC (SERTUC), The future of manufacturing: a strategy to support the development of manufacturing in London, the South East and the East of England, SERTUC, 2001, page 31.

[34]. On the EU's 'liberalisation' programme for the energy supply industries, see page 161, Michael Calingaert, 'Creating a European market', Chapter 8, pages 153-73, in Laura Cram, Desmond Dinan and Neill Nugent, editors, Developments in the European Union, Macmillan, 1999. For a useful summary of our energy industries' needs, see Nicholas Costello, Jonathan Michie and Seumas Milne, Beyond the casino economy: planning for the 1990s, Verso, 1989, pages 195-8.

[35]. See William Robson, Nationalized industry and public ownership, Allen & Unwin, 2nd edition, 1969, page 440. Other scholars reached similar conclusions, for instance, Richard Pryke, Public enterprise in practice, New York: St Martin's Press, 1979, page 103, and William Shepherd, Public enterprise: economic analysis of theory and practice, Lexington Books, 1976, page 110.

[36]. See Gar Alperovitz and Jeff Faux, Rebuilding America: a blueprint for the new economy, Pantheon Books, 1984, page 246; see their pages 245-6.

[37]. See Wyn Grant, Duncan Matthews and Peter Newell, The effectiveness of European Union environmental policy, Macmillan, 2000, pages 126-8 and 133.

[38]. See the Independent on Sunday, 17 September 2000, page 1. See also Wyn Grant, Duncan Matthews and Peter Newell, The effectiveness of European Union environmental policy, Macmillan, 2000, pages 130-1 and 133.

[39]. Daily Telegraph, 1 January 1980, cited page 218, Charles Docherty, Steel and steelworkers: the sons of Vulcan, Heinemann, 1983.

[40]. See Justin Greenwood, Representing interests in the European Union, New York: St Martin's Press, 1997, page 65.

[41]. For more on the steel industry, see David Osler, Labour Party plc: New

Labour as a party of business, Mainstream Publishing Company, 2002, pages 145-9.

[42]. See Terrence Guay, At arm's length: the European Union and Europe's defence industry, Macmillan, 1998, pages 142-6.

[43]. See Terrence Guay, At arm's length: the European Union and Europe's defence industry, Macmillan, 1998, page 117; see also his pages 144-6. British Aerospace is now called BAE Systems.

[44]. Page 161, Michael Calingaert, 'Creating a European market', Chapter 8, pages 153-73, in Laura Cram, Desmond Dinan and Neill Nugent, editors, Developments in the European Union, Macmillan, 1999; on telecommunications, see his pages 160-1. On the need for a unified national system of telecommunications, see Nicholas Costello, Jonathan Michie and Seumas Milne, Beyond the casino economy: Planning for the 1990s, Verso, 1989, pages 148-61.

[45]. John Peterson and Elizabeth Bomberg, Decision-making in the European Union, St Martin's Press, 1999, page 217.

[46]. See The Times, 22 September 2000, page 27.

[47]. See Andy McSmith, Kenneth Clarke: a political biography, Verso, 1994, pages 125-7.

[48]. Independent, 4 September 1994. For more on Thatcher's rundown of our shipbuilding industry, see Anthony Burton, The rise and fall of British shipbuilding, Constable, 1994, and Bo Strath, The politics of de-industrialisation: the contraction of the West European shipbuilding industry, Croom Helm, 1987, 'United Kingdom', Chapter 5, pages 116-54.

[49]. Mitchell Smith, page 172, in '"The Commission made me do it": the European Commission as a strategic asset in domestic politics', Chapter 9, pages 170-89, in Neill Nugent, editor, At the heart of the Union: studies of the European Commission, Macmillan, 2nd edition, 2000. On the shipyard closure, see his pages 171-2, 177-82 and 186-8.

[50]. For a useful account of the aerospace industry, see Nicholas Costello, Jonathan Michie and Seumas Milne, Beyond the casino economy: planning

for the 1990s, Verso, 1989, pages 176-81.

[51]. For more on aerospace, see David Osler, Labour Party plc: New Labour as a party of business, Mainstream Publishing Company, 2002, pages 149-50.

[52]. See Andrew McLaughlin and William Maloney, The European automobile industry: multi-level governance, policy and politics, Routledge, 1999, pages 2-3. For a useful summary of the industry's needs, see Nicholas Costello, Jonathan Michie and Seumas Milne, Beyond the casino economy: planning for the 1990s, Verso, 1989, pages 181-9.

[53]. See McLaughlin and Maloney, The European automobile industry: multi-level governance, policy and politics, Routledge, 1999, page 86; see their pages 84-6.

[54]. Cited page 198, McLaughlin and Maloney, The European automobile industry: multi-level governance, policy and politics, Routledge, 1999.

[55]. See Page 1, McLaughlin and Maloney, The European automobile industry: multi-level governance, policy and politics, Routledge, 1999. For more details on the privatisation, see their pages 145-52.

[56]. The Times, 31 July 2000, page 24.

[57]. See McLaughlin and Maloney, The European automobile industry: multi-level governance, policy and politics, Routledge, 1999, page 152.

[58]. See McLaughlin and Maloney, The European automobile industry: multi-level governance, policy and politics, Routledge, 1999, page 154.

[59]. For more on the motor industry, see David Osler, Labour Party plc: New Labour as a party of business, Mainstream Publishing Company, 2002, pages 143-5.

[60]. See McLaughlin and Maloney, The European automobile industry: multi-level governance, policy and politics, Routledge, 1999, page 81; see their pages 81-3.

[61]. See Gar Alperovitz and Jeff Faux, Rebuilding America: a blueprint for

the new economy, Pantheon Books, 1984, pages 125-6. See also Nicholas Costello, Jonathan Michie and Seumas Milne, Beyond the casino economy: planning for the 1990s, Verso, 1989, pages 189-95.

[62]. Justin Greenwood, Representing interests in the European Union, New York: St Martin's Press, 1997, page 257.

[63]. See the union campaign website www.safeskies.co.uk For more on air traffic control, see David Osler, Labour Party plc: New Labour as a party of business, Mainstream Publishing Company, 2002, pages 131-3.

[64]. See Roger Freeman, page vii, 'Preface', pages vii-ix, in Roger Freeman and Jon Shaw, editors, All change: British railway privatisation, McGraw-Hill, 2000.

[65]. See Christopher Booker and Richard North, The castle of lies: why Britain must get out of Europe, Duckworth, 1997, page 154.

[66]. Cited page 1, Railtrack 'failed to repair track', Guardian, 20 October 2000.

[67]. See Ben Webster, Railtrack's fall to cost public £5 bn, The Times, 7 February 2002, page 27.

[68]. For an excellent account, see Andrew Murray, Off the rails: Britain's great rail crisis - cause, consequences and cure, Verso, 2001. See also Ian Jack, The crash that stopped Britain, Granta Books, 2001, and David Hare's play, The permanent way or la voie anglaise, Faber, 2003.

[69]. For an explanation of why it behaved like this, see David Osler, Labour Party plc: New Labour as a party of business, Mainstream Publishing Company, 2002.

[70]. Interview with the Financial Times, 28 March 2002, page 1.

[71]. John Edmonds, page 57, Chapter 3, 'Creating Railtrack,' pages 57-81, in Roger Freeman and Jon Shaw, editors, All change: British railway privatisation, McGraw-Hill, 2000.

[72]. See Martin Mayer (the GEC member for Passenger Services, TGWU),

Exposed: Labour's opposition to public ownership of public transport, The Democrat, January 2002, Number 58, pages 8-9.

[73]. See Driven to death, TUC report, 2000.

[74]. Robert Kuttner, Everything for sale: the virtues and limits of markets, New York: Alfred A. Knopf, 1998, page 308.

[75]. Robert Kuttner, Everything for sale: the virtues and limits of markets, New York: Alfred A. Knopf, 1998, page 307.

[76]. For more on the PPP plan for London Underground, see David Osler, Labour Party plc: New Labour as a party of business, Mainstream Publishing Company, 2002, pages 133-6 and 140-1. See also Christian Wolmar, Down the tube: the battle for London's underground, Aurum Press, 2002.

[77]. Brussels green light for tube changes, Guardian, 1 October 2002, page 5.

[78]. Available at http://www.dti.gov.uk/support/textile.htm

Chapter 7: Agriculture, fisheries and services

Section 1: Agriculture

Section 2: Fisheries

Section 3: Public services

A.   National Health Service

B.   Education

C.   Pensions

D.   Taxes

E.   Conclusion

Section 1: Agriculture

Because of the small numbers employed in farming, only 2.2% of the population, it does not always receive the care and attention that it merits. But it is the foundation of our industrial ability: without food and drink, we could not survive to produce. Our farming has many advantages: our climate is temperate, our soil rich and fruitful and our agriculture is socially advanced and more mechanised than on the Continent.

Yet now, despite huge public spending, British farming is failing to do its job of feeding us. In 2000, we produced only 56% of the food and animal foodstuffs we needed, compared with 62% in 1990. The Labour government does not see farming as necessary, stating, "The role of rural England as the food provider for the nation is no longer an essential one."[1]

But many different industries depend on producing goods for farmers: farm machinery and equipment, agrochemicals like pesticides, herbicides, insecticides and fungicides, fertilisers, animal feed, seed supply, veterinary medicines and other pharmaceutical products, specialist loans and insurance services, specialist education, training and advisory services, and specialist farming publications and programmes. Britain's chemical industry has developed increasingly safe pesticides (early pesticides contained arsenic and mercury!), and are developing natural microbial pesticides, insecticides like Menazon that target aphids but not bees or ladybirds. These technological advances have improved food and plant production; self-sufficient food production is within reach.

The chemical industry is also developing insecticides that target the insects responsible for virulent tropical diseases like malaria, sleeping sickness and elephantiasis. R&D is working towards producing vaccines for tropical infectious diseases.[2]

The EU opposed biotechnology, although biotechnology is not new – people have been using fermentation for centuries to produce alcoholic drinks![3] Under pressure from animal rights and environmental groups, the European Parliament rejected draft legislation on patenting new plants and genetically improved animals.[4] The EU held up the use of BST (bovine somatotropin), produced by bacteria through recombinant DNA technology, which increases milk yields by 15% per lactation.[5] We should not oppose, not the GM knowledge and technology, but the big firms' monopoly of exclusive patents and their theft of people's intellectual property rights.[6]

In the Nice Treaty, the EU adopted the conservative precautionary approach which anticipates hazards that have not been documented but that could conceivably occur. By contrast, the US government adopted the preventive approach, which builds on our knowledge of proven adverse impacts from earlier products.[7] The EU's restrictive regulations have limited the availability of genetically modified foodstuffs and the amount of genetic experimentation within the EU. So billions of research dollars have left Europe and gone to the USA. High value-added jobs have been created in the USA rather than the EU and the USA now far exceeds the EU in the number of biotechnology patents. More US products are coming to market, generating more money for research and encouraging further innovation and discovery. This has given the USA a competitive advantage in perhaps the most important field of technology for the future.[8]

The Common Agricultural Policy is the cause of farming's problems, damaging it in many different ways.[9] The EU spends more than half its budget on a policy that does not help to sustain rural life, increases food prices for consumers and damages the land. Its costly, clumsy administration offers all too many opportunities for large-scale fraud, for which we all have to pay.

The CAP forces up land prices and cuts working farmers' incomes. It pushes workers out of the industry and out of the countryside. During the 1980s, 20,000 farmers and 50,000 farm workers, 20% of the agricultural workforce, lost their jobs. Between 1995 and 2000, 5,000 dairy farms closed down. Between 1990 and 2001, 100,000 agricultural workers left the land. In 1985, a quarter of land workers worked part-time or seasonally; now it is two thirds.

There is no land tax on big landowners and no tax on land sales. The rest of us pay £10 billion a year land tax in the form of council tax. Land prices have doubled since 1993, benefiting landowners but doubling tenant farmers' rents.

The EU, through the CAP, gives £2 billion a year to farming but most goes to landowners not to working farmers.[10] In Britain in 2003, 224 large estates received £47 million in cereals subsidies alone, an average of £210,000, £575 every day. The CAP gives the Duke of Marlborough £1 million every year and the Duke of Richmond £900,000. In 2004, the Duke of Westminster got £448,472, the Duke of Bedford £365,801, the Duke of Northumberland £450,740 and Lord de Ramsey more than £500,000. (These figures are only estimates because the 1979 Agricultural Statistics Act allows landowners to withhold all 'information relating to any particular land or business', so they can keep secret how much public money they get.)

Tate & Lyle gets £120 million a year, helping to keep sugar's price up at £320 a ton, five times the world price. The CAP benefits rich farmers, giving them £550 million a year, while penalising African exporters by imposing a 200% tariff on them.

Labour, in alliance with the Countryside Landowners' Association, has regularly rejected the proposed reform of capping subsidies to individual landowners at £187,500, because Britain has Europe's biggest landowners. Recent changes to the CAP will only add to the subsidies paid on the basis of landownership, not output.

The CAP's imposition of intensive monocultures reduces landscape diversity and depletes soil and water tables. It promoted over-intensive production and creates prairie fields, which erode the soil and destroy hedgerows.[11] Over 70% of our downlands have been ploughed up. Heaths, wetlands, water meadows and ponds have been obliterated.

The CAP also harmed animals' welfare. Between 1990 and 1994, the EU ordered over 300 abattoirs to be closed, destroying jobs and causing needless suffering to animals that had to be transported ever further for slaughter.

The CAP also harms the world's poorest farmers in Asia, Africa and Latin America by monopolizing some of their best land to produce food for the EU, depriving them of land on which they could grow food for themselves.[12] It robs them of life-saving income and deprives us of cheap food by stopping them from selling us their produce.[13] Further, the CAP's export subsidies undercut the prices of their products, destroying their domestic production. In 2005, the EU announced its decision to cut sugar subsidies by 39%. This will damage many of the world's poorest countries in Africa and the Caribbean, especially Jamaica and Guyana. For the last 30 years, they have benefited from an agreement giving them preferential access to EU markets, but the EU wanted to end this. All 18 countries in the African, Caribbean, Pacific group of states attacked the EU decision. The decision gave the states affected little time to diversify economically and was taken with scant consideration for the effects in regions where sugar is of critical economic importance. "No-one cares and they are not listening" said Bharrat Jagdeo, President of Guyana. All nations would benefit from moving towards agricultural self-reliance through land reform and we should set a good example.[14]

The CAP pays farmers not to produce food, to keep food prices high.[15] In 1994, just seven British arable farmers got £500,000 each for setting aside good land. During the 1980s, EC food prices were on average 70% higher than those in the world market. But when the British government vetoed higher farm prices in 1982, this veto was itself vetoed! We were then told that it was only a 'supposed right of veto'.[16] In 1995-98, the most recent years for which figures are available, the CAP puts an extra £800 a year, £16 a week, on the food bill of a household of four. It transfers wealth from the majority to the richest landowners and farmers.[17]

It costs us £3.9 billion a year to support the CAP. In 2004, it cost the

EU £29.3 billion, just under half its entire budget. The mass of the people do not run, or gain from, the CAP. The public interest does not figure in the CAP governance regime.[18] Nor do most farmers gain from the CAP. Farming accounts for 5.4% of the jobs in the EU and for 1.8% of GDP, but for 19.7% of household consumer spending.[19] Working farmers get all too small a share of the values they produce. British farm incomes have fallen every year since 1995, on all kinds of farms.

The large firms that rule food processing and retailing add value, but take most of the difference in profit: retail makes more profit than growing the goods. Only the very largest farms gain from the CAP. Subsidies, like the high prices, benefit the richest farmers at the expense of the mass of the people. 80% of subsidies go to the 20% richest farmers, diverting huge sums away from much-needed industrial investment, reducing our economic growth.[20] The CAP has cost Britain, Germany, Italy and France up to 2.5% of potential gross output, up to 6.2% of exports and 860,000 jobs, mostly in Britain and Germany. Of all the EU's members, Britain loses the most.[21]

Can the CAP be reformed, given that EU governments, especially the French, gain so much from it? The CAP was one of the EEC's original building blocks: its failings are part of the EEC's basic structure. The French majority on the EU's Agricultural Committee has blocked all efforts at reform. The Ministry of Agriculture, Fisheries and Food in 1995 detailed the CAP's failings but concluded, "most other EU governments appear strongly attached to the CAP in its present form." The first effort to reform the CAP, the Mansholt Plan, failed in 1968, just six years after the CAP began. Other EEC members do not want to change the CAP's rules to cater for the very different nature of British farming. If they had done so, the CAP would not have suited their agricultures' needs!

In 1998, Blair said about the CAP, "It is time to grasp fully the nettle of reform." Ever since, it has been one of his main themes, in his effort to con us into accepting the EU. In 2002 the EU made a deal on agriculture spending which is to last until 2013: this was an agreement not to reform the CAP. Blair signed and endorsed it in December 2003. It was impossible to reform the CAP, although all Parliamentary parties endlessly pledged to do so.

Each country needs a farm support system that suits its own needs.

This means food sovereignty, returning to national governments the powers to run their own farming industry.

The British government and the European Commission badly mishandled the BSE crisis, doing huge damage to our beef industry.[22] The Commission suspended BSE veterinary inspections from 1991 to 1994. It thwarted research into the BSE/CJD link and it only banned the use of mammal proteins in food for ruminants six years after being warned of the dangers.

The British government and the European Commission also damaged our agriculture in 2001's foot-and-mouth crisis, particularly by banning the use of life-saving vaccines. European Council Directive 85/511/EEC (as amended by Directive 90/423/EEC), article 13 (1), said, "member states shall ensure that the use of foot and mouth vaccines is prohibited." This prevented Britain from vaccinating, which had controlled Holland's outbreaks in less than two weeks.[23] The Commission also dictated the government's day-to-day management of the epidemic. MAFF turned down the US government's 9 March offer of a simple reliable test that could have avoided the needless slaughter of more than two million healthy animals.[24] (MAFF admitted that only 1% of the culled animals may have actually caught the disease.)

We need to create and support rural industries, particularly forestry and papermaking. Yet despite the fact that the Maastricht Treaty specifically excluded forestry policy from its remit, the EU tries to control the forestlands of EU members, threatening those countries seeking to produce more wood. Reforestation funds were used in Spain to fell intact natural forest and replant with monocultures like eucalyptus trees. EU reports show that forests' conditions are worsening.[25]

We need to keep our ancient forests, encourage the replanting of broad-leaved woodlands, and use domestic pulp to make paper. This would create many jobs in rural areas. Britain's wood production provides only 15% of our needs for wood and wood products, largely for furniture, fencing and garden equipment. Wood imports are one of the largest drains on our trade balance. Since 1945, we have lost more than half our ancient woodlands, while conifer plantations have quadrupled.[26]

In 2000, the paper industry, our fifth biggest manufacturing sector, employed 23,000 highly skilled workers. We produce 6.2 million tonnes of paper and board a year and import 6.6 million tonnes, 85% from EU countries. Investing in forestry here could reduce the need for such large amounts of expensive imports.

We need to gear our farming to our people's health needs. Presently, under CAP the demands of the big food firms determine what is produced and consumed. The CAP, in keeping with its market orientation, has no explicit health or nutrition aims. Our needs for the best possible foods should drive our farming. Health considerations should prevail over commercial food interests.[27]

The only way to improve our agriculture is to leave the CAP. Then we could plan farming policy properly.[28] SAFE (Sustainable Agriculture, Food and Environment), a body supported by the TGWU's rural workers' section, said that Britain should be 'self-sufficient in produce suitable to its climate and soil'. Costs would be lower and the food would come fresher to the table, because it would be shipped over a shorter distance. We could train farm workers, replant orchards and ban imports of foods that we can grow here. We could stabilise food and land prices and support farmers' incomes. SAFE estimated that these changes would create and support 60,000 new jobs.[29] We could grow 80% of what we need. We are already self-sufficient in beef, poultry, milk and wheat; we could easily be self-sufficient in fish, potatoes and butter.

In place of the CAP, we should have a more labour-intensive and skill-based agriculture, using technological advances and using more extensive farming styles for cattle. Outside the CAP, we could keep land prices down, reducing housing costs and ending speculative profits from land development, enabling us to plan the provision of affordable housing for all.[30] We need Local Development Plans to rebuild the rural economy and rural society. We need to plan investment in agriculture, in local industries and in rural infrastructure - transport, Post Offices, local bank branches, schools, medical practices and libraries.

Section 2: Fishing

Fish is a major part of our national diet. The more fish we eat, the healthier our hearts are. Since cardiovascular disease is now one of the major killers, restoring our fishing rights would save lives and reduce NHS costs. Fishing is the livelihood of thousands of British workers, and indirectly of thousands more: for every fisherman at sea, there were seven jobs ashore.

When we entered the Common Market, a senior civil servant in the Scottish fisheries department advised ministers not to go into detail on the damage caused to the fishing industry: "The more one is drawn into such explanations, the more difficult it is to avoid exposing the weaknesses of the inshore fisheries position, the only answer to which may be that in the wider context they must be regarded as expendable."

The Common Fisheries Policy (CFP) allots catches annually on a fixed percentage basis to the fishing fleets of the EU countries with no regard to territorial waters. Quotas are allocated for different species within a largely free-access system, pressing fishermen into catching as many fish as possible, as fast as possible. Foreign operators now own between a quarter and a third of Britain's quota. The system of national quotas that expired at the end of 2002 led to the rundown of the British fishing fleet.[31]

The Special European Permits System that replaced it allows all the EU's fishing fleets to fish all of Europe's fishing grounds, including our 12-mile coastal belt. This is theft of our sovereign waters. Each year the CFP makes us hand over to other countries £5 billions' worth of fish. Britain has more than 75% of the fish in EU waters, but we are allowed to catch only 30%. Consequently, British fishermen provide only 59% of our fish supplies. Since we joined the EU, the amount of fish that British vessels land fell by 40%, while imports more than doubled.

In November 2000, the EU announced that it would impose a one-year ban on cod fishing in all 'EU waters', including the North Sea, a crushing blow to Scottish trawlermen. Fisheries Minister Elliott Morley said that the government would 'reluctantly' back this call.

Shetland Skipper Magnie Stewart, of the appropriately named "Defiant", wrote, "The recent imposition of a cod ban in the North Sea, while thousands of tonnes of good edible fish are allowed to be caught as an industrial fisheries by-catch, and thousands more tonnes are dumped, due to an insane quota system, is further proof (if any more were needed) what an absolute farce and conservation disaster, the now thoroughly discredited, politically inspired, "Common Fisheries Policy" (Equal Access to a Common Resource) and the present 1983/2003 derogation from it, are. For politicians, bureaucrats and Civil Servants to portray the present derogation and the coming and real, and far more deadly Common Fisheries Policy, in which the fact that British waters provide over three-quarters of the fish, will not entitle British fishermen to any better treatment than 'European' fishermen from Austria, who provide not a single fish, to portray all this as a conservation tool, is an insult to all working fishermen. Up here, in Shetland, we - while our factories go hungry for raw material - have been forced to dump thousands of tons of good, marketable fish, all within sight of Shetland's coastline, all, supposedly, in the name of fish stock conservation. The present derogation, and the forthcoming regime of equal access to a common resource by all 'European' fishermen, is nothing more than a cynical political tool in the creation of a European Superstate, which will see a Single European Fishing Fleet, containing only a few British vessels. Shame on those in Westminster who have sold out our once proud fishing fleet for the sake of 'European' integration."[32]

There is no international law to conserve fish stocks, largely because the EU refuses to agree to any proposals. The EU still ignores UN resolutions banning drift nets longer than 1.5 miles. Since 1991, British governments, which in 1989 backed the UN Resolution banning such nets, have supinely followed the EU and refused to impose a ban. The EU repeatedly broke international conservation decisions and it backed the Spanish and Portuguese vessel owners who breached even the EU's overgenerous quotas. Italian fishermen ignored the EU ban on the ten-mile long nets they used to catch swordfish and tuna, nets that also ensnared and killed the Mediterranean's dolphins. The EU used the GATT commitment to free trade to overturn the USA's ban on importing tuna caught with these nets.[33] In 1996, the World Conservation Union had to put cod and haddock on their red list of endangered species after EU trawlers had fished out first the North Sea, then the Grand Banks off Canada and the USA and then the Barents Sea.[34]

The EU has 25 access agreements with countries in Africa and the Indian Ocean, allowing 4,000 trawlers, largely from the huge Spanish fleet, to fish in these countries' 200-mile Exclusive Economic Zones which are amongst the world's richest fishing grounds.[35] Exploiting the poverty and indebtedness of African governments, the EU pays them £127 million a year to let EU trawlers plunder their waters. These trawlers deplete the stock, destroy local fishermen's jobs and reduce local people's consumption of fish, their main source of protein. Spanish freezer trawlers scoop up hundreds of thousands of tons of fish, tossing it all back dead into the sea, keeping only the big African prawns which fetch a high price in Western European restaurants, while the local fishermen in their dugout canoes can barely feed their families.

Consequently, West Africa's fisheries are collapsing.[36] Under an EU agreement, Mauritania's government has to ban local fishermen from catching their traditional harvest of sardines. In return, it got £380 million over six years to allow unlimited fishing of its waters.

Namibia refused to accept the fisheries agreement that the EU proposed and told all foreign fleets to stop fishing in their waters. Spanish trawlers carried on regardless, until the Namibian authorities seized five Spanish vessels in 1990. Namibia has taken control of its own fishing industry and used its marine resources for its people's benefit. Fisheries have become its main engine of economic growth.[37] In early 2002, the EU demanded that South Africa allow EU industrial trawlers into its rich fishing waters. But the South African government refuses to allow access because it fears, quite rightly, that these trawlers would exploit the waters in an unsustainable manner. There is a Spanish majority on the EU's Fishing Committee so reform is unlikely.

Britain is well suited to producing fish and France is well suited to producing wine. But nobody seriously suggests that France's vineyards should become a 'common European resource' or proposes that the European Commission should give a huge chunk of French land to British wine producers.

John Ashworth, an experienced fisherman, wrote, "The Common Fisheries Policy has been, and continues to be, an environmental disaster, but is it any wonder? Instead of sensible fisheries management, it has been driven by the politics of integration, of creating the one European Union fishing fleet, and fishermen have been forced into still being hunters instead of becoming harvesters. Where else can one find the insanity of dumping prime fish back dead into the sea to pollute the seabed, and where every encouragement is given to catch and land baby fish, because the Commission, with the blessing of the Council of Ministers, abolished the 'Minimum Landing Size' (the smallest size allowed to be landed) for eleven species of fish? This to please the Spaniards, who regard tiny fish as a delicacy. Developing fishing gear to take the species and size you want is incredibly slow in the EU. It makes one wonder if the Commission wants fish stocks to decline, because it makes integration easier, as Northern EU vessels are got rid of in the name of conservation to make room for the Southern and possible future Eastern fleets. The present North Sea "Cod recovery" programme is a crude sham. The problem is not the lack of Cod, but the lack of feed for the Cod, and other fish such as Haddock, Coley and Whiting. It is a known fact that there is a very good brood of 2-year-old Cod in the North Sea, but last summer they did not grow as they should, for lack of feed. Why is their natural diet not available? Because industrial fishing for fertiliser has gone unchecked. This has happened before, in the Barents Sea, where the recovery of the larger fish such as Cod was achieved by restoring the food supply, by not catching the small species such as sandeel and pout."

A meeting of fishermen in Plymouth in January 1995 issued a statement on the CFP: "This agreement represents the culmination of over a decade of systematic destruction of the fishing industry of this country. We no longer see any future for us within the framework of the Common Fisheries Policy. We therefore demand that this Government withdraw from the Common Fisheries Policy forthwith." They wanted to ensure "that the fish around our shores within our sovereign waters are managed and conserved in such a way that there will be a fishing industry in this country for generations to come."

The EU's conservation policy has been a disaster.[38] The EU has squandered the opportunities to reduce catches of small fish and the high rates of fishing.[39]

In 2004, the EU aimed to create an EU-wide Common Fisheries Agency. This would police agency catches, inspections, vessel sizes and licences and it would report to Brussels, further diminishing our sovereignty. In a referendum held at Billingsgate, London's fish market, in 1998, market workers, traders and drivers voted overwhelmingly to leave the CFP. Outside the CFP, we could fish our own waters, rebuild our fleet and renew our ports.

Section 3: Public services policy

Public spending makes good economic sense, since it provides the investment in health, education and welfare that we need to flourish as healthy and educated people.[40] But the EU does not support social provision through public services. It continues to try to open up all public services (including health) to the 'controlled competition model' that gave us Railtrack.[41] It uses the EU's competition law to defeat national laws protecting public services.[42] The services market is worth an estimated $1.2 million a year

The EU member governments decided to meet the Maastricht Treaty's criteria for EMU, even though they knew that this would mean less public spending, more unemployment, higher taxes, less growth, lower wages and worse public services across the EU. The EU's increasing integration is eroding public finances and public sectors.[43] For instance, in France, the Juppe government tried to impose an EMU-driven austerity package of social service cuts and increased taxes, provoking a great wave of public sector strikes in November and December 1995. The strikers succeeded in forcing the government to renegotiate the whole package, withdrawing some proposals and changing others.[44] There were also widespread strikes in Spain (1994 and 1996), Italy (1996), Greece (1996 and 1997) and Belgium (1997). In Germany, meeting the Maastricht criteria meant massive social spending cuts and a public sector pay freeze. Its austerity programme (Sparpaket) cut public spending by £30 billion (70 billion DM), the biggest single fiscal retrenchment in economic history.[45]

To meet EMU's convergence criteria, the Major government cut public spending and raised taxation, cutting the rate of growth in pay and cutting labour's share of national income. The 1994 and 1995 budgets took £15 billion off public spending. The election of a Labour government in 1997 made no difference. As we noted earlier, the EU's Council of

Ministers secretly ordered that the new government 'strictly implements its budgetary policy' and commit itself to 'maintaining a rigorous control of public expenditure'. (It was secret because by Article 104c(7) of the Maastricht Treaty, the Council's instructions 'shall not be made public'.) So for three years Gordon Brown maintained the public spending squeeze that the Conservative government had imposed. As a result, the public sector shrank from 41% of GDP in 1996/97 to 37.7% in 1999/2000. The Institute for Fiscal Studies reported that the Blair government's record on public investment was the worst of any government since 1945.[46] This meant the loss of thousands of public sector jobs.

The Maastricht Treaty and the consequent Stability Pact exerted downward pressure on public spending.[47] The Growth and Stability Pact came under increasing pressure as it delivered only stagnation. France openly said that she would not be bound by it. Germany and Portugal imposed spending cuts to reduce their deficits below the Pact's ceiling of 3% of GDP, but failed. And to the dismay of his Commissioners, Romano Prodi punctured all confidence in the Pact by saying (the day after Blair had praised the euro as 'economic sense'), "I know very well that the stability pact is stupid, like all decisions that are rigid."[48] The European Central Bank responded by stating that the Pact was indispensable! However bad the Pact was, since its birth in 1996 it had been part of the EU's acquis, so all member governments would have to agree before it could be changed.

The Labour government speeded up the Conservative policy of privatisation.[49] (Incidentally, it was Mussolini, not Thatcher, who pioneered privatisation - he privatised Italy's utilities and railway service early in his rule.) Increasingly, people can see that privatisation does not make the industry or service more efficient, but then it was never designed for that purpose. As Dr Madsen Pirie, President of the Adam Smith Institute and one of privatisation's leading promoters, wrote, "The purpose of privatisation is not to make state operations competitive but to make them private."[50] Only by this test does privatisation 'work'.

The Labour government fostered Private Finance Initiatives (PFIs) to offload spending into the private sector, in order to avoid going over the EU-imposed limits on public spending. PFIs were no answer to the lack of investment. They were more costly and less efficient than public provision. Private borrowing is dearer and the risks are not transferred to the private sector. Labour has arranged public spending data and NHS accounts to hide the huge amounts of public money going straight through the NHS to private companies.

As the TUC stated, "the Private Finance Initiative … has persistently failed to deliver. … Payments to private contractors are set to rise and over the medium term the total cost of PFI service contracts may outweigh the costs that would have been incurred through additional public borrowing." London Health Emergency said, "the only appeal for the government is that the cost of the hospital does not appear as an immediate lump sum in the public expenditure figures. Capital advanced by the private sector as a PFI transaction is not counted as public sector 'borrowing' requirement, although the hospitals will effectively be paying off a high-cost mortgage for decades to come. This enables the government to stick within the single currency strait jacket … The cheaper alternative, building hospitals with public money financed through government borrowing, is ruled out by the Maastricht criteria."

City accountants Chantry Vellacott DFK estimated that PFI contracts cost 5% more than if the Treasury borrowed the money directly. This, if anything, understated the long-term cost differences: for example, a new hospital in Swindon was built and equipped at a cost of £135 million, but it will cost us £596 million over the next 30 years.[51] Under privatisation, profits could only be made by cutting costs, mainly staff costs, so it usually worsened the wages and conditions of the workers involved.[52] The first fourteen hospitals operated under PFI cut clinical staff by 20% and beds by 30%. The Andersen Report on PFI, the only report to conclude that PFI works, was compromised by Andersen's links with PFI contracts.

In 2004, Labour lifted the ceiling on health administration costs, which had already doubled, cutting clinical care budgets so that there are fewer beds in PFI hospitals. Labour excludes doctors, nurses and health professionals from hospital management, while welcoming failed businessmen. Surgery performed in private hospitals costs 40% more than in NHS hospitals, because of higher costs and the overriding need to return a profit to the shareholders.

In 2002, Labour privatised practice premises through the

introduction of Local Improvement Finance Trusts, which shifted control of primary care services from GPs to corporations. And Labour has forced local authorities to divest themselves of all their social service assets, including long-term care for the elderly, ending equal access to equal quality of care for older people.[53]

The EU continually pushes for privatisation. Since 1998, the European Investment Bank has lent more than £1 billion to support PFI projects. At the World Trade Organisation, the EU, in alliance with US financial companies, successfully pressed for a General Agreement on Trade in Services (GATS) to allow private capital access to all our services. David Hartridge, a WTO official, explained, "Without the enormous pressure generated by the American financial services sector, there would have been no services agreement." American finance firms are particularly targeting the NHS and European countries' health services. Dean O'Hare, president of one of the world's biggest insurance companies, who led the lobbying in Washington, told Congress, "We believe we can make much progress in the negotiations to allow the opportunity for US businesses to expand into foreign healthcare markets."

The WTO expanded the concept of services to cover just about everything, including schools, hospitals, social services, energy, food supply and 157 other services. GATS is designed to stop governments from fostering native industries and to enforce privatisation of all services.

WTO rules would override national sovereignty and impose privatisation on all the processes of service delivery and throughout all service sectors, destroying publicly owned and accountable services, with no reference to any electorate.[54] The European Commission confirmed, "GATS is not something which exists between governments. It is first and foremost an instrument for the benefit of business."

GATS is supposed to be forever: if a government agrees to liberalise any service, it would have made an irrevocable commitment. In a few years, every voter in Britain might, for example, oppose US firms taking over British hospitals under WTO rules, but neither they nor their MPs would legally be able to do anything about it. The EU identified countries that resisted GATS and prepared to whip them into line. The Labour government fully approved. In June 2005, the EU agreed to reorganise its trade barriers to bring them into line with WTO rules.

The EU's secret memo 'Domestic Regulation: Necessity and Transparency' abandons the 'sovereign right of government to regulate services' that trade minister Richard Caborn promised MPs that GATS would observe. Labour's promise to spare public services meant little, as Caborn showed when he said that it only covered those services not in competition with private operators. Of course, private hospitals and schools already compete for custom in Britain, so health and education are clearly up for grabs.

Blair welcomed the EU's proposed new code for services, which it too defined widely, covering many industries. This code was devised by the European Services Network, a lobby representing fifty firms like Goldman Sachs, Barclays and HSBC Holdings which aimed to liberalise the services market. It enjoyed extraordinary access to the EU, especially to the Commission's 133 Committee, which decided EU trade policy. The Committee's proceedings were not open to the public, MEPs or the press. When non-governmental organisations asked about the EU's position on allowing big firms to privatise health and education, the EU told them that the information was a 'trade secret'. When Danish MPs asked their government to explain what was going on, it told them that elected ministers could not get access to Commission documents!

The EU demanded that all its trading 'partners' across the world end all restrictions on foreign ownership, all controls over foreign accounting firms and advertisers, and all rules over repatriating profits. They aimed to end national control of key industries and services like water, energy, sewerage, telecommunications, postal services and financial services. In the 2002 round of world trade talks, the EU demanded across-the-board privatisation of public services throughout the world. It wanted to force countries to scrap all rules banning foreign competition in and ownership of their services. The Labour government enthusiastically pushed this EU policy package. This was a direct attack on the national economies of all the countries of Asia, Africa and Latin America.

A. National Health Service

Implementing EU employment laws cost the NHS more than £100 million a year, soaking up most of the extra money that the government proclaimed it was giving to hospitals. As the NHS Confederation said, "We've seen the biggest cash increase into the NHS for years but almost all of it is being used to fund the new measures. Hospitals all over the country are going into the red because of them."[55]

At Addenbrookes Hospital in Cambridge, for instance, the Working Time Directive caused financial chaos, bed shortages, longer waiting lists and cancelled operations. "Our finances are being bled dry by all the new demands on us and, in the end, it is the patients who suffer most. We seem to spend most of our time looking after the bureaucrats", said one hospital source. In 2000, the hospital spent £629,000 on the Directive, employing extra staff, some merely to keep the new records straight! The Directive did not cover the two key groups of hospital workers, doctors and nurses, and the costs therefore were all on administrative staff. All routine admissions were cancelled and even spaces for emergency patients could not be guaranteed.

By far the biggest single cost in the NHS was the wage bill, 75% of the budget. In the country as a whole, wages increased by 4.6% in 2000. But Blair awarded the nurses and doctors just 3.6%, so their wages fell further behind, worsening staffing problems. Our doctors and nurses are still underpaid and overworked. Medical costs rose much faster than price inflation, making a 5% a year rise in health spending equal a 2.25% rise in real terms.

The NHS paid much more for drugs as a result of the EU. The EU made us take supplies in blister pack strips with each pill separate. (Usually there were 28 to a box, which did not work out if one needed three a day, as many patients did). Previously they were supplied in bulk to the chemist who transferred the correct quantity to cheap plastic bottles. The storage space needed for all this packaging was - in one case - 25 times as great. These strips were extremely difficult for arthritic hands to use, so many of the pills got broken and the powdered bits were lost, so the dose was reduced. What happened to prices? Look at two standard prescription drugs, Warfarin and penicillin. In June 2000, Warfarin cost £20 a thousand; by September, it was £61, a 205% rise. The price of penicillin soared from

£8 to £44, a rise of 450%. In June, a bottle of 100 junior aspirins was 95p; in September a strip pack of 28 was 85p over the counter - another massive rise, of 219.5%. The EU was taxing the ill.

Even before the British people voted on the euro, it cost the NHS millions of pounds as computers, printers, financial forms, stationery, and new machinery for car parks, cashiers and vending machines were made ready for a changeover that might never happen. The government told every NHS Trust to form a project group on conversion and report to its regional office by August 2000. NHS staff had enough work to do, especially after the reorganisation of the service following the creation of Primary Care. There were no known benefits of the euro to the NHS.

As part of the government's National Changeover Plan, a company selling medical billing software received a five-page questionnaire from the NHS about the euro compliance of their software. It then listed all the phases the NHS was supposed to go through until the dawn of the new age when we joined the euro. The 'EMU Phases' were as follows:

1. Decision (i.e. to join the euro 'in principle', but it did not say that).

2. Four months later, Referendum.

3. 12 to 15 months later, Britain joined the euro. Note that the government assumed the referendum produced the result that it wanted. Transition phase started.

4. 24 to 30 months after the referendum, euro coins were in circulation. Transition phase ended.

5. Six months later the process was complete, and sterling was abolished.

The EU was also likely to impose a common health policy - Britain had the only National Health Service in the EU, the only one free at point of use. The EU was opposed in principle to national health services: the Continental system is based on medical insurance and privatised health care. The Maastricht Treaty, ominously, called for an EU policy on health. Commissioner Pascal Lamy said he believed that health and education were 'ripe for liberalisation'. The Treaty made no guarantees against attempts to 'harmonise' our system with theirs. In 2005, a series of European Court of Justice rulings dictated that health care provision is subject to the rules of the EU's internal market, and therefore to competition, regardless of national policy.

Wherever it could, the EU imposed privatisation of health services, for instance in Albania, through its Phare programme and in collaboration with the World Bank. As a result, *The Lancet* judged, "the EU has a dismal record on public health."[56]

We in Britain believed that the market should have no place in health care because all experience showed that it damaged health care. We knew that the US market system was more costly, less equitable and less able to provide good health care.[57] Primary care must be universally and equally available and publicly funded.[58] We needed to plan public health promotion.[59]

The European Central Bank's Monthly Bulletin for April 2003 carried a revealing policy statement from the Bank, 'The need for comprehensive reforms to cope with population ageing'. (See www.ecb.int/pub/pdf/mb200304en.pdf, pages 39-51.) The Bank said, "A comprehensive institutional framework has been set up at the European level to co-ordinate and monitor ageing-related policies. ... This framework should be implemented in full to support governments in adopting appropriate policies at the national level." It told us what health policies to implement. "Reforms should place both public pension systems and health and long-term care arrangements on a sustainable financial footing by limiting the public sector's exposure, enhancing private funding and setting incentives for efficient service provision."

It demanded the 'promotion of long-term contracts between providers of health services and the cost-covering institutions'. It said that within public health services, 'market forces can help to move towards efficient solutions'. It demanded that public health systems 'should focus on providing core services'. It called for governments to differentiate between 'essential, privately non-insurable and non-affordable services' and those where 'private financing might be more efficient'. This would limit free health care to accident and emergency care. It said, "Greater private involvement in healthcare financing can be achieved, in particular, through patient co-payments, as already implemented in a number of countries." It called on governments to 'raise contribution rates, streamline services and secure private financing and funding'.

B. Education

Education systems are vital to nations' cultures and skills bases. So the EU is increasingly determined to gain control of education. Rebuilding an independent Britain requires an academic education system enabling children's minds to flower and a training/apprenticeship system that prepare people for work. In particular, production skills are vitally important: we need more engineers, fewer politicians and lawyers.

We need a national, public, comprehensive system of education, which means ending the private education sector, whose fraudulent charitable status costs the taxpayer dearly. We need more teachers, trained here to recognised common standards, and well-paid. By 2000, the pupil/teacher ratio in secondary schools was the worst since 1985, at 17.2 pupils per teacher (when Labour took office in 1997 it was 16.4/1).

'Faith schools', the confessional schools promoted by the EU, sustain race feeling by segregating people. We need community cohesion, not separatism, not ghettoisation.

Public spending cuts enforced by the EU hit local libraries especially hard. We should extend library opening hours and improve their staffing and resourcing. The EU threatens to extend VAT to books, magazines and newspapers, raising their costs. We should end VAT on the theatre and support free universal entry to all museums and galleries.

We should stop the sale of any more playing fields, which belong to schools and the public. We should create a British Sports Institute, with regional centres, each with excellent facilities and coaching. Sport should be available for all and schools should not let pupils of 14 and above opt out of it.

The EU has different goals and it funds costly projects to achieve these goals.[60] In 1995, it launched two education schemes, the Socrates and Youth for Europe programmes. Between 1995 and 1998, these projects cost £685 million. In 2002, the EU Court of Auditors revealed 'serious irregularities' in their finances cost overruns, projects receiving money before they had even begun, unrecovered spent money and fraud. So what was done? A true EU solution - the EU extended the schemes until 2006 and doubled their budgets.

The Maastricht Treaty, the first EU treaty to state that the EU could intervene in educational matters, called for education and training to be merged, to focus on satisfying the employer's needs.[61] GCSE and A-levels are under pressure to conform to the Continental Baccalaureate. The Blair government introduced new vocational qualifications, with competence-based assessment widely seen as mechanical and mind numbing. Our teacher training system is also under threat.

The European Commission uses its information services budget of £200 million a year, among other efforts, to promote the EU in schools, contrary to Section 407 of the 1996 Education Act which bans political propaganda in primary schools, and requires balanced treatment of controversial matters in secondary schools.

The EU wants a privatised, decentralised and denationalised education system. It aims to introduce a European dimension into national education, promoting attitudes more favourable to European unity.[62] They wanted to indoctrinate our children into a pro-EU set of ideas, which as we have seen are contrary to the British nation's democratic and independent traditions.

C. Pensions

Britain had £830 billion invested in private pensions, more than the rest of the EU put together. The other members have a £1.2 trillion shortfall in money invested for future generations: their pension costs are likely to rise from 10 per cent of GDP now to around 16 per cent by 2030. It was estimated that by 2040, our pension costs would be 10% of GDP, compared to Germany's 110%.[63] The House of Commons Social Security Select Committee concluded, "The extent of unfunded pension liabilities in certain of our European partner countries casts serious doubts upon the long term sustainability of their finances." The EU could well press us to pay taxes to fund the other members' pension schemes. Delors had warned, "All members of EMU would become liable for the debts of a single country."[64]

The solution is not to reduce pensions (Brown's way) but to get more people into jobs by increasing demand. Brown is abolishing by stealth the state earnings related pension scheme. In 1999, he mandated local councils to transfer part of their pension funds into the euro, losing council workers millions. Brent, for instance, lost £1.8 million.

In April 2002, the EU proposed a new accounting standard for pensions, the FRS17, which delivered a fresh blow to British pension schemes, leaving millions of savers out of pocket. It forced firms to ensure that their assets cover liabilities at all times: firms have to make up immediately any deficit shown. Under the British system, pension funds are allowed some leeway because their liabilities are long-term and liable to fluctuate. About half of FTSE 100 companies show pension deficits on the new standard. It forces firms to inject billions of pounds into their beleaguered pension funds overnight or wind up their pension schemes. The directive accelerates the demise of final-salary pension plans. However, because Britain's pensions did not have to be fully funded, members often received substantially less than they were expecting when schemes are wound up.

The European Central Bank's 2003 policy statement called for 'strengthening private involvement in pension and health insurance arrangements', the 'private management of pension assets'. It advocated 'reductions in public pensions' and 'measures to raise the effective retirement age'. With regard to existing pay-as-you-go systems, it said that 'overly generous provisions will need to be reduced'. It also called for 'the extension of working hours', the 'containment of labour costs and the abolition of overly rigid labour market regulations'.

What caused the current pensions crisis? In 1997 the government decided to abolish the annual £5 billion tax credit on dividends received by pension funds. The Treasury and independent actuaries warned Brown that this would push pension schemes into a £50 billion deficit, close down final guaranteed salary schemes for millions of workers and cut payments to pensioners. Brown ignored them.

By 2001 the ending of the credit and the inevitable fall of the stock market had wrecked the retirement plans of millions of workers. In response, Brown proposed a pension tax credit guaranteeing a minimum income predicting that it would cost £2 billion in 2004-5. His advisers pointed out that since half the population would immediately be eligible for the credit it would cost more like £10 billion a year. Treasury civil servants warned him that the state would not be able to fund this scheme.

Brown said, "We're only committed to pay the credit for the next five years. We can change it after that." The questions came, "But what about after? People save for 20 years for their pensions. They won't believe in you and they won't save. And what happens to their pensions after five years?" Brown ignored them.

By 2002, Britain's pension funds were paying pensioners on average 28% less than in 1997 and two-thirds of final salary pension schemes had been closed to new members.

D. Taxes

As well as threatening our ability to decide our spending, the EU also threatens our ability to decide our own taxes. The Commissioner for the Internal Market, Mario Monti, said, "Tax co-ordination is now an ordinary though difficult, subject which has a permanent place on the EU agenda." Duisenberg said, "fiscal consolidation needs to be pushed forward more aggressively." In 2000, France's Finance Minster, Christian Sautter, said that the French government supported a 'rapid' abandonment of the national veto on tax policy. The vice-president of the Commission, Loyola de Palacio, called for harmonised fuel taxes. The Dutch Finance Minister, Gerrit Zalm, called for harmonisation of pension tax systems. In March 2002, the pace quickened. Laming, the EU Trade Commissioner, said, "the ultimate goal should be the creation of a European corporate income tax." Chirac called for 'genuine fiscal harmonisation in Europe'. Jospin said, "in terms of corporate tax, the tax bases should be harmonised and a minimum rate should be fixed."

We should instead promote the idea that revenues should be earmarked to pay for certain services. This idea, combined with referenda that would enable us, not the government, to choose where our money goes, has great democratic potential.

Our basic rates of personal tax were the lowest in the EU. EU harmonisation of taxes would raise taxes and impose VAT on house purchases, food, public transport, children's clothing, books and newspapers. Gordon Brown admitted that within the EU the British government could not repeal VAT, saying, "I would prefer it to be removed altogether, but it can't be done."[65]

In December 1997, the EU's Finance Ministers, including Brown, adopted the Commission's proposals for a Code of Conduct for Business Taxation, to end 'unfair tax competition', that is, to end taxes that were 'unfairly' low for people and 'unfairly' high for firms. The EU has already imposed taxes on us under the guise of single market harmonisation measures which were subject to qualified majority voting, not unanimity, as required for tax measures. The Commission threatened to use this tactic again. It also sought to evade our veto by considering 'the use of alternative instruments as a basis for initiatives in the tax field'.

The EU's budget is growing rapidly, at about 11.7% a year, so it draws proportionately more out of national exchequers when they spend less on their own people. The EU wants a direct EU income tax, to be levied on all EU citizens. The Belgian Prime Minister, Guy Verhofstadt, who proposed this in May 2001, said that it was just his 'personal opinion', yet Jospin, Schröder, Prodi and the European Parliament all immediately chimed in that they backed the idea.

E. Conclusion

Public sector workers should continue to provide services and we should reject privatisation. But if privatisations are imposed, we should not accept this as a final defeat to our attempts to provide decent public services. Whether in the private or the public sector, our work goes on: what counts is how much we control our workplaces. The more that we control our workplaces and our industries, the closer we are to running our country, the real meaning of socialism.

The EU's rulers want to extend the single market to services. The Commission has said, "Liberalisation of services is an essential element in the Lisbon Strategy. The Commission hopes services will be liberalized. It is out of the question to withdraw the proposal." Brendan Barber, the TUC General Secretary, said, "The Constitution makes clear the EU's commitment to liberalisation." The EU's draft Directive on Services, the Bolkestein Directive, aims for the 'liberalisation and deregulation of all service activity in Europe'. The Directive would legitimize the worst practices, as when a Latvian construction firm recently got a job in Sweden and tried to pay its workers there at Latvian rates, which are a fraction of Swedish wages. It also tried to ban union activities from its sites. The British Medical Association warned that the Directive would "undermine every member state's right to decide what is in the best interests of its patients and its healthcare systems." The American Chambers of Commerce support the Directive because it "would lead to a huge reduction of costs for businesses functioning in Europe."

George Ross accurately summed up what the EU wants to do to Europe's labour markets and welfare states: "From the point of view of European citizens, therefore, renewed European integration meant declining ability to constrain and shape markets to promote desirable public goals in social and industrial relations policies, for example. Moreover, the new setting created additional incentives for business to promote labour market and social policy deregulation in the interests of the 'flexibility' needed to cope. ... All this means that the great pressures on governments to pursue rigid price stability and balance budgets, which have been closely correlated with rising unemployment in the 1990s, will be continued. EMU and the coming of the single currency will in themselves remove any possibility of national governments adjusting to changed economic circumstances through the traditional monetary techniques of currency revaluation and interest rate shifts. This means that adjustments will have to be accomplished through changing price and wage levels and manipulating state spending, largely in social protection areas. The implications are clear. EMU will act to exert strong pressures on European nations to 'Americanize' their labour markets and welfare states."[66]

The EU wants us to work harder, longer and for less, until we drop. It wants to end state pensions, tax-funded public welfare systems and long-term care.[67] It wants to destroy the NHS.[68]

Endnotes

[1]. From the first paragraph of 'The Government Rural White Paper', The Seventh Report of the Environment, Transport and Regional Affairs Committee, Volume 1, 2000.

[2]. See C. A. Heaton, editor, The chemical industry, Blackie, 1986. See also David Osler, Labour Party plc: New Labour as a party of business, Mainstream Publishing Company, 2002, pages 150-3.

[3]. See Wyn Grant, The Common Agricultural Policy, Macmillan, 1997, pages 15-9, 22, 26 and 176, and Desmond Dinan, Ever closer union: an introduction to European integration, Macmillan, 2nd edition, 1999, pages 550-1.

[4]. See Wyn Grant, The Common Agricultural Policy, Macmillan, 1997, page 176. See also Justin Greenwood, Representing interests in the European Union, New York: St Martin's Press, 1997, pages 23 and 191-2.

[5]. See Wyn Grant, The Common Agricultural Policy, Macmillan, 1997, pages 16-7, and Desmond Dinan, Ever closer union: an introduction to European integration, Macmillan, 2nd edition, 1999, page 550.

[6]. On biotechnology and the EU, see Michael Nollert, 'Biotechnology in the European Union: a case study of political entrepreneurship', Chapter 8, pages 210-43, in Volker Bornschier, editor, State-building in Europe: the revitalization of Western European integration, Cambridge University Press, 2000.

[7]. See the discussion by Lee Ann Paterson, pages 324-8, in 'Biotechnology policy: regulating risks and risking regulation', Chapter 12, pages 317-43, in Helen Wallace and William Wallace, editors, Policy-making in the European Union, Oxford University Press, 4th edition, 2000.

[8]. See Lee Ann Paterson, page 340, in 'Biotechnology policy: regulating risks and risking regulation', Chapter 12, pages 317-43, in Helen Wallace and William Wallace, editors, Policy-making in the European Union, Oxford University Press, 4th edition, 2000.

[9]. See Wyn Grant, The Common Agricultural Policy, Macmillan, 1997,

page 228. See also Desmond Dinan, Ever closer union: an introduction to European integration, Macmillan, 2nd edition, 1999, Chapter 12, pages 333-51.

[10]. Oxfam, Spotlight on subsidies: cereal injustice under the CAP in Britain, Oxfam Briefing Paper 55, January 2004.

[11]. See Wyn Grant, Duncan Matthews and Peter Newell, The effectiveness of European Union environmental policy, Macmillan, 2000, page 207.

[12]. See Guglielmo Carchedi, For another Europe: a class analysis of European economic integration, Verso, 2001, page 215.

[13]. See Richard Body, Our food, our land: why contemporary farming practices must change, Rider, 1991, pages 229-46.

[14]. See Gar Alperovitz and Jeff Faux, Rebuilding America: a blueprint for the new economy, Pantheon Books, 1984, page 201. On land reform, see their pages 201-2.

[15]. Desmond Dinan, Ever closer union: an introduction to European integration, Macmillan, 2nd edition, 1999, page 350.

[16]. Richard Corbett, The European Parliament's role in closer EU integration, Macmillan, 1998, page 33.

[17]. See Roger Henderson, European finance, McGraw-Hill, 1993, page 104.

[18]. Kenneth Armstrong and Simon Bulmer, The governance of the Single European Market, Manchester University Press, 1998, page 57.

[19]. See Wyn Grant, The Common Agricultural Policy, Macmillan, 1997, page 5.

[20]. See D. G. Demekas et al, page 141, The effects of the Common Agricultural Policy of the European Community: a survey of the literature, Journal of Common Market Studies, 1988, Volume 27, Number 2, pages 113-45.

[21]. See D. G. Demekas et al, page 141, The effects of the Common Agricultural Policy of the European Community: a survey of the literature, Journal of Common Market Studies, 1988, Volume 27, Number 2, pages 113-45.

Agriculture, fisheries and services

[22]. For a superb account of the BSE crisis, see Rob Baggott, 'The BSE crisis: public health and the "risk society"', Chapter 4, pages 61-78, in Pat Gray and Paul 't Hart, editors, Public policy disasters in Western Europe, Routledge, 1998. See also Wyn Grant, The Common Agricultural Policy, Macmillan, 1997, pages 123-9, and Desmond Dinan, Ever closer union: an introduction to European integration, Macmillan, 2nd edition, 1999, pages 344-5 and 549-50.

[23]. We are indebted to Dr Richard North, Research Director, EDD Group, for the following section.

[24]. For this paragraph, see US offer of test refused, Guardian, 25 April 2001, page 6.

[25]. See Claus-Peter Hutter et al, The eco-twisters: dossier on the European environment, Green Print, 1995, pages 177-9.

[26]. See Richard Body, Our food, our land: why contemporary farming practices must change, Rider, 1991, pages 93-4 and 292-3.

[27]. Ben Fine, The political economy of diet, health and food policy, Routledge, 1998, page 108.

[28]. On the need to plan agriculture, see Gar Alperovitz and Jeff Faux, Rebuilding America: a blueprint for the new economy, Pantheon Books, 1984, pages 199-201.

[29]. See Double yields, published by SAFE, 1998.

[30]. See Gar Alperovitz and Jeff Faux, Rebuilding America: a blueprint for the new economy, Pantheon Books, 1984, pages 212-23.

[31]. On the CFP, see Ella Ritchie and Anthony Zito, 'The Common Fisheries Policy: a European disaster?' Chapter 9, pages 152-74, in Pat Gray and Paul 't Hart, editors, Public policy disasters in Western Europe, Routledge, 1998. See also Christopher Booker and Richard North, The castle of lies: why Britain must get out of Europe, Duckworth, 1997, 'Worse than a blunder, a crime - the great fish disaster', Chapter 7, pages 77-90.

[32]. Thanks for this whole section to Eric Clements, Save Britain's Fish's

Trades Union Liaison Officer.

[33]. See Charlotte Bretherton and John Vogler, The European Union as a global actor, Routledge, 1999, page 82.

[34]. Martin Walker, Cod swims to oblivion as the EU flounders, Guardian, 3 June 1998.

[35]. See Charles Clover, The end of the line: how overfishing is changing the world and what we eat, Ebury Press, 2005, pages 37-46.

[36]. Paul Brown, The rich inherit the sea, Guardian, 16 October 1998. See also Michael McCarthy, European fishing fleets plundering west African stocks, Independent, 18 March 2002, page 12.

[37]. See Charles Clover, The end of the line: how overfishing is changing the world and what we eat, Ebury Press, 2005, page 45.

[38]. See Charles Clover, The end of the line: how overfishing is changing the world and what we eat, Ebury Press, 2005, pages 12-14 and 265-71.

[39]. See Mike Holden, The Common Fisheries Policy: origin, evaluation and future, Fishing News Books, 1994, page 167.

[40]. See Nicholas Barr, The economics of the welfare state, Stanford University Press, 3rd edition, 1998.

[41]. See the Commission's report COM (2000) 580, 'Services of a General Interest'.

[42]. See Fritz Scharpf, Governing in Europe: effective and democratic, Oxford University Press, 1999, pages 59-60.

[43]. See John Grahl, After Maastricht: a guide to European Monetary Union, Lawrence & Wishart, 1997, page 189.

[44]. See Kim Moody, Workers in a lean world: unions in the international economy, Verso, 1997, pages 15-8.

[45]. See Paul Teague, Economic citizenship in the European Union: employment relations in the new Europe, Routledge, 1999, page 167.

[46]. See Larry Elliott and Charlotte Denny, Scorn for EU pleas on spending, Guardian, 31 January 2002, page 2.

[47]. See Colin Crouch, editor, After the euro: shaping institutions for governance in the wake of European Monetary Union, Oxford University Press, 2000, page 2.

[48]. Euro rules 'stupid', says Prodi, Financial Times, 18 October 2002, page 1.

[49]. For a superb attack on privatisation, see Robert Kuttner, Everything for sale: the virtues and limits of markets, New York: Alfred A. Knopf, 1998, especially pages 98, 273 and 358-60. He also demolished 'Public Choice Theory', the intellectual underpinning of the privatisation mania, see his pages 22-3, 34, 236, 287, 332, 333-42 ('The Market as Anti Democratic Theory') and 346.

[50]. Madsen Pirie, Privatisation: a conceptual framework, Wildwood House, 1988.

[51]. See Allyson Pollock, A new NHS built on debt, Observer, 28 April 2002.

[52]. See Daniel Wincott, page 93, in 'The Court of Justice and the legal system', Chapter 5, pages 84-104, in Laura Cram, Desmond Dinan and Neill Nugent, editors, Developments in the European Union, Macmillan, 1999.

[53]. See Allyson Pollock, NHS plc: the privatisation of our health care, Verso, 2004.

[54]. See Allyson Pollock and David Price, Rewriting the regulations: how the World Trade Organisation could accelerate privatisation in health-care systems, The Lancet, 9 December 2000, Volume 356, Number 9246, page 1995. For a full account, see the whole article, pages 1995-2000.

[55]. Cited Daily Mail, 17 July 1999.

[56]. Editorial, Trading public health for private wealth, The Lancet, 9 December 2000, Volume 356, Number 9246, page 1941.

[57]. Robert Kuttner, Everything for sale: the virtues and limits of markets, New York: Alfred A. Knopf, 1998, page 158. His Chapter 4, pages 110-58 destroys the case for introducing the market into health. See also Gar Alperovitz and Jeff Faux, Rebuilding America: a blueprint for the new economy, Pantheon Books, 1984, pages 205-12: they called for a US NHS. Richard Evans' wonderful book, Death in Hamburg: society and politics in the cholera years, 1830-1910, Clarendon Press, 1987, showed how useless laissez faire policies were in public health. He concluded that the 1892 epidemic "demonstrated, with a graphic and shocking immediacy, the inadequacy of classical liberal political and administrative practice in the face of urban growth and social change." Page 565. Richard Titmuss's famous study, The gift relationship: from human blood to social policy, Allen & Unwin, 1970, proved that in health care altruism worked far better than commercialism.

[58]. On health, see Richard Titmuss, Essays on the welfare state, Unwin, 1958, John Westergaard, Who gets what? The hardening of class inequality in the late 20th century, Polity, 1995, Richard Wilkinson, Unhealthy societies: the afflictions of inequality, Routledge, 1996, and Richard Smith, Unemployment and health, Oxford University Press, 1987.

[59]. On the vital role of health promotion, see Theodore MacDonald, Rethinking health promotion, Routledge, 1998.

[60]. See Desmond Dinan, Ever closer union: an introduction to European integration, Macmillan, 2nd edition, 1999, pages 429-30.

[61]. See Renaud Dehousse, The European Court of Justice: the politics of judicial integration, Macmillan, 1998, page 166.

[62]. See Tamara Hervey, European social law and policy, Longman, 1998, 'Education and training', Chapter 6, pages 109-34.

[63]. See Clive Archer, The European Union: structure and process, Continuum, 3rd edition, 2000, page 95.

[64]. Cited page 113, Adrian Hilton, The principality and power of Europe: Britain and the emerging Holy European Empire, Dorchester House, 2nd

edition, 2000.

[65]. Budget speech, Hansard, 2 July 1997, cited page 157, Adrian Hilton, The principality and power of Europe: Britain and the Holy European Empire, Dorchester House, 2nd edition, 2000.

[66]. George Ross, pages 177-8, in 'European integration and globalization', Chapter 10, pages 164-83, in Roland Axtmann, editor, Globalization and Europe: theoretical and empirical investigations, Pinter, 1998.

[67]. See Paul Teague, Economic citizenship in the European Union: employment relations in the new Europe, Routledge, 1999, page 165.

[68]. See Ben Daniels, The euro, UNIFI, 2001, page 31.

Chapter 8: Yes to independence and sovereignty – out of the EU!

1: Sovereignty or dependence?

2: The Constitution for Europe

3: The Constitution campaign

4: An independent Britain

*   "Sovereignty did matter! Countries which had it would grow faster than countries which did not." (Economic historian Shahid Alam)

*   "The EU Constitution is the birth certificate of the United States of Europe." (Germany's Minister for Europe, Hans Martin Bury)

1: Sovereignty or dependence?

Opposing the euro is not xenophobic, although the EU's rulers say that it is, just as the British Empire's rulers always called national liberation movements xenophobic. The Empire's rulers also described as 'little Englanders' those who rightly opposed their world-ranging greed and wars. Now the EU's rulers describe as 'little Englanders' those who oppose the empire building of their EU state.

Asserting sovereignty is the root of wisdom for a country, just as joining a trade union is for workers. For each it is the birth of dignity; for neither is it an end in itself. What matters is what you do with it. We have been careless of our inheritance so now both trade unionism and British sovereignty are under attack. To assert and fight for the sovereignty of Britain should be as natural to workers as joining a trade union. Both have the same aim: to keep our freedom. Asserting our right to decide what happens in Britain parallels asserting the right to have a say in our wages and conditions of work. Nobody has a right to interfere in Britain's affairs, any more than we have a right to interfere in any other country's affairs.

How should Europe's nations behave to each other? The principles of peaceful coexistence should govern relations between all nations - respect for other nations' sovereignty, economic independence and territorial integrity, non-interference in their internal affairs, non-aggression, economic relations of equality and mutual benefit, and settling disputes by negotiation. The basis of good foreign policy is respect for the equal sovereignty of every nation, that all nations have the right to self-determination. As in Charles de Gaulle's idea of the Europe of the Nations, each nation should take its own decisions and make its own relations with other countries.[1]

Trade unions have always worked for international cooperation, so they have been tempted by the EU claim that it is creating a new international brotherhood of man. But the EU is really creating a state, whereby previously independent countries become subordinate parts of a larger whole. Similarly, EMU is not a simple, self-contained economic matter: its economic guise covers (not very well!) a political agenda. Just as, for an individual, taking out a loan does not mean giving up all control over your own affairs, so for a country making a decision about money should not mean losing all control over the currency. Living amicably with your neighbours does not mean giving them either your front door key or access to your bank account. Nations, like individuals, should always read the small print.[2]

EU supporters usually mentioned the issue of sovereignty only to dismiss it quickly. Some said that Britain would lose its sovereignty as the EU proceeded, but only in the distant future. Others said that we would lose our sovereignty soon, but that it did not matter because we would get something better - pooled sovereignty, meaning that we would lose control over our own country but gain a small measure of control over others. What sort of deal is that? Consider it in relation to trade union membership. It would be like swapping union membership for membership in, say, an International Fellowship for Social Advance. The former is limited in scope, specific and grounded in real life. The latter is vast in scope, vaguely impressive and (of course) fictitious. Equally fictitious is the idea of pooling national sovereignty. As Robert Worcester put it, "Shared sovereignty is lost sovereignty in my view."[3]

Our sovereignty is for us to use to achieve economic self-reliance, political independence, strategic autonomy and constitutional democracy. What democracy we have is tied to and depends upon nation-states. As Douglas Jay wrote, "if you ... join supranational (as opposed to international) institutions, you involve yourself in an inescapable dilemma. If the supranational authority responsible for decision and for legislation is not accountable to, and representative of, the people so governed, then you are in breach of the most fundamental of democratic principles: that people should not be coerced by laws or decisions made by a body which they had no part, even indirect, in selecting. On the other hand, so far as you make the legislative authority elected by, and responsible to, an electorate outside your own country, then you so far cease to be an independent sovereign state. With a supranational authority, that dilemma is inexorable. With an international body, it does not arise. That was, and is, the kernel of the political choice confronting the UK by the EC in its present form as designed by Monnet and his followers."[4]

The people are the source of all legitimate authority. But only a sovereign people can secure a sovereign nation. The people should be really running society for it to be an independent country. The EU claims to be democratic, but doesn't democracy mean reflecting people's wishes, that society goes where people want it to go? The EU cannot allow us either democracy or sovereignty. Jacques Santer said, "There will be monetary union and Britain will be a member", but the decision on whether we joined was for us, not him.[5] The EU's sanctification of its treaties is a triumph of dogma over experience, of theory over practice, of the word over life. The British experience, on the other hand, is that no decision is irreversible; the people can always repeal any acts or treaties; we can neither bind, nor be bound by, future governments; we can always overrule the executive; and we can always choose a better road.

The trade union movement has always worked for democracy, for the maximum accountability in the workplace and political spheres. British history shows that trade unions were always at the forefront of struggles to extend the franchise so that everyone of 18 and over, regardless of gender or wealth, can vote in general elections for a parliament of their choice and in local elections for local government.

National sovereignty is vital. No country run from outside ever amounted to anything. Sovereignty has been one of the great dynamics of human development - if a country does not run its own affairs, those who control it prioritise their own interests, at the expense of the country's interests. Losing economic sovereignty to international capital markets denies citizens the right to have their choices on economic policy implemented.[6] A single EU state would weaken democratic constraints on market forces.[7]

The economy is the root of sovereignty. As the economic historian Shahid Alam wrote, "Sovereignty did matter! Countries which had it would grow faster than countries which did not. The logic of it is simple. Colonization of lagging countries led, via forced integration, to the loss of manufactures, a shrinking comparative advantage in primary production, and the displacement of indigenous capital, skills and enterprises; it also led to monopolization and direct appropriation of their resources. Only sovereign lagging countries - free to structure their integration into the world economy - could avoid or minimize the adverse consequences of integration. Ergo, loss of sovereignty retarded economic growth. ... In the long run, sovereign countries will structure their international relations to develop manufactures and indigenous capital, enterprises and technological capabilities; they will impose at the outset, or gradually, policies that regulate the entry of imports and foreign capital, labor and enterprises. On the other hand, the quasi-colonies and colonies will implement policies which facilitate the free entry of imports and foreign factors; the establishment of foreign monopolies over their markets; and direct expropriation of their resources. These asymmetries ensure that loss of sovereignty will produce lower levels of industrialisation, lower levels of productivity in the subsistence sector, lower levels of human capital, lower rates of taxation and public expenditure and, finally, lower growth rates of per capita income."[8] He summarised, "All other things remaining the same, the loss of sovereignty retarded industrialisation, human capital formation and economic growth. ... The results showed a strong positive correlation between sovereignty and industrialisation."[9]

Economic sovereignty works in practice. For instance, India and China avoided the economic disaster of 1997-98 largely because they had not opened up their money markets. China also had a big trade surplus and massive reserves, of more than $100 billion, so it had avoided the dependence on short-term foreign loans to finance a deficit which had afflicted Indonesia, Malaysia, Thailand, the Philippines and South Korea.[10]

Many Latin American countries gave up their economic sovereignty to the USA and suffered the consequences. For instance, in 1998 Argentina pegged its peso so tightly to the dollar that the dollar became legal tender and its bank became an 'Exchange Board' with no independent policy. By 2002, the country was bereft of industry, its agriculture failing and its people unemployed and desperate.

Keynes held that economic sovereignty was vital; that national authorities should control the domestic rate of interest and the currency so that the country could pursue full employment as the key domestic economic goal. To achieve full employment, governments had to socialise investment, control money markets to reduce deflationary pressure, control imports through state trading agreements and adopt a steady cheap money policy for investment. He showed how full employment reduced the dangers of international conflict. "If nations can learn to provide themselves with full employment by their domestic policy there need be no important economic forces calculated to set the interests of one country against that of its neighbours."

He said in 1944, "We are determined that, in future, the external value of sterling shall conform to its internal value as set by our own domestic policies, and not the other way round. Secondly, we intend to retain control of our domestic rate of interest, so that we can keep it as low as suits our own purposes, without interference from the ebb and flow of international capital movements or flights of hot money. Thirdly, whilst we intend to prevent inflation at home, we will not accept deflation at the dictate of influences from outside."[11]

Current disillusion with politics results from the way our rulers have emptied our system of democratic content. Parliamentary democracy thwarts real democracy. It was designed to prevent, not enable, the people to rule and has led to turnabout despotisms by party leaders. A system that delivered 22 years of Thatcherism, when only a minority of people ever voted for it, does not deserve popular support. As a result, the number of people who believed that 'the system works well' fell from 48% in 1973 to just 22% in 1995.

Without economic sovereignty, what have we got? One million industrial jobs have gone since 1997. Growth is lower than under Major: between 1990 and 1997 it averaged 3.2% a year, since 1997, 2.4%, between 2000 and 2004, 2.3%. How do we rebuild industry when universities have closed 46 engineering departments, 28 physics departments and 28 chemistry departments since 1996?

Unemployment is officially 1.5 million, intolerably high. 8 million people are classed as either unemployed or as having withdrawn from job search (economically inactive), in 2005, up by 124,000 since 2003. The economic inactivity rate for 16-17 year olds rose from 40% in 1997 to 47% in 2003. 2.7 million people are on incapacity benefit, a threefold increase since 1990, costing £16 billion a year.

Under Major, productivity rose 2.4% a year, under Blair 1.4%. We have less capital invested per worker than in France, the USA and

Germany, so output per hour worked is 25% higher in France, 16% higher in the USA and 8% higher in Germany.

Investment in Britain's manufacturing industry is just 1.3% of Gross Domestic Product, the lowest level since the Office for National Statistics' series on business investment started in 1965. Corporate investment was 11% of GDP in 1997, 9.5% in 2004. Investment is 13.4% lower than the average of the G8 countries. Investment in R&D was 2.2% of national income in 1995, 1.8% now. Labour has cut corporation tax and taxes on shares and property, and still the capitalists do not invest in Britain.

They have other priorities, which the government has done nothing to stem. Chief Executive Officers give themselves vast salary increases (up by 16% in 2004), golden handshakes, golden hellos, bonuses unrelated to performance, huge pensions and offshore tax havens. To nobody's surprise, income inequality and wealth inequality have risen since 1997.

A fifth of job vacancies, 135,000, are unfilled, due to skills shortages. Eight million people still lack basic skills. Only 30% of British workers have craft, skilled craft or vocational qualifications compared to 65% in Germany and 51% in France. Fewer than 25% of young workers take up places on apprenticeship schemes compared to more than 60% in Germany. 252,900 people started on work-based learning in 1999/2000, just 239,300 in 2002/2003. One million young people are not in education, training or employment.

Even with two incomes, households have to eat into their savings and borrow more just to stay afloat. Personal savings are falling: in 2003, households saved just 4.8% of their disposable income, in 1997, 9.4%. Household debt is a colossal £1 trillion. In 1997 taxation took 35.4% of national income, now it takes 36.3%. Taxes have risen faster than in any other European country.

The public sector deficit has risen from £25 billion in 2002 to £36 billion in 2003 and £34 billion last year. Public borrowing will rise by £102 billion more than Brown forecast over the next five years. The public debt incurred thanks to the Private Finance Initiatives is £35.5 billion.

What do the British people want? Most of us want to keep the pound and want import controls to protect our economy. Most of us believe that Britain, not the EU, should decide our policies on taxes, health, welfare, education, culture, the law, immigration, defence, rights at work and agricultural production. Most people want to keep passport controls between EU countries. Most of us want to keep Britain united and oppose separatism.[12] People want to control the money markets (some who supported the euro did so in the optimistic hope that the euro would control these markets). People want to live in a society based on full employment, a society that aims to raise living standards. No parliamentary party represents these aspirations.

We need to put all our people to work. This can be done with the political will. It may cost £100,000 to create a job, but how much does it cost not to? How much does it cost to keep five million workers unemployed and underemployed? We have the money anyway: if we can auction off mobile phone licences once, we can do it again. Come to that, why auction them off at all? Let's run the thing ourselves, and keep and use all the revenue that would bring.

We need to invest in the future. We can show that American, Japanese and German companies are not the only ones that can develop new industries and rebuild old ones. With the same investment in research and development we can match their achievements. We are one of the largest economies on the planet, with a diverse range of trading arrangements throughout the world and with most of our GDP involved in supplying the domestic or world markets. Our scientists, technicians and engineers remain at the forefront of many of the most advanced new industries, whether biogenetics or e-commerce. We have a dearth of opportunities to apply our discoveries and too many unskilled workers living in poverty.

We need to get our hands on our own money, and we need to control its investment. Pensions are deferred wages, and pension funds alone are enough to rebuild substantial sections of British industry. Add to that our ability to generate more savings, and dead capital can be brought to life.

We need to stop them running away with the family silver. Thatcher's first act was to end exchange controls, allowing capital to be freely removed from Britain (using the argument that this would allow it freely to flow in too). We can reimpose these controls and ensure that profits made in Britain stay in Britain. We could also alter the monetarist brief given to the Bank of England and the consequent high rate of the pound. We could even stop the irresponsible speculation with our gold reserves that Brown started, and by refusing to sign up to the euro we would retain our gold reserves rather than give them all away. We could reimpose import controls and stop the undercutting and devastation of our staple industries.

Except of course we could not reimpose these controls, or do a lot of other things we need to do, while we remain members of the European Union. So we need to leave the EU.

2: The Constitution for Europe

The EU's leaders have long wanted a single constitution for Europe. They used the Charter of Fundamental Rights to prepare the way. In September 2000, Antonio Vitorino, the Justice and Home Affairs Commissioner, said that the Charter "will mark a turning point in the integration of Europe, moving it away from the essentially economic logic of its origins to become a real political union."[13] By February 2002, the Blair government backed making the Charter mandatory and supported the proposed Constitution.[14]

To force through its agenda, the EU set up a Convention on the Future of Europe, chaired by Valery Giscard d'Estaing. Giuliano Amato, Italian Prime Minister and Vice-President of the Convention, said, "In Europe one needs to act 'as if' – as if what was wanted was little, in order to obtain much, as if States were to remain sovereign to convince them to concede sovereignty … The Commission in Brussels, for example, should act as if it were a technical instrument, in order to be able to be treated as a government. And so on by disguise and subterfuge."[15]

Gisela Stuart, a Labour MP whom the government appointed to serve on this Convention, noted, "The Convention was riddled with imperfections and moulded by a largely unaccountable political elite set on a particular outcome from the very start."

Blair had no mandate to sign the 'Treaty establishing a Constitution for Europe'. None of the proposed changes ever appeared in any party's manifesto. No MP had any right to vote for this Treaty. The Act ratifying the Constitution, authorising the government to sign this Treaty on our behalf, was ultra vires. A Constitution is no ordinary Treaty, an agreement between sovereign governments. It is a set of rules for an organisation, in this case a supranational body that is giving itself new powers.[16] Our sovereign national rights are not Parliament's to give away.

The Constitution would

1. ... set up a single new European state, ending the separate independent existence of its member states. Article IV-437 says, "This Treaty establishing a Constitution for Europe shall repeal the Treaty establishing the European Community [the Treaty of Rome], the Treaty on European Union [the Maastricht Treaty] and ... the acts and treaties which have supplemented and amended them [the Nice and Amsterdam Treaties]." So it is not 'consolidating', 'building on' or 'tidying up' the existing Treaties. It is repealing them all. It is establishing a new, different EU. As Article I-1 says, "this Constitution establishes the European Union." The EU would no longer be based on treaties agreed by sovereign member states. It would become a supra-national state based on its own Constitution (Article I-1). The Constitution would make the EU the sole sovereign legal and political power, the sole, independent source of all legal authority in all the member countries.[17] This was new - all the EU's earlier Treaties left sovereignty in the hands of 'the High Contracting Parties'; that is, the member nations were each the sole source of all legal authority in their countries.

Under 'the principle of conferral' (Article I-11), the last exercise by states of their sovereign independent powers would be to give these powers to the Union. If the Constitution were put in place, no future government would be able to amend it because we would all be bound by international treaty to abide by it. This is how the states of Germany, the USA, Canada and Australia were built. Members would have to change their national Constitutions to transfer sovereignty to the EU. Member states would be reduced to provinces of the EU state.

If states ratified the Constitution, they would formally strip themselves of their constitutional sovereignty as independent nation states and subordinate themselves to the authority of a supranational entity that has all the attributes of a state save two, military and taxation powers. Its proponents are confident that the EU will soon get these two. Prodi said, "After 2006 no more decisions can be taken by unanimity."[18]

Article I-6 says, "The Constitution and laws adopted by the institutions of the Union in exercising competences conferred on it shall have primacy over the laws of the Member States." For the first time, an EU Treaty states that the EU shall have primacy over all the national, including constitutional, laws of member states. Previously, only the European Court of Justice had asserted the primacy of EU law.

For the first time the EU would have legal personality to make legal agreements in its own right (Article I-7), which Romano Prodi describes as a 'gigantic leap forward'. We would no longer be just notional citizens of an EU that has no legal personality or standing. If we ratified the Constitution, we would become citizens of the EU state and our Union citizenship would become our primary citizenship and obligation. We would owe the EU state the first duty of citizenship, to obey one's state's laws. Article I-10 says, "Every member of a Member State shall be a citizen of the Union ... citizens of the Union shall enjoy the rights and be subject to the duties provided for in the Constitution."

2. ... create a full-time EU President (Article I-22) with a two and a half year term of office, renewable once, who would be far more powerful than the existing six-monthly rotating Council president. The Council, in secret, would appoint the President who would be the Union's head of state, with a leading role in the state's foreign policy. The Commission President would be responsible for the state's internal policy.

The Commission President and the Council jointly appoint all the other Commissioners. The Commission is inherently undemocratic – how many of us would have chosen Peter Mandelson as a Commissioner? Membership of the Commission would be rotating and the number of Commissioners would be a third less than the number of member states. So member states would have no representative for five years of every 15.

The unelected Commission would keep its monopoly as the only source of law (Article I-26) and would have that power extended to important new policy areas (Article I-26.2). The European Parliament would still be unable to initiate any laws. The Constitution gives the Commissioners more powers to "provide the Union with the necessary impetus for its development and shall define the general political directions and priorities thereof." The Commissioners, dominated by the Chief Executive Officers of multinational corporations through the European Roundtable of Industrialists, would run the EU in the EU's interests, overriding national interests.

The 25-member Council of Ministers, irremovable as a group, would get increased powers to make EU laws on the basis of the Commission's proposals (Article I-23). Article I-18, the 'flexibility' clause, empowers the Council of Ministers to 'adopt the appropriate measures' where the Council decides that its existing powers under the Constitution are inadequate. The Constitution's Article IV-444, the so-called passerelle or escalator clause, would give the Council new powers to change the Treaty with no need of new Treaties and without recourse to national governments. So the EU could end remaining national vetoes for the many policy areas set out in Part III of the Constitution.

National parliaments, far from having a 'greater role', could only register concerns about EU proposals. They can propose amendments to laws being considered by the Council, but would remain unable to impose these amendments on either the Council or the Commission. The 'emergency brake' means only a brief delay before the EU enforces laws that we could not veto. If we ratified the Constitution, we would be subjecting ourselves to a new executive power, accountable to nobody, under a new, unelected President, more like Charles I's government than anything seen since in Britain.

3. ... give the EU the power to 'define and implement' a single foreign, security and defence policy (Article I-12). Article I-15 creates this single policy, overriding the policies of individual countries: "1. The Union's competence in matters of common foreign and security policy shall cover all areas of foreign policy and all questions relating to the Union's security, including the progressive framing of a common defence policy, which might lead to a common defence. 2. Member States shall actively and unreservedly support the Union's common foreign and security policy in a spirit of loyalty and mutual solidarity and shall comply with the acts adopted by the Union in this area. They shall refrain from action contrary to the Union's interests or likely to impair its effectiveness." The Commission

and the Council would jointly appoint an EU Foreign Minister, with a five-year term of office, responsible for conducting this policy (Article I-28). The EU has already started creating a new European External Action Service (diplomatic corps). Another escalator clause, Article I-40.7, allows a shift from unanimity to majority voting on the CSFP without national parliaments having a veto.

The EU is creating a single European army 'to deal with trouble spots in and around Europe and in the rest of the world', as the Constitution says, an open avowal that EU foreign policy would be aggressive. Yet Blair wrote in The Times, "There is no such concept called a European army." (13 October 2003). All member states would have to provide military resources to the EU and increase their military spending. This single EU army would raise the tensions between the three large trading blocs over access to dwindling mineral resources and oil and gas pipelines, and between the EU and the countries of Asia and Africa.

4. ... remove our elected government's right to make laws unless the EU decides not to. The EU would have exclusive competences over the movements of capital, goods, services and persons, including a common asylum and immigration policy, over commercial policies, including international agreements, over competition policy for the single market, over monetary policy for the eurozone, and over fisheries.

Article I-12 says, "The Member States shall exercise their competences to the extent that the Union has not exercised, or has decided to cease exercising, its competence." In every area, we would only be allowed to make decisions where the EU chose not to. Member states' rights are residual and on sufferance.

Article I-14 would forbid our elected government to make laws in 'shared competence' areas which would be subject to Qualified Majority Voting. These include the single market, social policy, communications networks, industrial policy, R&D, space exploration, policing, economic and social cohesion, regional aid, agriculture and fisheries, environment, consumer protection, transport, energy, 'freedom, security and justice', and 'common safety concerns in public health matters'.

This would allow Brussels to control our oil and gas reserves, 90% of the total in the EU. Under the Constitution the EU could impose its rules on energy to create an EU oil reserve, allowing it to ration our oil EU-wide. Thirty years after Heath gave away our fisheries, and having virtually finished off our coal industry, Blair was scheming to give away our energy reserves.

Article I-17 gives the EU the power to take 'supporting, co-ordinating or complementary action' in a further range of loosely-defined areas including the 'protection and improvement of human health', industry, culture, education, youth, sport, vocational training, 'civil protection' and 'administrative co-operation'. If we ratified the Constitution, we would lose the power to make our own laws.

5. ... give the EU new powers to 'co-ordinate' all its policies (Article I-1), especially its economic, employment and social policies (Article I-15). It would make the basic principle of laissez-faire - free competition across national borders on the basis of free movement of capital, goods, services and labour - into a Constitutional obligation (Articles I-3 and 4, Articles III-130, 156, 166 and 167). The Constitution refers to 'the market' 92 times. It puts into words the EU's capitalist reality, its overriding commitment to the 'free market' earlier spelt out in the Thatcher-inspired Maastricht Treaty.

Article I-3 says, "The Member States and the Union shall [not 'may'] act in accordance with the principles of an open market economy with free competition." So if we decided that we wanted to renationalise our rail industry, the ECJ could deem this a breach of our Constitutional obligation to conduct 'an open market economy with free competition'.

Article III-156 decrees that there shall be no control over the movements of capital either within the EU or between the EU and the rest of the world - even though such controls can serve the public interest. The Constitution forbids social controls on capital. It forbids public enterprises and state aid to serve national social purposes (Articles III-161, 162, 166 and 167).

The European Central Bank's sole brief in setting interest rates and controlling the eurozone's money supply is to ensure price stability, not rebuild industry, achieve economic growth or create full employment (Article III-185). The EU would decide which countries would have which industries, which would stop us working as an independent economy.

If we ratified the Constitution, we would be accepting the Constitutional obligation to adopt the euro. Article I-8 says, "The currency of the Union shall be the euro." Our 'opt-out' from the euro has mysteriously vanished. The Protocol on the Euro-Group (No. 12) – an integral part of the Treaty – refers to currencies in the EU 'pending the euro becoming the currency of all Member States of the Union'.

Article III-147 allows the EU to enforce 'liberalisation' and privatisation of public services including health, education, social services, housing, water, and cultural services. It says, "A European framework law shall establish the measures in order to achieve the liberalisation of a specific service." Article III-148 says, "The Member States shall endeavour to undertake liberalisation of services beyond the extent required by the European framework laws adopted pursuant to Article III-147(1), if their general economic situation and situation of the economic sector concerned so permit. To this end, the Commission shall make recommendations to the Member State concerned."

Article II-96, 'Access to services of general interest within the limits of Union law', says, "The Union recognises and respects access to services of general economic interest as provided for in national laws and practices, in accordance with the Constitution, in order to promote the social and territorial cohesion of the Union."

Article III-122 gives the EU new powers to lay down the 'economic and financial' principles and conditions under which 'services of general economic interest' are provided 'in compliance with the Constitution' by for example the Bolkestein Directive on Services. The drafters of the Constitution rejected the use of the term 'public services', because this would create a presumption in favour of services being provided by the public sector. They also rejected proposals to call them 'services of general interest' and 'services of general economic and social interest'.

Article III-166 gives the EU the power to decide by majority vote what counts as a public service and which areas of public education and health services could be opened to private sector competition.

"1. In the case of public undertakings and undertakings to which Member States grant special or exclusive rights, Member States shall neither enact nor maintain in force any measure contrary to the Constitution, in particular Article I-4(2) and Articles III-161 to III-169.

2. Undertakings entrusted with the operation of services of general economic interest or having the character of an income-producing monopoly shall be subject to the provisions of the Constitution, in particular to the rules on competition, insofar as the application of such provisions does not obstruct the performance, in law or in fact, of the particular tasks assigned to them. The development of trade must not be affected to such an extent as would be contrary to the Union's interests."

Article III-210 lists the almost unlimited areas of social policy where the EU would have the right to 'support and complement' the activities of member states. Article III-315 gives the Trade Commissioner more power to conclude deals with other countries which could impose liberalisation of their health, education and social services.

Article II-88 provides that workers have rights only 'in accordance with Union law and national laws and practices'. This makes Thatcher's anti-union legislation a constitutional obligation. We can expect no employment or trade union laws meeting our aspirations. As Jack Straw told the CBI, "We will insist that … the Charter of Fundamental Rights creates no new rights under national law, so as not to upset the balance of Britain's industrial relations policy." EU employment laws have not prevented the unemployment of 30 million European workers.

The Constitution does not include key trade union demands for the right to work, the right to take secondary industrial action, the application of employment rights from day one in all workplaces or rights to housing, free education and free health care. Our National Health Service free at the point of need is not compatible with the EU model, as Brussels has repeatedly said. If we ratified the Constitution, we would lose our economic independence.

6. … abolish 69 national vetoes, greatly increasing the EU's powers. The Nice Treaty transferred 35 policy powers, the Treaty of Amsterdam 19. The EU is not about sharing or cooperation between sovereign governments. It is supranational not inter-governmental. The dividing line is the veto. Where there are vetoes, there is inter-governmentalism. Without vetoes, there is only a supranational state beyond the control of governments or peoples. Prodi said on 19 December 1999, "As long as the veto exists, the

EU will be like a soldier trying to march around with a ball and chain around its leg." The EU wants to abolish every veto.

Nation states, governments and parliaments could be left in place - but they would be subordinated to a supranational state in a slow-motion coup d'etat, a rolling programme towards 'ever closer union' that the Treaty of Rome called for and that the Constitution reaffirmed. If we ratified the Constitution, the EU would decide for us that we must do whatever its majority decided.

7. ... allow movement towards a criminal justice system through harmonisation of national laws and mutual recognition of judicial and extra-judicial decisions (Article I-42) and the power to set common definitions of criminal offences and sanctions (Article III-271). The Constitution strengthens the role of Eurojust from 'co-ordination' of criminal prosecutions to their 'initiation' and permits the extension of its 'structure, operation, field of action and tasks' (Article III-273). An EU Public Prosecutor's Office is proposed (Article III-274). Article III-276 gives the EU the right to extend the powers of the rapidly-expanding police force, Europol, whose officers are immune from criminal prosecution.

Most EU members lack habeas corpus (the right to be brought before a judge to have your detention legally and publicly justified), the presumption of innocence, single jeopardy, the right to silence and trial by jury. Now the EU wants to impose on us this system (corpus juris), its own prosecution service and its mode of policing. Under the European arrest warrant, prosecuting authorities from any EU member country can order the arrest of a citizen of any other EU country. Under the Constitution, the EU takes the power of extradition over British citizens. If we ratified the Constitution, we would lose our traditional rights under the rule of law.

8. ... includes the Charter of Fundamental Rights, making it legally binding on member states and their citizens. Article II-112 sinisterly allows 'limitations' of all rights 'if they are necessary and genuinely meet objectives of general interest recognised by the Union'. Similarly, the constitution of Germany's Weimar Republic in the 1920s gave its President the powers to suspend any or all individual rights if public safety and order was seriously disturbed or endangered. This proved an irresistible temptation to every subsequent German government. Eventually Hitler persuaded President

von Hindenburg to suspend all such rights permanently. Article II-114 forbids any political campaigning to reverse any aspects of the Charter. The Charter, far from extending, or even protecting, our rights, would reduce them. No people would be able to change their rights without permission from the EU state.

This would, for instance, allow the EU to block anti-EU policies, as Joschka Fischer recommended in March 2000, "We and our partners cannot accept that a party whose politics are directed against Europe can get into a position where it can block the further integration of Europe."[19]

It could also justify the European Commission's attempts to silence critics. In 1999, it tried to silence Bernard Connolly, who had written 'The Rotten Heart of Europe', a stinging critique of EMU, after serving from 1989 to 1996 as head of the Commission's unit for 'EMS, National and Community Monetary Policies' in Brussels. The ECJ's lower court, the Court of First Instance, ruled then that 'the general interest of the Communities' overrode the right to freedom of speech. On 19 October 2000, the ECJ's Advocate General argued - in Case C-274/99 P - that political criticism of the EU was akin to blasphemy and so could be legally limited. He ruled that any EU governing body could legitimately limit any 'fundamental right' in order to protect its reputation.

A fixed Constitution is reactionary in nature. Under the USA's written Constitution, the Supreme Court can only make its judgements by harking back to the Founding Fathers' presumed intentions and to presumptions of what they would have thought if they had to face today's circumstances. 1776's standards of thought determine today's judgements.

Giving the EU a human rights competence would be a big step towards a 'harmonized' legal system in which EU members would become provinces of an EU state. The historical experience of federations showed that a single standard of human rights enforced by a Supreme Court is a powerful weapon in subordinating national and local courts and constitutions to central rule. It would mean a huge increase in the judicial power of the EU and its Court. These institutions, supported by the planned EU army, could prevail over elected national authorities. The Constitution would transfer power from national parliaments to unaccountable judges. The European Court of Justice would become our Supreme Court and the repository of sovereignty. If we ratified the Constitution, we the British people would no longer have sovereignty over our own affairs.

9. ... give all these new powers to the EU fundamentally altering its nature and hugely centralising the powers of the EU oligarchy, while setting in stone the EU's current undemocratic structure. The unelected European Commission would keep the sole right to propose new EU laws (Article I-26). The European Central Bank would remain unaccountable since MEPs, EU officials and national governments are obliged 'not to seek to influence the ... European Central Bank' (Article III-188).

The Constitution would end our democracy, because the EU is intrinsically undemocratic, since it opposes all national, popular and democratic interests. The Constitution is all too similar to Bismarck's 1871 Constitution for the German Reich. Under both Constitutions, the Parliament has no power to elect or dismiss the government. The powers to declare war and to run the army are reserved to the executive. Government ministers are beholden to the executive not to the people or to Parliament.

Almost everybody agrees that this Constitution is of extraordinary importance. German Foreign Minister Joschka Fischer said that the Treaty was 'anything but minimalistic ... it creates the prerequisites for the completion of the unity of Europe' and, "This is the most important treaty since the formation of the European Economic Community." He also said, "Creating a single European State bound by one European Constitution is the decisive task of our time."[20] Prodi said, "The Single Market was the theme of the 80s; the single currency was the theme of the 90s; we must now face the difficult task of moving towards a single economic and political unity."

Former Italian PM Lamberto Dini said, "The Constitution is not just an intellectual exercise. It will quickly change people's lives." Spanish Foreign Minister Miguel Angel Moratinos said, "Does accepting the European Constitution mean a surrender of Member States' sovereignty? Absolutely ... we are witnessing the last remnants of national politics." Former Spanish Foreign Minister Ana Palacio said, "This is a legal revolution without precedent." Italian Foreign Minister Franco Frattini said that the Constitution is 'a historic step in the integration process'. French Foreign

Minister Dominique de Villepin said it created 'a new political age'. Its supporters said, "A Constitution will foster clarity and truth by putting an end to the fiction of the abiding intact sovereignty of the member states."

Guy Verhofstadt, the Belgian Prime Minister, said, "The Constitution is the capstone of a European Federal State." He also said that some countries "want an inter-governmental Europe; others, like us, want a federal Europe. We have to choose, once and for all." Germany's Minister for Europe, Hans Martin Bury, said, "The EU Constitution is the birth certificate of the United States of Europe."[21]

Giscard d'Estaing said, "Our Constitution cannot be reduced to a mere treaty for co-operation between governments. Anyone who has not yet grasped this fact deserves to wear the dunce's cap." He also said, "It wasn't worth creating a negative commotion with the British. I rewrote my text with the word federal replaced by communautaire, which means exactly the same thing."[22]

Roger Liddle, Blair's special advisor on Europe for seven years, said that the Constitution would hand over 'more and more' powers to Brussels. Peter Hain said on 22 March 2003, "Our task is nothing less than the creation of a new constitutional order for a new united Europe" and on 1 April, "I am not saying it has no substantial constitutional significance, of course it will have." Hain also reported that Blair had said, "The outcome of the convention is absolutely fundamental. It will define the relationship between Britain and the rest of Europe, the prospects for the euro, and it would last for generations. He said it was more important than Iraq." But by May 2003, Hain had shifted to saying, "This is more of a tidying-up exercise."

Accepting the Constitution would bind the hands of all later governments, contradicting Britain's tradition of sovereignty that no parliament can bind the hands of its successor. This revolutionary idea has no parallel in any continental country's constitution. In the definitive case of Bradford v. the Attorney General, Lord Justice Sir Robert Megarry ruled, "The Courts of England hold it as a matter of law, that Parliament is omnipotent in all things save the power to destroy its own omnipotence." Parliament is not allowed to cede sovereignty to a source of power and authority outside Britain, or beyond the British people. John Locke wrote of parliament's power, "It being but a delegative Power from the People, those who have it cannot pass it over to others."

But what happens if parliament chooses to pass this power to others? We cannot now rely on parliament to defend our sovereignty. Ever since we joined the EEC, it has failed to defend its own powers against the EU. By voting for the Constitution it has committed suicide as an independent legislature – but we must not let it drag us down with it. We only ever lent it its powers. Britain's sovereignty, the last word, belongs to the British nation. When Parliament betrays Britain, we the omnipotent people must retrieve our power from parliament and sovereignly decide to save Britain.

What were we doing about the EU's unprecedented attack on our democracy and sovereignty? We have done all too little, as yet. We have indeed increasingly opposed the EU in our trade unions and in the country at large: every poll has shown at least a 2-to-1 opposition to the EU and all its works. But if our response stays passive, the EU and its quislings will get their way.

Will the British working class survive as an independent, sovereign and democratic nation? The Constitution for Europe is the biggest threat to our independence and democracy.

3: The Constitution campaign

The vast majority of the British working class consistently demanded a referendum on the EU Constitution so that we could vote against it. Blair, opposing this, was isolated and desperate. Our class won an important victory by forcing him to concede a referendum.

The government's European Union Act started the government campaign to get us to accept the Constitution. The Act did not set a date for the referendum or even indicate when it might be held. This is important because until the date is set the government, EU bodies and campaign organisations can spend as much as they want. This is one reason why the government is delaying announcing the date for the referendum.

The proposed referendum question is, "Should the United

Kingdom approve the Treaty establishing a Constitution for the European Union?" This only presents one option and it asks us to 'approve' the treaty. The Electoral Commission's guidelines for a fair question warned against using this word, "Words such as 'new' and 'approve' may in some instances imply that something is a positive concept."

The referendum question is about 'the Treaty establishing a Constitution for the European Union' when the Treaty's real title is 'the Treaty establishing a Constitution for Europe'. The title in the question implies that the Treaty merely creates a body of rules for the existing EU. The Treaty's real title implies that the Treaty is creating a constitution for Britain as part of the new state of Europe. By contrast, the question put to Dutch voters in their 1 June 2005 referendum was - "Are you for or against the Netherlands agreeing to the treaty establishing a Constitution for Europe?" This presented both options, avoided using loaded words and got the title right.

Its European Union Act allowed the government to combine the referendum with another vote, for example with the local elections due in May 2006. The Electoral Commission recommended against this, saying, "We believe that referenda on fundamental issues of national importance should be considered in isolation. Cross-party campaigning on a fundamental referendum could cause significant confusion amongst the electorate if combined with normal party election campaigning. There is a risk that the dominance of the referendum issue would influence other polls to an extent that may compromise the electorate's will in those other polls."

The government has created a team at the Foreign and Commonwealth Office to promote the Constitution. Fourteen civil servants are working full-time on the FCO's 'EU Constitution Team' with a budget of £613,000. Staffing and spending are expected to increase as the referendum draws closer. Their remit covers 'policy on the EU Constitutional Treaty' and 'communications work'. The government admitted that civil servants would police themselves on the neutrality of the information they provide in the referendum campaign and that the only way to complain would be to seek a judicial review. Denis MacShane said that the government would ensure that its publicity would be 'objective [and] explanatory' but insisted that it would also 'be in line with and support Government policy'.

The government also appointed a 'partnership marketing' agency, Iris, and aimed to appoint an 'e-communications' agency too. The contract would cost a six-figure sum, on top of the £40,000 initial fee already paid to Geronimo PR to promote the Constitution.

Early in 2005, the European Commission announced that it was going to spend eight million euros on information campaigns on the Constitution. The Commission has two different funds. Five million euros would be spent according to member states' populations, so Germany would get around 900,000 euros while Malta would get about 5,000. In a 'second wave', three million euros would go to member states according to the Commission's criteria: the quality of the projects proposed, people's level of knowledge of the Constitution and whether parliament or people take the decision.

The countries whose people know least about the Constitution would get most. In the most recent Eurobarometer survey, these were apparently Cyprus (35%), Britain (50%) and Greece (51%). States deciding by referendum will also get more. Us again!

The Commission earmarked more than €650,000 for us, but the government was frightened to accept the money. "We don't want any of this money spent in the UK. It would clearly be utterly counterproductive," an official said. It pledged that "not a single penny" of EU money would be spent in the campaign. A Commission spokesman said, "We have every right and obligation to promote information about our activities, and we will continue doing that. We are not going to shy away from our duty."

The government did not stop the Commission's 'pro-constitution propaganda' of seminars, leafleting and theatre activities across schools, libraries, think-tanks, local government and pro-EU pressure groups. The Commission continued to fund the Europe Direct Information Network here with €840,000 a year to 'raise local and regional awareness of the Union's policies and programmes' and the 'Spring Day for Europe' to celebrate the Constitution. It spends more than €1 million a year on a network of think-tanks and pressure groups that promote the EU state, including the International European Movement, the Union of European Federalists, Friends of Europe, Young European Federalists, the Centre for

European Policy Studies and the European Policy Centre.

The Commission gave €10,551 to Hull University to 'raise awareness and understanding' of the Constitution, €25,000 to Liverpool Hope University College to help school pupils and students to find out about it, €38,318 to the Foreign Policy Centre for a conference, €48,601 to the Institute for Citizenship in London for a series of seminars, €27,291 to Yorkshire Forward, the regional development agency, to fund a conference called 'Europe Alive with Opportunity', €18,233 to Europaworld, a Welsh company, to set up a website to 'educate' people about the Constitution and to send information to secondary schools and €42,005 to the Federal Trust, a think-tank, to promote EU enlargement, including producing 100,000 'information' cards. The Trust's advisory board included Blair's policy adviser Andrew Adonis.

The EU has decided that we must accept the Constitution. Jean-Luc Dehaene, former Belgian Prime Minister and Vice-President of the EU Convention, said, "if the answer is No, the vote will probably have to be done again, because it absolutely has to be Yes."[23] Even before the result, they were already saying that a No vote in France would not really be a rejection of the Constitution, only a gesture against Chirac. Some said that if France voted No there would be no need for a referendum in Britain. But we have every right to make our voice heard, whatever happened in France or Holland or any other country.

Early in March 2005, the Commission identified "the components of a structured communication and information strategy on the Constitution to support the ongoing ratification process".

"The Commission has made it clear that it will not: issue propaganda on the Constitution; campaign during election periods or breach national rules on referenda or distribution of information.

"The Commission will seek to ensure that Europe's citizens are able to take informed choices on the Constitution. To do so, it has become increasingly clear that the Commission needs to do more to demonstrate the benefits of Europe.

"The Commission will be more pro-active in setting out the political case for the adoption of the Constitution - and demonstrate its concrete benefits to citizens. The entry into force of the Constitution would enhance the ability of the European Union to deliver on its strategic objectives over the next five years. The Commission and individual Commissioners cannot therefore stand on the sidelines or refrain from entering the political debate.

"The Commission approach will be guided by three objectives:
Getting people informed;
Getting people mobilized;
Respect for national and regional specificities.

"1) Wider distribution of the Constitution text for free. The Commission will not charge citizens that make a specific request for a copy of the Constitution text.

2) A new website on the Constitution so that citizens can easily obtain the text of the Constitution; the position of the Commission, details of the ratification process; key speeches and rebuttal of the main myths on the Constitution.

3) Informed Journalists: The Commission will increase the number of training seminars for national and regional journalists.

4) Roundtable discussions with civil society. Each Commission Representation Office will organize roundtable discussions on the Constitution with civil society

5) Engaging Europe's students. The Commission will produce a 'Constitution Pack' for distribution to Universities, Colleges and voter age students. The Commission will further promote the Spring Day initiative for schools.

6) Audiovisual. Radio and Television programmes will be produced to inform citizens about the Future of Europe.

7) Constitution Direct. The Commission will respond to questions on the Constitution at the EuropeDirect call centre. An advertising campaign will promote the Constitution Direct free phone number.

8) Mobilising the network of multipliers. Within each policy area a network of multipliers exists that can promote the benefits of the Constitution. The Commission will mobilize these information networks at regional and local level (e.g. TeamEurope, information relays, European documentation centres). The Commission will work with the Member States to mobilize the Youth Convention network created by the Convention on

the Future of Europe.

9) Accurate research and polling. The Commission will work with Member States to undertake detailed opinion poll analysis and focus group research.

10) Making PRINCE work. The Commission will intensify its contacts with Member States to speed-up delivery of country allocations under the PRINCE programme."

So no propaganda at all!

But the plans for creating a single EU state met an immovable obstacle – the peoples of Europe's nations. In May 2005 the French working class decisively rejected the proposed Constitution by 55% to 45% on a 70% turnout. 80% of blue-collar workers and 60% of white-collar workers voted No. In June, the Dutch voted against by 61.6% to 38.4% on a 62.8% turnout.

After the votes, various EU oligarchs showed their contempt and loathing for democracy. Lord Kinnock described the Dutch people's vote as 'a triumph of ignorance'. The European Green Party stated, "No in France and Holland does not mean no to the European Constitution." Liberal Democrat MEP Andrew Duff said that the No votes were not a brake on the European project, but were "proof that we are not going sufficiently fast".

The EU tried to impose the Constitution anyway, overriding the opposition of the nations. Valery Giscard-d'Estaing said, "What we'll say at the end, is that those who have not voted for the Constitution, we will ask them to revote." Peter Mandelson said, "No single member state has a veto over a constitutional treaty of this sort. France will have to consider its position: whether it is going to maintain a No or whether it is going to revisit the question and possibly come forward with a different view." MEP Elmar Brok said, "In the end there will be the Constitution because there is no alternative in Europe" – a familiar tune! Lord Patten said that parts of the Constitution should be implemented under the existing treaties: "the job for the UK in the presidency will be to pick out the bits of the Constitution which don't require treaty change." Baron Brittan agreed, saying that the EU should now 'cherry pick' parts of the Constitution and implement them.

John Monks, Secretary General of the European Trade Union Congress, said, "the treaty is not dead. I think that by suspending the referendum, Blair acted with opportunism – or with realism. He knows that, if there had been a referendum in Great Britain, he would have lost it … Keeping the referendum would have been suicidal. … In six or twelve months the 25 could publish a political declaration and put it to ratification, with the Constitution – eventually modified."

The EU had never wanted to put its Constitution to referenda. As Dutch foreign minister Bernard Bot said, "We always said that this subject matter was far too complex to be made the subject of a referendum." They had to risk referenda because, in the 2005 general election, the Labour government promised the British people a referendum in order to prevent its unpopular pro-Constitution policy being an issue in the election. They continued to make this promise even after the election. For example, on 20 April 2004, Blair told the House of Commons, "The referendum should go ahead in any event. Of course it should." He said on 18 April 2005, "I've always said we'll have a vote on the Constitution. It doesn't matter what other countries do; we'll have a vote on the Constitution." And on 13 May 2005, "Even if the French voted No, we would have a referendum. This is a government promise."

But after the French and Dutch referenda, Blair wanted to drop the promised referendum, in order to try to keep the Constitution alive. He wanted to stop any other peoples from voting to reject the Constitution. The fewer countries that held referenda, the easier it would be for the EU to impose the Constitution, in whole or in part. Six countries, the Czech Republic, Denmark, Ireland, Poland, Portugal and Britain, have postponed their referendums.

Blair had promised us a referendum in order to get out of one fix; then he broke the promise in order to get out of another. In Le Monde of 24 June 2005, he argued that voters in France had not actually reject the EU Constitution, but voted instead on other issues. Asked if the Constitution was dead, he said, "I continue to think that the Constitution is a set of rules perfectly apt for Europe to function better. We will have to reflect on it again. The problem is that the people have said to the politicians: we will not let you adopt this text until you begin to respond to our daily problems."

After Luxembourg's Yes vote in July 2005, 13 governments had ratified the Constitution. Commission President Jose Manuel Barroso said the result was "a strong signal because it means that a majority of member states consider that the constitutional treaty responds to their expectations". Luxembourg's Prime Minister Jean-Claude Juncker said, "The message that has come out and which is addressed to Europe and the world is that the Constitution is not dead after the votes in France and the Netherlands. As Luxembourg has said 'yes' the process can go ahead. There is a way for the European constitution to be adopted." The Finnish Prime Minister said, "None of the EU leaders has questioned the need for a Constitution. But it also became clear that further 'no' decisions are not needed."

The Constitution said (in Article IV-443) that if, after two years from the Treaty being signed, i.e. by October 2006, twenty member states had ratified it and others 'have encountered difficulties', the "matter will be referred to the European Council." So the European Council (the heads of state and government of the member states and the Commission's President, which takes its decisions in secret) wanted to decide for us what to do next.

A Mori poll held after the French and Dutch referenda found that 67% of the British people wanted a referendum on the Constitution and an ICM poll showed that 64% would vote against the Constitution and just 20% for. In June 2005, Unison's annual conference voted unanimously to welcome the French and Dutch no votes and to recommit the union to opposing the EU's "liberalisation and marketisation policies". Unison also decided to launch a high profile campaign against the 'Bolkestein' directive on services, the directive that the government so passionately supported. The RMT conference voted to oppose the Constitution and to keep up the campaign to oppose privatisation of public services across Europe, in particular to oppose the services directive.

Every nation affected by a Treaty has the right to veto it. Even the Treaty's Article IV-447 says it cannot enter into force until all 25 EU members have deposited their 'instruments of ratification'. The French and Dutch votes meant that the French and Dutch governments could not, as things stood, ratify the Treaty, so it could not enter into force. The French and Dutch peoples had wounded the Constitution, but it was not dead.

Blair had signed Britain up to the Treaty Establishing the Constitution for Europe, without asking us, on 29 October 2004. We were stuck with it, until we said that we were not. It would not be dead until we made the EU's leaders withdraw it completely. We in Britain must have the promised referendum so that we can nail the Constitution.

Unless we destroy the Constitution the EU will act as though it is in force. Regardless of the French and Dutch votes against the Constitution the EU is moving quickly to establish institutions and implement policies which only the Constitution, if adopted, would legitimise. Several institutions with no legal basis outside the Constitution have been, or at the time of writing, are being created. These include the European Defence Agency whose remit is to harmonise arms procurement, a mutual defence clause which makes the NATO alliance redundant, the deployment of EU uniformed troops in Macedonia, the Congo and Bosnia, A Foreign Minister, an EU diplomatic force representing the EU in other countries and international institutions, a European Space Programme, a Charter of Fundamental Rights and a Rights Agency, an EU criminal code and an EU wide asylum policy and External Borders Agency. Such developments show the EU entering a new phase of anti-democratic activity, it is lumbering ahead without mandate or accountability, purely in the interests of capital and regardless of the will of the people in their referenda.

4: An independent Britain

Britain is today, and has been for nearly a thousand years a sovereign country in the sense that the decisions that matter are taken here not abroad. Sovereignty in Britain belongs and throughout this time has belonged to the people who live in Britain. No foreign power has held sway here. This makes us different from the other EU countries, all of which have been occupied and run by foreign powers in the last two centuries: France, Belgium, Holland, Denmark, Greece, Austria, Sweden, Finland and Luxembourg by Nazi Germany, Italy, Germany, Spain and Portugal by Napoleonic France, Ireland by Britain.

Sovereignty has nothing to do with the 'sovereign' monarch.

Ever since Magna Carta tamed King John and still more since Charles I's execution in 1649, the monarch here has been head of state in name only (all head, no body) and a warning has been posted for any would-be tyrant. Sovereignty also has little to do with the attempts through parliamentary democracy to tailor rule by the people to other needs, but it has everything to do with the real democracy that we have where we live and work. From the village councils of the Middle Ages to modern trade unionism, invented by British workers and won against the employers' opposition, people's rule has prevailed in Britain. That we the people, the vast majority of the country, have entrusted the day-to-day conduct of affairs in this country to those who form governments does not change this basic truth - we gave them the authority to govern Britain and we can withdraw that authority. The sovereignty, the final veto, rests with us.

The British nation was not created by its rulers or by any economic system. Rather, the British people founded the nation, indeed became the nation, very early in our history.

Britain's democracy and sovereignty, our power to decide what goes on in our country, is at stake. If we became a province in a European state, we would lose at one fell swoop our sovereignty and our democracy. We must defeat those who would dissolve Britain into a European state.

Our trade unions have to reassert their historic role of upholding and extending our democratic processes. All of us, especially our trade unions, must oppose the Constitution for Europe, uphold our nation's sovereignty and take responsibility for our country's future. The opposition to the Constitution by the TUC Congress in 2005 was just a start.

Endnotes

[1]. See Jean Lacouture, De Gaulle the ruler 1945-1970, HarperCollins, 1991, and Regis Debray, Charles de Gaulle: futurist of the nation, Verso, 1994.

[2]. See Doug Nicholls, The euro: bad for trade unions, Congress for Democracy, 1999. See also Will Podmore and Phil Katz, Sovereignty for what? Why stopping EMU is just the start. Introduction by Joe Marino, General Secretary of the Bakers, Food and Allied Workers' Union, Tribune,

1997.

[3]. Roger Beetham, editor, The euro debate: persuading the people, Federal Trust, 2001, page 15.

[4]. Douglas Jay, pages 124-5, in his masterly brief essay, 'The free trade alternative to the EC: a witness account', pages 123-33, in Brian Brivati and Harriet Jones, editors, From reconstruction to integration: Britain and Europe since 1945, Leicester University Press, 1993.

[5]. Financial Times, 2 December 1996.

[6]. See Valerio Lintner, page 120, in 'Controlling Monetary Union', Chapter 6, pages 117-38, in Catherine Hoskyns and Michael Newman, editors, Democratizing the European Union: issues for the twenty-first century, Manchester University Press, 2000.

[7]. See Larry Siedentop, Democracy in Europe, Allen Lane, 2000, page 34.

[8]. M. Shahid Alam, Poverty from the wealth of nations: integration and polarization in the global economy since 1760, Macmillan, 2000, pages 10-11.

[9]. M. Shahid Alam, Poverty from the wealth of nations: integration and polarization in the global economy since 1760, Macmillan, 2000, pages xi and 13.

[10]. See Susan Strange, Mad money, Manchester University Press, 1998, page 112.

[11]. For details of how the financial system could be controlled democratically, see Nicholas Costello, Jonathan Michie and Seumas Milne, 'Taming the City of London', Chapter 6, pages 115-45, in Beyond the casino economy: planning for the 1990s, Verso, 1989.

[12]. See the Social and Community Planning Research, British and European Social Attitudes: How Britain Differs: the 1998/99 Report, Ashgate Press, 1999.

[13]. Cited page 17, Daily Telegraph, 14 September 2000.

[14]. See Brian Groom, London is open to rights charter being added to an EU

constitution, Financial Times, 18 February 2002, page 2.

[15]. Interview with Barbara Spinelli, La Stampa, 13 July 2000.

[16]. See Trade Unionists say No to the EU Constitution, TUAEUC, 2005.

[17]. See Trevor Hartley, Constitutional problems of the European Union, Oxford: Hart Publishing, 1999, page 179.

[18]. Cited in La Stampa, 1 November 2000.

[19]. Cited page 29, Roberto de Mattei, The Charter of Fundamental Rights' totalitarian spirit, European Journal, June 2001, Volume 8, Number 7, pages 28-30.

[20]. Daily Telegraph, 27 December 1998.

[21]. Die Welt, 25 February 2005.

[22]. Wall Street Journal Europe, 7 July 2003.

[23]. Irish Times, 2 June 2004.

Index

Accession, Treaty of (1972), 141
Acheson, Dean, 7-8
Acquis communautaire, 133, 141
Action Committee for a United States of Europe, 6
Adam Smith Institute, 252
Addenbrookes Hospital, 256
Adenauer, Konrad, 7, 113
Adonis, Andrew, 295
AEEU, see Amicus
Africa, 1, 6, 54, 101-2, 107, 110, 242, 243, 248-9, 255, 284
Agriculture, 108, 216, 240-6
Aid, 107-8
Air transport, 227-8
Aircraft industry, 210-11, 222, 224-5
Alam, Shahid, 272, 275-6
Albania, 258
Allot, Philip, 136
Amato, Giuliano, 280
American Chambers of Commerce, 134, 264
Amicus, 197-8
Amsterdam, Treaty of (1997), 2, 47, 57, 109, 180, 182, 225, 281
Andersen Report, 253
Anderson, Benedict, 21
Anderson, Paul, 77
Andreasen, Marta, 143-4
Annan, Kofi, 101
Apprenticeships, 219, 259, 278
Argentina, 276
Arient, 102
Armstrong, Kenneth, 148
Ascherson, Neal, 114
Ashdown, Paddy, 67

Ashworth, John, 249-50
Asia, 53-4, 99, 107, 108, 190, 220, 243, 255, 284
Association des Constructeurs Europeens d'Automobiles, 225
Association for Monetary Union, 134
Association of London Government, 120
Association of South East Asian Nations (ASEAN), 53, 99
Asylum, 68, 72, 109-10, 284
Atkins, Robert, 227
Australia, 94
Austria, 71, 102, 214, 248, 300

Baker, Dean, 188
Ball, George, 8
Balsom, Denis, 78
Bank of England, 19-22, 73, 169, 170, 177, 181, 192, 212, 279-80
Banks, 53, 171, 176-9
Barber, Brendan, 263
Barclays, 255
Barclays Capital, 174
Barroso, Jose Manuel, 52, 299
Bassam, Lord, 74-5, 75-6
Bay of Pigs, 8
Bea, Cardinal, 113
Bedford, Duke of, 242
Belgium, 5, 71, 101-2, 111, 190, 300
Berliner Zeitung, 58
Berthold, Norbert, 184
Bevin, Ernest, 5
Bilderberg Group, 4, 8, 52
Billingsgate, 250-1
Biotechnology, 215, 241
Birmingham, 227

Index

Bismarck, Otto von, 290
Blair, Tony, 2, 64-6, 69-72, 73, 77, 78, 79, 90, 92, 95, 96, 100-1, 103, 104-5, 106, 107, 115, 138, 151, 153, 170, 173, 181, 182, 183, 191, 207, 211, 217, 221-2, 223, 226, 227, 228, 229, 231-2, 244, 252, 255, 256, 260, 277, 280, 284, 285, 291, 292, 295, 298, 300
Blessing, Karl, 9
Blockades, 16, 107
BMW, 225
Bolkestein Directive, 263-4, 286, 299
Borders, 93, 100, 108-9, 111, 149, 184, 187-8, 285
Bosnia, 100, 300
Bot, Bernard, 298
Bradford v. the Attorney General, 291
Brandt, Willy, 12
Brazil, 224
Bretherton, Charlotte, 196-7
Breuer, Rolf, 177
Britain in Europe, 66, 72
Britain into Europe, 13
British Aerospace, 222, 225
British Bankers Association, 176
British Broadcasting Corporation (BBC), 13, 76
British Empire, 21, 54-5, 273
British Home Stores, 231
British Medical Association, 264
British Shipbuilders (BS), 224
British Telecom (BT), 222
British Union of Fascists, 4
Brittan, Leon, 72, 297
Brittan, Samuel, 171
Brok, Elmar, 105, 297
Brown, Gordon, 65, 77, 170, 171, 172, 181, 182, 183, 195, 229, 252, 260-3, 278, 280
Brussels, 135, 137
Bruton, John, 56-7
BSE crisis, 245
Buchan, James, 172

Buckby, Simon, 72
Building industry, 212
Buiter, William, 73
Bulmer, Simon, 148
Bundesbank, 9, 15, 56, 219
Bunyan, Tony, 97
Bury, Hans Martin, 272, 291
Business for Sterling, 45, 173-5, 180, 181
Butler, R. A., 49
Butler, Richard, 101
Byers, Stephen, 176
Byrne, David, 197

Caborn, Richard, 255
Calingaert, Michael, 222-3
Callaghan, James, 63
Campaign against Euro-federalism (CAEF), 28
Campaign for English Regions, 118
Capital, 1, 14, 15-6, 23, 54, 176-9, 208, 209, 216-20, 223-4, 253, 254, 275-9, 284, 285
Capital export, see Investment, foreign
Capitalism, 49, 101, 220, 285
Caribbean, 243
Carter, President Jimmy, 13
Castle, Barbara, 11, 46
Caucasus, 101
Cecchini Report (1988), 16-7
Central banks, 25, 29, 54, 56, 177
Central Intelligence Agency (CIA), 6, 7, 13, 75
Central Office of Information, 13
Chabot, Christian, 194, 196
Chantry Vellacott DFK, 253
Charles I, King, 283, 300-1
Charter of Fundamental Rights, 72, 280, 287, 288-9, 300
Chemical industry, 210-1, 240-1
Children, 101, 153, 259-60, 262
Chile, 29
China, 230, 276

305

Chirac, President Jacques, 69, 98, 104-5, 262, 295
Christopher, Warren, 31
Churchill, Winston, 5, 8, 49-50
Ciampi, Carlo, 59
Citizenship, 23, 30, 55, 142, 150, 187, 282, 295
City of London, 17, 176-9, 182
Civil Aviation Authority, 227
Clark, David, 77
Clarke, Charles, 79
Clarke, Kenneth, 18, 29-31, 64, 65
Class, 21, 46-55
Clinton, President Bill, 31, 100, 107
Clothing and footwear industry, 210, 219, 231
Coal, 5, 7, 23, 218, 219, 220, 285
Cockfield, Lord, 152
Colley, Linda, 21
Commerce, see Trade
Committee of Independent Experts, 143
Common Agricultural Policy (CAP), 9-10, 61, 144-5, 153-4, 173, 208, 212, 241-6
Committee of Permanent Representatives of the Member States (COREPER), 143
Committee of the Regions, 114
Common Fisheries Policy (CFP), 211, 246-51
Common law, 95
Commonwealth, 5, 8, 208
Communications, see Telecommunications industry
Community and Youth Workers' Union, 49
Competition, 8, 17, 24, 63, 68, 109, 140, 148, 150, 153-4, 176-7, 187, 192, 193, 217, 222-3, 229, 230, 231, 251, 255, 257-8, 263, 284, 285, 286, 287
Confederation of British Industry (CBI), 13, 17
Congo, 102, 300
Congress for Cultural Freedom, 8

Congress for Democracy, 76
Connolly, Bernard, 289
Conservative Party, 10, 13, 15, 17, 18-9, 23-4, 30, 31, 46, 49-50, 67, 75, 76, 79, 91, 97, 105, 115, 139, 216, 252
Constitution for Europe, 1,2,273-301
Cook, Robin, 72, 74, 102
Corbett, Gerald, 17, 228
Corporatism, 16, 47, 94, 221
Corpus Juris, 91-3, 95
Corruption, 1, 143-6, 153, 259
Cot, Pierre, 152
Council of Europe, 5, 10
Council of Ministers, 10, 131, 133, 136, 171-2, 221, 227, 250, 251-2, 283
Countryside Landowners' Association, 242
Court of Auditors, 143, 144, 145, 259
Court of First Instance, 140, 289
Cram, Laura, 196
Craxi, Bettino, 75
Crime, 111
Croatia, 100, 114
Crouch, Colin, 183, 197
Cuba, 8, 102-3, 107, 224
Currency unions, 6, 7, 9, 11, 12, 190
Cyprus, 294
Czechoslovakia, 100, 113-4

Daily Express, 13
Daniels, Ben, 176-7, 183, 184
De Charette, Herve, 57
De Gaulle, General Charles, 9, 10, 273
De Grauwe, Paul, 192
De Palacio, Loyola, 262
De Ramsey, Lord, 242
De Silguy, Yves-Thibault, 59
De Tocqueville, Alexis, 6-7
De Villepin, Dominique, 290
Decline, 1, 8, 17, 20, 184, 188-9, 208, 212-3, 214, 220
Defence, Ministry of, 231-2

Index

Defence industry, 222
Defence policy, 23, 103-7, 283-4
Deflation, 29, 63, 169-70, 173, 179-80, 182, 188-98, 212-3, 276-7
Dehaene, Jean-Luc, 27, 295
Deindustrialisation, 208-12, 213-4
Delors, Jacques, 5, 23, 27, 48, 131, 260
Delors Committee, 17
Democracy, 1, 22, 28-9, 30, 31-2, 50, 54, 103, 121, 131, 136, 139, 149-52, 155, 273-92, 297, 300-1
Denman, Roy, 73
Denmark, 18, 30, 45, 73-4, 300
Denton, Geoffrey, 150
Derby, 227
D'Estaing, Valery Giscard, 280, 291, 297
Development, 107-8
Devolution, 114-8
Dinan, Desmond, 150, 184, 186, 196
Dini, Lamberto, 290
Dividends, 189, 209, 216, 261
Dollar, 170, 171, 174, 179, 276
Donoughue, Bernard, 13
Douglas-Home, Alec, 9
Drugs, 111
Duff, Andrew, 297
Duisenberg, Wim, 25-6, 27, 59, 168, 182, 262
Dulles, John Foster, 8
Dyson, Kenneth, 192

E-commerce, 279
Eastern Europe, 1, 4, 52, 99-100, 111, 153-5
Economic and Monetary Union, 3, 12, 14, 19-32, 49-51, 55-63, 63-7, 68, 154-5, 168-98, 251-2
Economic and Social Committee, 142, 169
Economy, 14, 19-20, 25, 48, 53, 169, 182, 188-98, 207-20, 273-80
Eden, Anthony, 5, 6, 8

Edmonds, John, 183
Education, 215, 218-9, 229, 254, 255, 257-8, 259-60, 278-9
Eichel, Hans, 104
Eisenhower, President Dwight, 8
Election Commission Committee, 74
Electoral Commission, 293
Elliott, Larry, 182
Employers, 2, 14, 15, 48, 49, 50, 51-5, 109, 134, 142, 153, 183, 184, 185, 188, 191, 221, 300, 301
Endo, Ken, 150
Energy, 23, 71-2, 74, 101, 107-8, 174-5, 190, 220-1, 254, 255, 284-5
Energy industry, 174-5, 190, 220-1
Engels, Frederick, 95
Engineering industry, 210-5, 217, 222, 224, 277
Enlargement of EU, 71, 100, 102, 111, 153-5, 196-7, 295
Environmental Action Programmes, 134-5
Ernst & Young Item Club, 195-6
EU legislation, 27, 133
EU state, 14-5, 22-32, 55-63, 67-73, 90-129, 130-55, 275-301
Euro, 2, 3, 19-32, 63-7, 73-80, 168-98, 232, 285-6
Eurojust, 91, 288
Europe Direct Information Network, 294
European army, 96, 103-7, 284
European Atomic Energy Community (EURATOM), 8
European Central Bank, 19-22, 23, 25-9, 32, 168, 169, 173, 181, 191, 193, 194, 196, 198, 252, 258-9, 261, 285, 290
European Coal and Steel Community (ECSC), 7, 140
European Commission, 10, 14, 16, 17, 32, 60, 75-6, 112, 115, 131-5, 136, 137, 196, 221, 282-3, 290, 294-6
European Council, 25, 137-9, 185, 299

European Court of Justice (ECJ), 67, 68, 75, 140-2, 257-8, 282, 289
European defence Agency, 300
European elections, 13, 66, 137, 139
European Federation of Iron and Steel Industries, 221
European Investment Bank, 254
European Movement, 5, 6, 13, 142
European Parliament, 19, 137-9, 145-6, 282, 290
European People's Party (EPP), 30, 138, 139
European Rapid Reaction Force, 96, 106-7
European Regional Development Funds, 114-5, 117
European Roundtable of Industrialists, 14, 15, 130, 134, 283
European Security and Intelligence Force, 96-8
European Services Network, 255
European Space Programme, 300
European Trades Union Congress (ETUC), 47-8, 142
European Works Council Directive, 47-8
European Youth Campaign, 7
Europol, 95-6, 288
Eurostat, 144
Exchange controls, 14, 15-6, 220, 277
Exchange rate, 3, 12, 16, 17-20, 26, 31, 50, 63, 169, 171, 175-6, 179, 181, 187, 192-3
Exchange Rate Mechanism, 17-20, 26, 63, 174, 189, 191
Exploitation, 54-5
Exports, 17, 195
External Borders Agency, 300
Fabian Society, 79
Fabius, Laurent, 59
Faith schools, 259
Falconer, Lord Charles, 116
Featherstone, Kevin, 192
Federal Trust, 114
Federalism, see EU state

Feldstein, Martin, 196
Fella, Stefano, 150
Finance, 176-9, 181, 213
Financial Times, 134, 171, 181-2, 197, 230
Finland, 300
Fischer, Joschka, 57-9, 62, 103, 289, 290
Fishing industry, 175, 194, 216, 219, 220, 223, 246-51, 284
Five tests, 50-1, 79, 173-82
Fontaine, Nicole, 62-3
Food, 2, 107-8, 219, 240-6
Foot and mouth epidemic, 245
Ford, 13
Ford Foundation, 6
Forestry, 245-6
Foreign Office, 6, 11, 94, 293
Foreign policy, 23, 98-103, 273, 283-4
France, 1, 2, 5, 7, 9, 10, 18, 101-2, 190, 251, 252, 277-8, 297, 298, 299, 300
Frankfurt Stock Exchange, 177-8
Frattini, Franco, 290
Friedman, Milton, 29
Full employment, 23, 26, 27, 29, 48, 49, 109-10, 116, 185, 189, 191, 193, 194-5, 218, 219, 276-7, 278, 279, 285

G8, 1
Galleries, 259
Garcia, Miguel Angel, 193
Gasperi, Alcide di, 113
Gates, Paul, 231
Geddes, Andrew, 150
General Agreement on Tariffs and Trade (GATT), 16, 53, 230
General Agreement on Trade in Services (GATS), 254-5
General Motors, 48
George, Eddie, 22, 73, 176, 191
Germany, 5, 7, 9, 99-100, 101-2, 109, 139, 154-5, 175, 180, 188, 190, 251, 252, 277-8, 281, 288, 294, 300

Index

Giddens, Anthony, 48
Gil-Robles, Jose-Maria, 91
Globalisation, 16, 52-5, 100, 192, 254-5
Gold Standard, 31
Goldman Sachs, 255
Gonzalez, Felipe, 45, 55-6
Grahl, John, 198
Grant, Wyn, 150
Greece, 153, 189, 294, 300
Green, Pauline, 144
Greens, 56, 116, 217-8, 297
Grinols, E. L., 208
Guantanamo Bay, 102-3
Guardian, 73, 77, 78, 196
Gulf States, 6
Guyana, 243

Habeas corpus, 69, 91-2, 288
Haider, Jorg, 102
Hain, Peter, 16, 24, 28-9, 154, 191, 291
Hallstein, Walter, 10, 55
Hartridge, David, 254
Haskins, Lord, 119
Hattersley, Roy, 152
Health, 228, 246-7, 253-9, 262, 287
Heath, Edward, 2, 5, 8, 10, 11, 12, 13, 75, 105, 141, 147, 209, 285
Helms-Burton Act (1996), 107
Hennessy, Peter, 151
Heseltine, Michael, 15, 52, 65, 136, 149-150
Heywood, Jeremy, 77
Hitler, Adolf, 4, 49-50, 112, 288
Hix, Simon, 184
Hobsbawm, Eric, 21
Holland, Martin, 148, 152
Holmes, Oliver Wendell, 92
Holy Roman Empire, 4
Home Office, 133
Hongkong and Shanghai Banking Corporation (HSBC), 255
Hoon, Geoff, 106

Housing, 218, 246, 286, 287
Hutton, Will, 48
Hunke, Heinrich, 117

IBM, 13, 214
ICI, 13
Identity cards, 93-5
Imports, 17, 207-11
Independent, The, 195, 197
India, 99, 221-2, 230, 276
Indonesia, 276
Industrial Relations Act (1971), 46
Industry, 1, 3, 14, 17, 18, 23, 26, 50-1, 68-9, 115, 119-20, 170-1, 179-82, 194, 197-8, 207-32, 275-6
Inflation, 18, 21, 25-7, 29, 169-70, 172, 181, 191, 193-4, 196, 218, 256, 277
Institution of Professionals, Managers and Specialists (IPMS), 227
International Chamber of Commerce, 52
Interest rates, 18-20, 21-2, 25-6, 31, 169, 175-6, 179-81, 193, 194, 198, 276-7, 285
International law, 30, 110, 248-9, 299
International Monetary Fund (IMF), 9, 52, 170, 174
Investment, domestic, 1, 18, 23, 194, 208-20, 251-2, 275-80
Investment, foreign, 54, 153, 170-1, 174, 176, 181, 189, 197-8, 207, 218
Iraq, 101
Ireland, 18, 70-1, 172, 175, 189, 193-4, 300
Irish Confederation of Trade Unions, 71
Iron and Steel Confederation, 221
Irvine of Lairg, Lord, 93
Issing, Otmar, 27, 29
Italy, 5, 18, 183-4. 300

Jacobs, Michael, 79
Jagdeo, Bharrat, 243
Jaguar Cars, 225
Jamaica, 243

Japan, 99, 214, 224-6
Jay, Douglas, 209, 274
Jebb, Gladwyn, 6
Jenkins, Roy, 10
Jimeno, Juan, 185-6
Jobs, see Full employment and Unemployment
John, King, 300
John XXIII, Pope, 113
John Paul II, Pope, 113
Johnson, Alan, 226
Johnson, President Lyndon, 10
Jospin, Lionel, 103-4, 106-7, 262, 263
Juncker, Jean-Claude, 299

Kennedy, Charles, 114, 116, 173
Kennedy, President John, 8, 31
Keynes, John Maynard, 28, 29, 276-7
Kinnock, Lord, 72-3, 132, 143, 297
Kirkhope, Timothy, 97
Kissinger, Henry, 10
Kitson, Michael, 212-3
Kohl, Chancellor Helmut, 55, 56, 58, 75, 95, 98, 100
Korea, 214, 276
Kosovo, 96-7, 100
Kosovo Liberation Army (KLA), 100

Labour Committee for Europe, 13
Labour Euro-Safeguards Campaign, 76
Labour market, 15-6, 168, 182-8, 263-4
Labour movement, see Trade unions
Labour Party, 10, 17, 18-9, 63-7, 76, 79, 80, 104, 139, 175, 221, 229
Laffan, Brigid, 152
Lafontaine, Oscar, 25-6, 56
Lamers, Karl, 56
Lamfalussy, Alexandre, 170
Lamont, Norman, 18
Lamy, Pascal, 152, 257
Lancet, The, 258

Land reform, 240-6
Laos, 8, 9
Latin America, 53-4, 102, 107, 243, 255, 276
Latvia, 263-4
Lawson, Nigel, 15, 170
Lazenby, Mike, 169
Leonardo Programme, 144
Levene, Lord, 178
Liberal Democrat Party, 13, 17, 18-9, 75, 78, 79, 116
Liberalisation, 16, 52, 53, 221, 222, 227, 257, 263-4, 286-7, 290
Liddle, Roger, 73, 291
Lintner, Valerio, 99, 184, 208
Lithuania, 114
Livingstone, Ken, 63, 191
Lloyd George, David, 51
Local Improvement Finance Trusts, 253-4
Locke, John, 291-2
Lome Convention, 107
London, 119-20
London Health Emergency, 253
London Underground, 229, 230
Lucas, Caroline, 193
Lutzenberger, Jose, 53
Luxemburg, 5, 108, 111, 137, 140, 180, 299, 300

Maastricht Treaty (1992), 17, 22-31, 55, 131-2, 138, 142, 191, 198, 220, 245, 251-2, 253, 257-8, 260, 281, 285
Macedonia, 300
Machine tools industry, 210-1, 214-5
Macmillan, Harold, 5-6, 8, 188-9
MacShane, Denis, 293
Magna Carta, 114, 300
Major, John, 2, 17-8, 19, 29-30, 222, 251
Malaysia, 6, 276
Malta, 294
Mandelson, Peter, 132, 230, 282, 297

Index

Mann, Michael, 179
Mansholt, Sicco, 107, 131, 189-90, 244
Manufacturing, see Industry
Marconi, 223
Marks & Spencer, 231
Marlborough, Duke of, 242
Marr, Andrew, 76, 114
Marshall, Matt, 25
Marshall, Peter, 77
Mauritania, 249
Maxwell Fyfe, David, 11
McCormick, John, 147
McKay, David, 147
McCreevy, Charlie, 57
McNamara, Kathleen, 150
Medicines, 256-7
Megarry, Sir Robert, 291
Members of the European Parliament (MEPs), 137-9, 145-6
Menon, Anand, 134
Mercosur, 53
Mexico, 53
Michel, Louis, 51
Michie, Jonathan, 212-3
Microsoft, 214
Migration, 15-6, 102, 108-11, 153-4, 184, 187-8, 192, 278-9, 284
Mitterand, Francois, 75, 190
Monetarism, see Deflation
Monks, John, 50, 51, 66, 297-8
Monnet, Jean, 5, 6, 7, 33, 135, 148, 149, 150, 274
Montenegro, 101
Monti, Mario, 262
Moore, Lynden, 208
Moratinos, Miguel Angel, 290
Morley, Elliott, 247
Morris, Bill, 3, 29, 50
Mortgages, 172, 178
Moscovici, Pierre, 60
Mosley, Oswald, 4, 30

Motor industry, 210, 225-6
Museums, 259
Mussolini, Benito, 112, 252

Naisbitt, John, 224
Namibia, 249
Napoleon, 4
Nation, 122, 260, 264, 273-6, 281-3, 290, 298, 300-1
National Air Traffic Services (Nats), 227
National Changeover Plan, 65, 257
National Health Service, 229, 254-8, 264, 287
National Institute for Economic and Social Research (NIESR), 195
National liberation movements, 21, 99, 273
National Referendum Campaign, 13
Nationalism, 99, 122
Neill Commission, 74-6
Netherlands, 1, 2, 5, 110, 245, 293, 295, 297, 298, 299, 300
New Zealand, 94
Nice Treaty (2000), 67-73, 136, 139, 241, 281, 287
Nicholls, Doug, 21-2
Nixon, President Richard, 10
Nkrumah, President Kwame, 101
Nolling, Wilhelm, 154-5, 192-3
North American Free Trade Agreement (NAFTA), 53, 99
North Atlantic Treaty Organization (NATO), 6, 9, 99-100, 105-6; 300
war against Yugoslavia (1999), 100
Northumberland, Duke of, 242
Norway, 190, 195
Nugent, Neill, 148, 196

O'Hare, Dean, 254
Oil, 100, 101, 174-5, 190, 220-1, 284-5
O'Neill, Con, 5
Opinion polls, 45, 77, 78, 292, 294, 299

311

Owen, David, 10, 69-70, 74, 105, 151
Oxfam, 108

Palacio, Ana, 290
Palast, Gregory, 221
Paper industry, 245-6
Paris, Treaty of (1951), 7
Party of European Socialists, 72
Patten, Lord, 132, 297
Pension funds, 215, 279
Pensions, 2, 180, 260-2, 264, 279
Pepsi-Cola, 48
Philippines, 276
Pilkington, Colin, 147
Pirie, Madsen, 252
Pius XII, Pope, 112-3
Plaid Cymru, 75, 78, 79
Playing fields, 259
Poland, 114, 153-4, 190
Police, 95-8, 288
Polish Stock Exchange, 100-1
Political Parties, Elections and Referendums Act, 74
Pompidou, Georges, 9-10, 12
Pond, Chris, 93-4
Porritt, Jonathon, 217-8
Portugal, 153, 248, 252,300
Postal services, 23, 223
Potsdam, Treaty of (1945), 99
Pound, 3, 12, 18-9, 21-2, 27, 30-1, 50, 63, 69, 77, 170, 172, 174, 178, 179, 194, 198, 212, 257, 276-7
Poverty, 1, 109, 116, 188, 213, 249, 279
Prescott, John, 119
Prices, 17, 18, 26, 51, 108, 181, 189, 193, 197, 208, 211, 241-6, 256-7
Private Finance Initiative, 252-4, 278
Privatisation, 28, 47, 52, 134, 153, 169, 220-2, 224, 226-9, 252-5, 257-8, 263-4, 269, 279, 286, 299
Prodi, Romano, 52, 60, 104, 135, 139, 144, 183-4, 185, 217, 252, 263, 281-2, 287-8, 290
Productivity, 53, 154, 180, 184, 189, 193, 212, 218, 276, 277
Profits, 53, 54, 171, 189, 210, 214, 219, 246, 253, 255, 279
Propaganda, 260, 293-7
Proportional representation, 138
Public services, 1, 3, 16, 18, 28, 31-2, 50, 171-2, 185, 189, 212, 214-5, 218, 229, 251-64, 284-6, 299
Putzhammer, Heinz, 193

Qualified Majority Voting (QMV), 14, 23, 24, 64, 67-9, 136, 285-6
Quinn, Ruairi, 56

Race, 110-1
Racism and Xenophobia Directive, 94
Radice, Giles, 193
Rail, Maritime and Transport Workers (RMT), 299
Railtrack, 227-8
Railways, 23, 226-9, 285
Ranger, Terence, 21
Rank, 13
Raynsford, Nick, 119
Reagan, President Ronald, 15
Recessions, see Slumps
Reder, Melvyn, 187-8
Referendum (1975), 2, 12-3, 74, 75
Referendum on the Constitution, 292-301
Referendum on the euro, 64, 65, 73-80
Regional Development Agencies, 116, 295
Regional Development Agencies Act (1999), 115
Regionalisation, 114-8
Religion, 111-4
Research and Development, 215-6, 231, 241
Resistance, 4

Index

Respect, 138
Ribbentrop, Joachim, 4
Richard, Alain, 106
Richardson, Jeremy, 187
Richardson, Keith, 130, 185
Road haulage, 229-30
Roberts, John, 223
Rocard, Pierre, 57
Rolt, L. T. C., 215
Roman Catholic Church, 24, 32, 71, 112-4
Roman Empire, 4
Rome, Treaties of (1957), 8, 10, 14, 16, 141, 146, 281, 288
Ross, George, 150, 264
Rover Group, 225-6
Ruding, Onno, 171
Ruling class, 53, 99, 151-2
Rumania, 221-2
Russia, 100, 101
Rwanda, 102
Rwandan Patriotic Front, 102
Ryanair, 146

Sanctions, 101
Santamaki-Vuori, Tuire, 187
Santer, Jacques, 59, 75, 183, 185, 275
Sautter, Christian, 262
Scarman, Lord, 141
Schengen Agreement, 108, 109, 111
Schlesinger, Helmut, 56
Schmidt, Helmut, 154
Schroeder, Gerhard, 61-2, 72, 98, 217, 263
Schuman, Robert, 7, 113
Scott of Foscote, Lord, 92
Scottish National Party, 75, 78, 79, 220
Second World War, 4, 99
Self-determination, see Sovereignty
Serbia, 101
Shell, 13
Shipping, 223-4
Shore, Cris, 148-9, 150-1

Shore, Peter, 65
Simonazzi, Annamaria, 186-7, 188
Single European Act (1986), 2, 14
Single European Market, 14-7, 23, 24, 67, 108-9, 134, 187, 191, 217
Slovenia, 100
Slumps, 20, 21, 29, 169, 170, 189, 198, 209
Smith, John, 10, 19, 175
Social Charter, 30, 47, 141-2
Social Contract (1974-76), 46
Socialism, 1, 263
Socrates Programme, 259
Solana, Javier, 97, 105
Soros, George, 213
Soul for Europe, 111-2
South Africa, 110, 249
South West TUC, 198
Southern and Eastern Regional Council of the TUC (SERTUC), 220
Soviet Union, 4, 21, 99, 114
Sovereignty, 6, 11-2, 15, 20-2, 24-5, 26, 27, 28, 29-30, 31, 55-63, 64, 95, 103, 107, 120, 140, 147, 172, 219-20, 272-301
Spaak, Paul-Henri, 4, 10
Spain, 18, 102, 153, 190, 193-4, 245, 251, 300
Sport, 259
Stability and Growth Pact, 27, 51, 57, 173, 190, 252
Stabreit, Immo, 154
Steel, 5, 7, 218, 221-2
Sterling, see Pound
Stewart, Magnie, 247-8
Strange, Susan, 196
Strauss-Kahn, Dominique, 57
Straw, Jack, 71, 74, 78-9, 287
Stuart, Gisela, 280
Subsidiarity, 24-5, 112, 115
Sugar, 242-3
Sun, 64
Sunday Telegraph, 18

Sutherland, Peter, 16
Sweden, 18, 45, 180, 190, 214, 223, 263-4, 300
Switzerland, 109, 114, 195, 214, 216, 218

Tate & Lyle, 242
Taxation, 24, 26, 30-1, 31-2, 67, 171-2, 210, 211, 213, 218, 221, 228, 229, 230, 242, 251-2, 257, 259, 260-1, 262-3, 276, 278-9, 281
Telecommunications industry, 209-10, 211, 223
Terrorism, 93, 94-5, 114
Textile industry, 210, 230-2
Thailand, 276
Thatcher, Margaret, 2, 14, 15, 17-8, 21, 47, 50, 79, 103, 170, 182-3, 191, 207, 209-10, 215, 219, 221, 225, 252, 277, 279, 285, 287
Theatres, 259
Thirlwall, Tony, 193
Tietmeyer, Hans, 56
Times, The, 79, 284
Town-twinning, 117
Trade, 15-6, 52-3, 63, 68, 98, 99, 102, 107-8, 120, 148, 153, 170, 174, 179, 189, 194-5, 196, 208-21, 223-32, 243-6, 254-5, 275-7, 287
Trade deficits, 170, 189, 195, 208-16, 220
Trade unions, 4, 16, 18, 22, 46-55, 68, 109, 111, 182-8, 189, 273, 275, 287, 292, 299-301
Trades Union Congress, 2, 17, 21-2, 31-2, 49, 50-1, 66, 170, 216, 218, 219, 230, 253, 263
Transport and General Workers Union (T&G), 48, 230
Transport industry, 212, 216-7, 223-30
Travis, Alan, 78
Treasury, 19, 219
Trial by jury, 92-3, 288
Tribune, 77
Trichet, Jean-Claude, 57

Trilateral Commission, 52
Turkey, 154
Turner, Adair, 192

Ukraine, 114
Ulman, Lloyd, 187-8
Unemployment, 3, 14, 15, 16, 17, 18, 26, 27, 29, 45, 63, 69, 109, 168, 169-70, 179-82, 183, 185, 188-98, 208-10, 213, 218, 219, 226, 242, 251, 255-6, 264, 276-7, 278-9
Union of Industrial and Employers' Confederation of Europe (UNICE), 134
UNISON, 77, 299
United Kingdom Independence Party (UKIP), 76
United Nations, 53, 97-8, 248
United Nations Conference on Trade and Development (UNCTAD), 169
United States Chamber of Commerce, 134
United States Department of Commerce, 134
United States of America, 6-7, 31, 99, 102-3, 107, 122, 147, 174, 176, 190-1, 213-4, 216, 218, 220, 226, 241, 245, 248, 276-8, 281, 289
Universities, 277

Value Added Tax (VAT), 23, 259, 262-3
Van Buitenen, Paul, 144
Van den Broek, Hans, 98
Verhofstadt, Guy, 72, 93, 102, 104, 263, 291
Veto, 9-10, 12, 15, 17, 23-5, 30, 57, 61, 64-9, 91, 136, 138, 243, 262-3, 283-8, 297, 299, 300,301
Vichy, 1, 7
Vietnam, 9
Villa, Paola, 186-7, 188
Vinals, Jose, 185-6
Vitorino, Antonio, 280
Vogler, John, 196-7
Volcker, Paul, 214

Index

Voltaire, 4
Von Hindenburg, President Paul, 288
Von Papen, Franz, 112

Wages, 3, 15, 17, 18, 26-7, 29, 45, 47, 48, 51-2, 53, 69, 101, 109, 153, 170-1, 179-80, 182-8, 192, 196, 198, 210, 214, 218, 251, 253, 256, 264, 273, 279
Waigel, Theo, 100
Walesa, Lech, 114
Wallace, William, 147-8, 152
Wallstrom, Margot, 99
Weale, Martin, 194
Welfare services, 16, 168, 185, 188, 251-64
Weimar Republic, 288
Welteke, Horst, 27
Werner Report (1970), 11
West European Union (WEU), 106
West Indies, 6
Westminster, Duke of, 242
Wicks, Nigel, 192
Wilkinson, John, 107
Williams, Shirley, 10, 113
Wilson, Harold, 2, 10, 12, 13
Winters, Alan, 208
Wolf, Martin, 181-2
Women, 112, 142, 153, 185
Woodin, Mike, 193
Worcester, Robert, 76-7, 274
Working class, 48-9, 71, 103, 220, 292, 297
Working Time Directive, 46, 256
Works Councils, 47-8
World Bank, 52, 108, 183, 258
World Business Council for Sustainable Development, 52
World Economic Forum, 53
World Trade Organization (WTO), 16, 52, 98, 108, 195, 254
Wright, David, 176

Yalta, Treaty of (1945), 99

Yen, 179
Yes4Yorkshire, 119
Yorkshire Forward, 295
Young, Hugo, 73, 77, 169
Young, Lord, 15
Youth for Europe, 259
Yugoslavia, 99, 112, 113-4
Yugoslavia, NATO's war on (1999), 1, 100

Zalm, Gerrit, 262
Zimbabwe, 110

315

The EU Bad for Britain

Index